Introduction to Compiler Design
An Object-Oriented Approach Using Java®

John I. Moore, Jr.
The Citadel, Charleston, SC

ii

Oracle and Java are registered trademarks of Oracle and/or its affiliates. Other names may be trademarks of their respective owners.

The programs presented in this book and on the accompanying web site have been included for their educational value and are not guaranteed for any particular purpose. The author does not offer any warranties nor accept any liabilities with respect to the programs.

Table of Contents

Preface

Many compiler books have been published over the years, so why another one? Let me be perfectly clear. This book is designed primarily for use as a textbook in a one-semester course for undergraduate students and beginning graduate students. The only prerequisites for this book are familiarity with basic algorithms and data structures (lists, maps, recursion, etc.), a rudimentary knowledge of computer architecture and assembly language, and some experience with the Java programming language. Most undergraduate computer science majors will have covered these topics in their first two years of study. Graduate students who have never had a course in compilers will also find the book useful, especially if they undertake some of the more challenging project exercises described in Appendix B.

A complete study of compilers could easily fill several graduate-level courses, and therefore some simplifications and compromises are necessary for a one-semester course that is accessible to undergraduate students. Following are some of the decisions made in order to accommodate the goals of this book.

1. The book has a narrow focus as a project-oriented course on compilers. Compiler theory is kept to a minimum, but the project orientation retains the "fun" part of studying compilers.

2. The source language being compiled is relatively simple, but it is powerful enough to be interesting and challenging. It has basic data types, arrays, procedures, functions, and parameters, but it relegates many other interesting language features to the project exercises. Most undergraduate students will find it challenging just to complete a compiler for the basic project language without any additional features. Graduate students will want to extend the basic project language with features outlined in the exercises.

3. The target language is assembly language for a virtual machine with a stack-based architecture, similar to but much simpler than the Java Virtual Machine (JVM). This approach greatly simplifies code generation. First, it eliminates the need to deal with general-purpose registers. And second, relative addresses for branch instructions are handled by the assembler, simplifying the amount of work that needs to be done by the compiler. Both an assembler and an emulator for the virtual machine are provided on the course web site.

4. No special compiler-related tools are required or used within the book. Students require access only to a Java compiler and a text editor, but most students will want to use Java with an Integrated Development Environment (IDE) such as Eclipse, NetBeans, or IntelliJ IDEA. Compiler-related tools such as scanner generators or parser generators could simplify certain tasks involved in building a compiler, but I believe that the approach used in this book makes the structure of the compiler more transparent. Students who wish to use compiler-related tools are welcome to do so, but

they will need to look elsewhere to learn how to use these tools. Examples of freely available compiler-related tools include ANTLR, Coco/R, Flex/Bison, Lex/Yacc, JavaCC, and Eclipse Xtext. In addition, while the presentation of the book uses Java, students are free to select an alternative implementation language. Languages that support recursion and object-oriented programming will work best with the approach used in this book. Examples include C++, C#, Python, Kotlin, Scala, and Swift.

5. One very important component of a compiler is the parser, which verifies that a source program conforms to the language syntax and produces an intermediate representation of the program that is suitable for additional analysis and code generation. There are several different approaches to parsing, but in keeping with the focus on a one-semester course, this book emphasizes only one approach, recursive descent parsing with one symbol lookahead.

> In his book *Language Implementation Patterns* [Parr 2010], Terence Parr offers this statement about recursive descent parsing, "This pattern shows how to implement parsing decisions that use a single token of lookahead. It's the weakest form of recursive-descent parser but the easiest to understand and implement. If you can conveniently implement your language with this pattern, you should do so."

6. Missing from the book are a lot of favorite compiler topics such as finite automata, bottom-up parsing, attribute grammars, heap management, register allocation, and data-flow analysis. What remains fits nicely into a one-semester, project-oriented course for undergraduate students and beginning graduate students.

The Course Project

This book discusses the implementation of a compiler for a relatively small programming language named CPRL (for Compiler PRoject Language), which was designed for teaching basics of compiler design. The target language is assembly language for CVM (CPRL Virtual Machine), a simple stack-based virtual machine. Together we will build a compiler slowly, one step at a time, with lots of template Java code in the book and even more on the book web site to guide you through the process. The book web site has even more Java code examples, which students are expected to download and study as part of their learning experience. The end result is likely the largest single program that most students will encounter.

Appendix A describes the decomposition of the overall project of developing a CPRL compiler into 8 smaller subprojects. Students should complete the subprojects in the specified order since each one builds on the previous.

Appendix B describes a number of extensions or variations to the basic compiler project outlined in this book. Some are more challenging than others. Ambitious undergraduate students and most graduate students will want to attempt one or more of these exercises.

Structure of the Book

The book chapters are organized in a natural progression from general concepts to step-by-step details for implementing the compiler project. Each chapter builds on the previous chapters, and forward references have been kept to a minimum. A few sections can be omitted or postponed without loss of continuity, but in general, the book is designed to be studied from front to back.

Chapter 1 introduces basic concepts and terminology in the study of compilers. Following [Watt 2000], it uses tombstone diagrams as a visual aid to explaining many of the concepts. Sections 1.2, 1.3, and 1.6 are required. The other sections can be omitted or postponed without impacting the material in subsequent chapters.

Chapter 2 presents an overview of the structure of a compiler. In a sense, it sets the context for the remaining chapters.

Chapter 3 provides an overview of how programming languages are defined, with detailed coverage of context-free grammars. The complete context-free grammar for CPRL, the source language for the compiler project, is defined in Appendix D.

Chapter 4 gives a brief overview of CPRL. A more complete definition of CPRL is provided in Appendix C.

Chapter 5 presents the details of implementing a scanner for CPRL, including an overview of several related classes found on the course web site.

Chapter 6 is the longest and most complicated chapter in the book. It includes a discussion of grammar analysis to compute first and follow sets plus details on the implementation of a recursive descent parser for CPRL. As defined in the compiler project, the initial version of the parser concentrates only on verification that a source program conforms to the syntax defined by the context-free grammar for CPRL.

Chapter 7 extends the parser developed in Chapter 6 to perform error recovery, so that multiple errors can be detected and reported.

Chapter 8 contains a detailed discussion of abstract syntax trees. Abstract syntax trees provide an intermediate representation for source programs that can be used for additional analysis and code generation. In this chapter, the parsing methods are modified to construct an abstract syntax tree for the source program.

Chapter 9 uses the abstract syntax trees from Chapter 8 to perform constraint analysis, with emphasis on checking conformance to CPRL's scope and type rules as defined for CPRL/0 a major subset of CPRL.

Chapter 10 gives a brief overview of the CVM, the virtual machine that serves as the target for CPRL programs. The CVM has a stack architecture that is similar to but much simpler than the Java Virtual Machine (JVM). Appendix E contains a more detailed definition of the CVM.

Chapter 11 modifies the abstract syntax trees to perform code generation for a subset of the CPRL language. The code generated is assembly language for the CVM. The book web site provides an assembler that can be used to generate the actual machine code.

Chapter 12 presents an overview of code optimization. None of the basic compiler projects require mastery of the material from this chapter, and therefore this chapter can be postponed if desired, but it should not be omitted.

Chapter 13 extends constraint analysis and code generation to handle subprograms. It includes a detailed discussion of scope and activation records.

Chapter 14 extends constraint analysis and code generation to handle arrays. Implementing arrays completes the basic compiler project, but students are always encouraged to attempt some of variations and extensions outlined in Appendix B.

Chapter Dependencies

As illustrated in the diagram on the next page, Chapters 2 and 12 can be covered any time after Chapter 1, and Chapters 13 and 14 can be covered any time after Chapter 11. Otherwise, most chapters should be covered in the order presented in the book.

Book Resources

The web site for this book at https://github.com/SoftMoore/CPRL contains a number of related resources as follows:

- Java source code that implements the CVM, the target machine for the compiler project.

- Java source code that implements an assembler for the CVM. The compiler project targets assembly language for the CVM rather than the actual virtual machine.

- Java source code for a disassembler; i.e., a program that takes CVM machine code and converts it back into assembly language. This program can be useful in trying to understand how machine code is laid out in memory.

- Java source code or skeletal Java source code for many of the classes described in the book so that students don't need to start from scratch to create their compilers. Much of the code for these classes reveal implementation ideas for other classes whose implementations are either not provided or are only partially provided. Students should begin each phase of their compiler project by trying to understand the related Java source code that is provided.

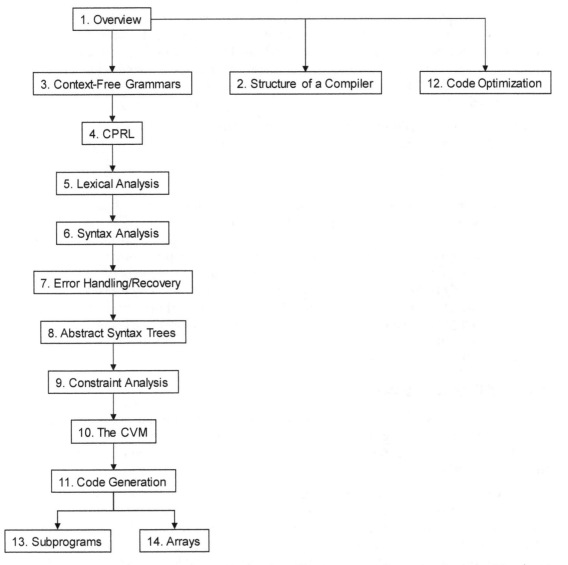

- Java documentation (javadoc) files for the full CPRL compiler as implemented by the author.

- Many examples of correct and incorrect CPRL programs that can be used to test a compiler. The final compiler should reject all incorrect CPRL programs with appropriate error messages, and it should generate semantically equivalent assembly language for all correct CPRL programs. Using the provided assembler and CVM emulator, all correct CPRL programs can be run to compare observed and expected results. Students are strongly encouraged to develop additional test programs.

- Sample Windows command scripts and Bash shell scripts for running and testing various stages of the compiler. For example, rather than trying to compile test programs one at a time, there are command/shell files for running the compiler on all CPRL source files in the current working directory. These command/shell files are useful for testing the compiler against collections of correct and incorrect CPRL programs.

Appendix A provides additional details about the resources available on the course web site and how those resources fit into the overall structure of the course compiler project.

Why Study Compilers?

Relatively few people write commercial compilers, but I believe that the study of compiler design is an important part of a computer science education since compilers and closely related language translators are the primary tools for software development. Having a fundamental knowledge of how compilers actually work can improve one's ability to write good programs. In addition, learning how to write a compiler gives experience on working with a moderately large program, and it makes an excellent case study for software engineering and good program design. And the techniques used in compiler design are useful for other purposes such as writing a test harness, a support tool for process control, or an interpreter for a small, special-purpose language. One of my former students applied compiler technology to a commercial tool for testing software.

Java and Object-Orientation

As indicated in the book's subtitle, the language used herein for implementing a compiler is Java, but other options are certainly possible. In fact, one of the project exercises listed Appendix B is to write the compiler in a different language, and some of my former students have done this.

Since Java is an object-oriented language, then every component of the compiler is structured in terms of classes and objects – the scanner is an object, the parser is an object, tokens are objects, etc. But the full power of "object-orientation" doesn't come into play until Chapter 8, where we introduce the details of abstract syntax trees. The approach used in this book for implementing abstract syntax trees fully exploits Java's object-oriented facilities for inheritance and polymorphism. As an example, consider that code generation for a list of statements looks like the following:

```
for (Statement stmt : statements)
    stmt.emit();
```

The list could include if statements, assignment statements, loop statements, etc., and therefore different statements generate code in different ways. But at the level of programming abstraction shown in this example, we only need to know that each statement has an emit() method that writes out the appropriate object code.

Similarly, the code to check constraints for a list of CPRL subprogram declarations looks like the following:

```
for (SubprogramDecl decl : subprogDecls)
    decl.checkConstraints();
```

Note that the subprogram declarations in the list could be either procedures or functions.

A Note from the Author About Formatting Source Code

Every programmer has his/her preferred way to format and indent source code. Should curly braces be aligned? Should code be indented 2, 3, or 4 spaces? What is the best way to format an `if` statement or a `while` loop? Sometimes arguments about how source code should be formatted seem to take on religious-like fervor. I avoid such arguments, for I have found the **one true way** that all Java source code should be formatted. ☺ But if you are a nonbeliever, please feel free to reformat the Java source code according to your personal tastes.

Acknowledgements

When I was first learning about computers as a young man, I was in awe of compilers. That awe evolved into curiosity, which led to a lot of thought and study about how compilers are constructed, which led to a lot of contemplation about how best to teach an introductory course in compilers, which eventually led to my writing this book. Along the way I was guided and influenced by a number of teachers, colleagues, students, and books. I would like to acknowledge those that have been the most influential on my thinking.

I was first introduced to compilers many years ago when I "unofficially" audited a course on compiler design given by Richard LeBlanc at Georgia Institute of Technology (a.k.a., Georgia Tech). For reasons I can no longer remember, I was unable to take the course for credit, but auditing it, especially under Richard LeBlanc, was enough to motivate me to learn more. I was fortunate enough to have Richard LeBlanc later on for another course on programming language design.

My next introduction to compilers came in a professional development course given by Frank DeRemer and Tom Pennello, with a guest lecture or two by Bill McKeeman. They will not remember me, but I am grateful to have learned more about compilers from teachers and researchers of their calibers.

I have also been inspired by several compiler books, especially two of them that took a pedagogical approach similar to this one. The first book is *Brinch Hansen on Pascal Compilers* by Per Brinch Hansen (Prentice Hall, 1985). That book is a little out of date now, but it had one of the most readable descriptions of compilers when it was first released. A second, much more modern book is *Programming Language Processors in Java: Compilers and Interpreters* by David A. Watt and Deryck F. Brown (Prentice Hall 2000). I followed their treatment of tombstone diagrams when explaining compilers and interpreters in Chapter 1. Years ago I used the Brinch Hansen book as a textbook in my compiler courses, and more recently I used the Watt-Brown book several times when it was first published.

It is important to acknowledge former students at Johns Hopkins University and The Citadel and to thank these institutions for allowing me to explore my ideas about writing compilers. I am particularly grateful to the following students who had the most influence on my thinking about how to teach compilers: Rob Ring, Scott Stanchfield, Zack Aardahl, Ben Hunter, Gordon Finlay, Josh Terry, Davis Jeffords, and Mike Dalpee. Some of the earlier students at Johns Hopkins suffered through my courses as I was trying to crystallize my approach to teaching compilers, and I am grateful for their feedback. They would barely recognize my course if they took it today.

I must also acknowledge Vince Sigillito, who served as Chair of the Computer Science program at the Johns Hopkins Part-Time Programs in Engineering and Applied Science, for first allowing me to teach a course on compilers many years ago. I remember telling Vince that I wanted to teach a course on compilers so that I could learn more about them. He had no objections and even indicated that he had done something similar in the past. Compiler Design has evolved into my favorite course.

I would especially like to acknowledge the following individuals who provided invaluable advice and feedback on the presentation and exposition in this book: Richard LeBlanc, Art Pyster, Shankar Banik, and George Rudolph. I am most appreciative and humble that they spent part of their valuable time to assist me with this effort. In addition, I am grateful to master graphic designer Kevin Metzger, who graciously donated his time and effort to the design of the book cover.

Finally, I would like to acknowledge Kayran Cox Moore, my wife of many years, for proofreading and providing invaluable feedback on several drafts of this book. She might not understand compilers or Java programming, but she has a deep understanding of English grammar and sentence structure, and she has no reservations about correcting my errors or improving my writing. Any grammatical errors remaining in this book are a result of my stubborn refusal to follow her advice. I also want to thank Kayran for being my anchor in life and the source for most of what is good about myself.

Chapter 1
Overview of Compilers and Language Translation

"... language is an instrument of human reason, and not merely a medium for the expression of thought ..." – George Boole

1.1 The Role of Programming Languages

Mathematicians have long understood the importance of a good notation for communication and understanding, and the same can be said for programming languages. Programming languages serve as a means of communication among people as well as between people and machines, and they provide a framework for formulating the software solution to a problem. Moreover, programming languages can influence how we think about software design by making some program structures easier to describe than others. As an example, consider the fact that recursion was not available in early versions of Fortran, making it difficult for a programmer to "invent" a recursive solution to a problem even when such a solution might be the most natural.

In addition, programming languages provide a degree of machine independence and portability as they raise the level of abstraction used in problem solving. A good programming language lets us concentrate more on the problem being solved rather than on mundane implementation issues, thereby making us more productive.

In the early days of object-oriented programming, I was often asked if one could "do" object-oriented programming in C. My response was that of course you could do it in C. You could even do it in assembly language. And if you were very, very patient, you could do it in 0's and 1's. The question is not *if* it can be done but how long it would take you to do it – how much support is provided by the programming language versus how much has to be implemented or simulated by the programmer.

1.2 Translators and Compilers

In the context of programming languages, a **translator** is a program that accepts as input text written in one language (called the source language) and converts it into a semantically equivalent representation in a second language (called the target or object language). If the source language is a high-level language (HLL) and the target language is a low-level language (LLL), then the translator is called a **compiler**.

The figure below shows a simplified view of the compile/execute process as a two-step sequence. In reality, there can be other intermediate steps involved in creating an executable program. For example, most compilers do not actually create an executable program, but rather a **linker** is used to combine several user-developed and system modules into an executable program. Compilers could be used to create the individual modules used by the linker. Additionally, another system utility called a **loader** would likely be used to copy the object program into main memory.

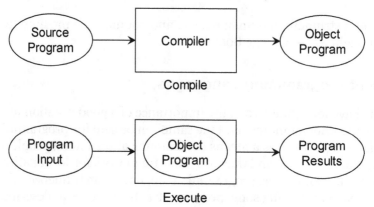

It is important to distinguish between the definition of a programming language and the implementation of that programming language in the form of a compiler. For example, some languages do not formally specify the maximum number of characters allowed in an identifier or the sizes for basic integer and floating point types. Instead, the compiler implementer is free to make these kinds of decisions, and implementation decisions are often driven by the compiler implementation approaches and the target hardware architecture; e.g., an integer could be the "natural" size of integer for the target machine, which means that it could be 16 bits on one computer, 32 bits on another computer, and 64 bits on yet a third computer.

The Role of Compilers

A compiler must first verify that the source program is valid with respect to the source language definition. If the source program is valid, the compiler must produce a **semantically equivalent** and reasonably efficient machine language program for the target computer. If the source program is not valid, the compiler must provide meaningful feedback to the programmer as to the nature and location of any errors. Feedback on possible multiple errors is usually desirable.

Other Language Processors

While the focus of this book is on compilers, it is important to recognize that there are a number of other language processors that perform similar functions. Following is a brief discussion of some related language processors. Most are implemented using approaches similar to those of compilers.

An **assembler** is a translator that translates symbolic assembly language into machine code. Since assembly language is essentially a low-level representation of machine code, then the implementation of an assembler is usually much simpler than that of a compiler.

A **high-level language translator** (a.k.a., a **transpiler**) translates from one high-level language to another. For example, since C compilers were rather ubiquitous at the time, Bjarne Stroustrup originally implemented C++ as a translator to C. C++ programs were first translated to C, and then the C versions of the programs were compiled. Such an approach not only simplified the implementation of C++, but it made C++ immediately available on a lot of different computer systems. Due to the popularity of JavaScript for internet applications, today there are many languages that provide an option for JavaScript as a target language – examples include Dart, TypeScript, Kotlin, and Scala. In addition, there exist third party translators to JavaScript from several other languages such as Ruby, Python, and Java.

A "pure" **interpreter** translates/executes source program instructions immediately (e.g., one line at a time). The interpreter does not analyze and translate the entire program before starting to run; rather, translation is performed one line at a time as the program is being executed, and translation occurs every time the program is run. The source program is basically treated as another form of input data to the interpreter. Whereas compilation can be viewed as a two-step process (first compile, then execute), interpretation can be viewed essentially as a one-step process (execute), as illustrated below.

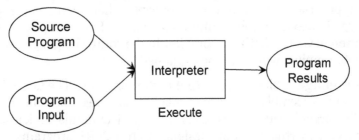

Examples of interpreters include most interactive command-line processors such as the bash shell (which can also run shell scripts), the Windows command line interpreter (which can also run command files), and relational database interpreters for SQL. Early versions of LISP and BASIC were interpreted, and many language implementations come with a read-eval-print loop that is essentially an interpreter for language expressions.

In general, compilers provide earlier and better error detection, and the compiled programs generally run much faster, while interpreters can provide more rapid feedback to the user. Interpreters are sometimes preferred for prototyping and for highly interactive systems if the performance penalty can be tolerated.

There are other variations on these themes. For example, Java is compiled to an intermediate, low-level form (Java byte code) that gets interpreted by the JVM. In addition, Java uses a **Just-In-Time (JIT) Compiler**, which translates Java bytecode into native machine code at run time. The translation is performed for methods that are called frequently, and thereafter the JVM uses the compiled code directly instead of interpreting it. Use of the JIT compiler is optional, but it is enabled by default. Additionally, profiling is used to discover methods (hot spots) where additional optimization can be performed. Performance improvements can be significant for methods that are executed repeatedly.

An **emulator** or **virtual machine** is an interpreter for a machine instruction set. The machine being "emulated" may be real or hypothetical. The JVM is an example of an emulator for a hypothetical Java machine. Similar to real machines, emulators typically use an instruction pointer (program counter) and a fetch-decode-execute cycle. Running a program on an emulator is functionally equivalent to running the program directly on the machine, but the program will experience some performance degradation on the emulator. A real machine can be viewed as an interpreter implemented in hardware. Conversely, an emulator can be viewed as a machine implemented in software.

Writing a Compiler

Writing a compiler involves 3 languages as follows:

1. The **source language**, which is the input into the compiler. Examples include C++, Java, or CPRL, the language that we will use for our compiler project.

2. The **implementation language**, which is the language that the compiler is written in. This book uses Java as the implementation language, but other languages would have been just as appropriate. One interesting concept is that, for many compilers, the source language is also the implementation language. For example, a C++ compiler might be written in C++. Writing a compiler in the source language uses an approach known as bootstrapping, which will be explained later.

3. The **target language**, which is the output of the compiler. The target language for a compiler is usually assembly language or machine language, possibly for a virtual computer. The target language for the compiler project in this book is assembly language for CVM, a virtual machine designed to run CPRL programs.

1.3 Tombstone Diagrams

Tombstone diagrams provide a convenient notation to illustrate the three languages involved in writing a compiler.

This first diagram illustrates that program P is expressed in language L. L could be a high-level language, or, after compiling the program, L could be a machine language.

The second diagram illustrates simply that we have a machine (computer) M.

The third diagram illustrates an S-to-T translator expressed in language L. If L is a high-level language, then, after compilation, we would have a second version of this diagram, with L replaced by a machine language.

The figures below show several specific examples of these diagrams with actual program names, programming languages, and machines.

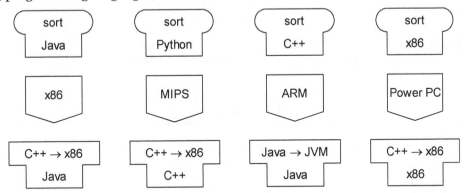

By themselves, these diagrams don't say a whole lot. The real power of these diagrams to illustrate concepts comes when we combine them. For example, suppose we have a program P that has been compiled to run on a particular machine M. We could illustrate the idea of a program running on a computer as follows:

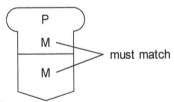

As indicated, the machine that the program has been compiled to run on must be the same as the machine actually running the program. So, for example, the combination below on the left is valid, but the combination on the right is not.

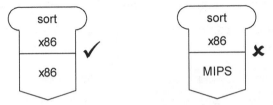

Now let's consider the idea of translating a program P, where the program is written in language S and the translator from language S to language T runs on machine M. The result of running the translator would be a semantically equivalent program in language T. If S were a high-level language and T were a low-level language, then the translator would, in fact, be a compiler.

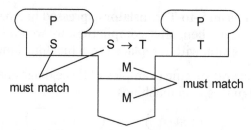

Let's illustrate with a sort program written in C++ using a compiler that targets an x86 computer. Then the two-step compile/execute process would look as follows:

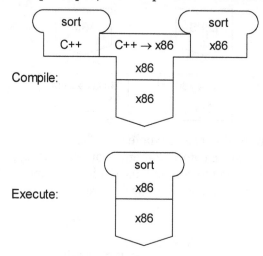

Cross-Compiler

A **cross-compiler** is a compiler that runs on one machine and produces target code for a different machine. The output of a cross-compiler must be downloaded to the target machine for execution. Cross-compilers are commonly used for embedded systems; for example, a small computer that might be embedded in a thermostat or an automobile engine. Cross-compilers are also common for developing applications for mobile phones.

Using tombstone diagrams, we can illustrate the idea of a cross-compiler as follows:

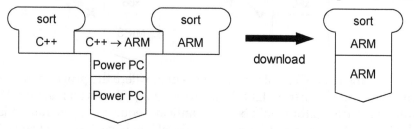

Two-stage Compiler

We mentioned earlier that Bjarne Stroustrup originally implemented C++ as a translator to C. C++ programs were first translated to C, and then the C versions of the programs were compiled. As shown below, we can visualize this process using tombstone diagrams as a two-stage compiler.

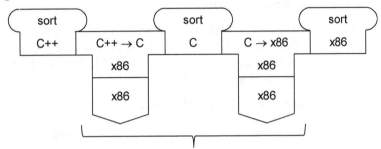

Functionally equivalent to a C++-to-x86 compiler

Note that the middle parts of the diagram could be viewed as being functionally equivalent to a C++-to-x86 compiler.

Similarly, a compiler that targets assembly language is essentially a two-stage compiler, where the first stage translates from the source language to assembly language, and the second stage translates from assembly language to machine code.

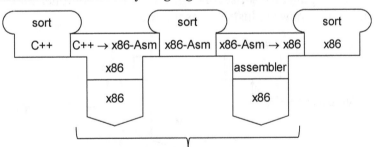

Functionally equivalent to a C++-to-x86 compiler

1.4 Bootstrapping a Compiler

It is common to write a compiler in the language being compiled; e.g., writing a C++ compiler in C++. Doing so has several advantages as follows:

- The compiler itself provides a non-trivial test of the language being compiled.

- Only one language needs to be learned by compiler developers.

- Only one compiler needs to be maintained.

- If changes are made in the compiler to improve performance, then recompiling the compiler will improve compiler performance.

For a new programming language, how do we write a compiler in that language? This appears to be "a chicken and an egg problem" in that we can't write a compiler for the new language unless we already have a compiler for the new language. The problem can be solved by a process known as **bootstrapping**.

Let's make the problem more specific. Suppose that we want to build a compiler for a programming language, say C#, that will run on machine M, and assume that we already have a compiler for a different language, say C, that runs on M. Furthermore, we desire ultimately that the source code for the C# compiler be C#.

The following tombstone diagrams illustrate this situation:

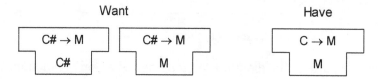

Bootstrapping a Compiler: Step 1

Start by selecting a subset of C# that is sufficiently complete for writing a compiler. We will call the subset C#/0 (i.e., the zero subset of C#). Now write a compiler for C#/0 in C and compile it. What we have now is illustrated as follows:

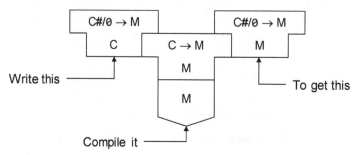

Bootstrapping a Compiler: Step 2

Now we write another compiler for C#/0, only this time we write it in the language C#/0. Then we compile our new C#/0 compiler using the compiler obtained from step 1.

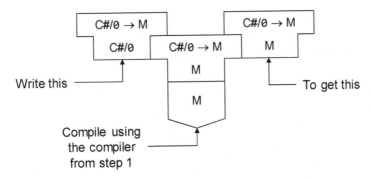

Write this —————

To get this

Compile using
the compiler
from step 1

At this point we no longer need the C compiler.

Bootstrapping a Compiler: Step 3

As a final step in the bootstrapping process, we write the full compiler for C# in C#/0, and then we compile it using the compiler obtained from step 2.

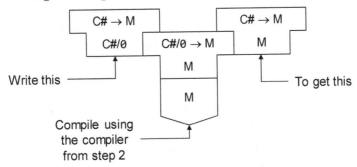

Write this —————

To get this

Compile using
the compiler
from step 2

At this point we have exactly what we wanted – a C# compiler for machine M written in C#.

Efficiency of a Compiler

When we talk about the efficiency or performance of a program, we commonly refer to the speed at which it executes. The speed can be in absolute terms such as 12.31 seconds, or it can be in be in terms of asymptotic growth based on the size of the input. The latter is usually expressed using the big-Oh notation such as $O(n)$ or $O(n \log n)$. Note that efficiency can also refer to the program's use of memory, and for application domains such as embedded systems, the efficient use of memory can be more important than the program's speed since it can affect product cost.

When we talk about the efficiency of a compiler, there are two aspects to consider: the efficiency of the compiler itself as a program and the efficiency of the object code generated by the compiler. For example, a compiler could run quickly but generate object code that is not very efficient.

Now suppose you have a compiler for a language (say C++) written in that language. If you modify the compiler to improve efficiency of the generated object code, then you can recompile the compiler to obtain a more efficient compiler. This idea is illustrated in the following diagram.

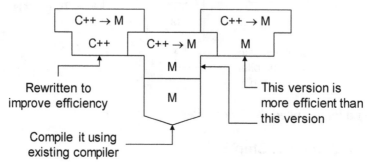

1.5 Interpreters

The tombstone diagram for an interpreter for language S expressed in language L is depicted as a simple rectangle. Note that L could be a machine language.

S
L

Here are three interpreter examples. The last two represent compiled versions that are ready to run on a specific machine.

Basic
Java

Lisp
x86

JVM
x86-64

The diagram on the right illustrates a Basic interpreter running on an x86 machine.

Basic
x86
x86

This is functionally equivalent to a "Basic" machine; i.e., a machine that executes Basic commands in hardware.

Basic

We can use the Basic interpreter to run a sort program written in Basic.

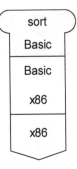

If we ignore just-in-time compilation, we can think of Java programs as essentially being interpreted by the JVM. Thus, the compile/execute steps involved in using Java can be illustrated as follows:

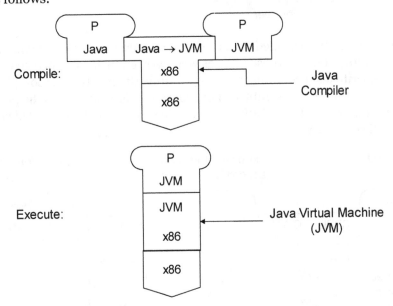

1.6 The Compiler Project

The compiler project outlined in this book uses a relatively small source language called CPRL (an acronym for for Compiler PRoject Language), which was designed for teaching the basic concepts of compiler design. The eventual target machine is a hypothetical machine called CVM (for CPRL Virtual Machine), but in order to simplify the process of writing a compiler, the target language for the compiler project is assembly language for CVM, not the actual machine language. It is easier to write a compiler for an assembly language than to write it for an actual machine, even a simple machine.

We denote the project's target language by CVM/A, where the "A" stands for assembly language. Thus, the project is to write a CPRL-to-CVM/A compiler in Java. When you

compile your compiler, you will have a CPRL-to-CVM/A compiler that runs on a Java
virtual machine. The process of writing and compiling a CPRL-to-CVM/A compiler is
illustrated as follows:

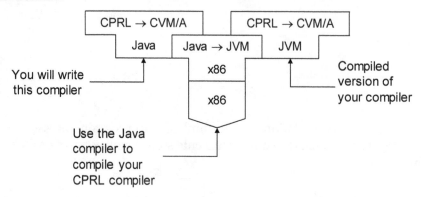

Two important utilities are provided with the book resources, a CVM assembler and a CVM
interpreter (emulator). Both of these utilities were written in Java. Once your compiler is
working, you can write test programs in CPRL, compile them with your compiler, and then
assemble them with the CVM assembler. The diagram below illustrates the process of
starting with a program written in CPRL and creating a compiled/assembled version of the
program that will run on CVM.

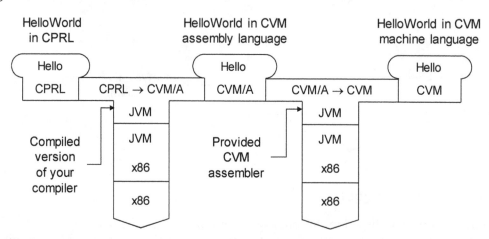

You can then execute your program using the CVM interpreter, as illustrated in the diagram
below.

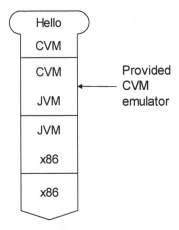

The program illustrated in the two diagrams above is the typical first program in a new language that prints "Hello, world." to standard output. Using the naming conventions outlined in the course project, the actual file names for the three versions of the program would be Hello.cprl (for the CPRL version), Hello.asm (for the assembly language version), and Hello.obj (for the CVM version).

1.7 Essential Terms and Concepts

assembler	bootstrapping
compiler	compile/execute process
CPRL	CVM
cross-compiler	efficiency of a compiler
emulator/virtual machine	high-level language translator/transpiler
implementation language (for a compiler)	interpreter
Java bytecode	JIT
JVM	linker
source language (for a compiler)	target language (for a compiler)
tombstone diagrams	translator
transpiler	two-stage compiler

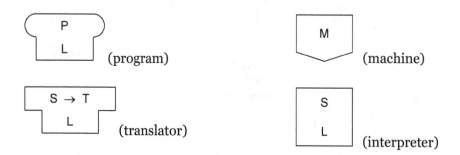

1.8 Exercises

1. Name and briefly describe the three languages involved in writing a compiler.

2. Describe several advantages of writing a compiler in the language being compiled (i.e., writing a C++ compiler in C++).

3. Explain the difference between a compiler and an interpreter. What are the relative advantages and disadvantages of each?

4. Draw a tombstone diagram representing a Fortran compiler for an x86 computer that is written in C++. Assuming that the C++ compiler runs on an x86 computer, draw a tombstone diagram for the "compiled" version of the Fortran compiler.

5. Describe the basic steps in bootstrapping a compiler. Assume that you have a C++ compiler for an x86 machine and that you want to write a Swift compiler for that machine. Use tombstone diagrams as part of your description.

6. A new computer called MACH-1 is being created, and you want to write a Kotlin compiler for the MACH-1. Assuming that you already have a C++ compiler for an x86 machine, explain how to use your existing C++ compiler to create a Kotlin compiler for a MACH-1 machine. Use appropriate tombstone diagrams as part of your explanation. Here are a couple to help you get started.

Hint: Review the concepts of cross-compiling and bootstrapping.

Chapter 2
Structure of a Compiler

The structure of a compiler generally has a form as illustrated in the diagram below. Details of the components or phases shown in this example will be covered in subsequent chapters, but here we present a general overview of this structure.

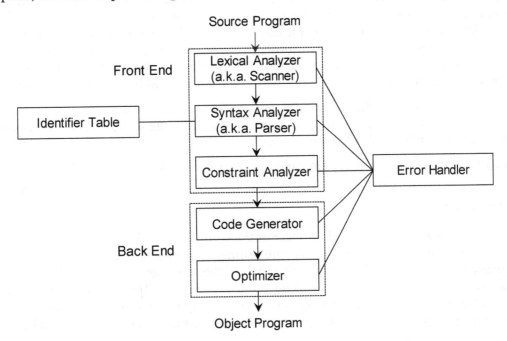

Think of the diagram as a general set of functions that have to be performed, and don't take the actual structure literally. Not every phase is required to be separated out as a distinct collection of code modules in the compiler; e.g., syntax analysis and constraint analysis might be intertwined. Also, optimization might actually be performed in several places within the compilation process.

Not shown in the diagram above is the fact that most compilers use one or more intermediate representations during the compilation process. Common intermediate forms include abstract syntax trees, which provide a high-level intermediate representation of the basic structure of the program, and low-level intermediate code similar to machine code but usually machine independent. Some compilers use both abstract syntax trees and low-level intermediate code. Note that some optimizations can be performed on the intermediate representations as well as on the final machine dependent object code.

The lexical analyzer, syntax analyzer, and constraint analyzer – the first three components shown in the diagram – are collectively called the "front end" of the compiler. The front end performs analysis of the source code to determine whether or not the source code is valid according to the definition of the language being compiled. If the source code is valid, then the front end must determine its intended effect. The front end is heavily dependent on the source language but relatively independent of the target machine. The front end can include some high-level optimizations, but most optimizations are handled later in the compilation process.

The code generator and optimizer – the last two components shown in the diagram – are collectively called the "back end" of the compiler. The role of the back end is to generate efficient machine code that is semantically equivalent to the source code. The back end is heavily dependent on the target machine but relatively independent of source language. Most compiler books would reverse the order of code generator and optimizer from that shown in the above diagram, but this diagram reflects the compiler project as outlined in this book, where the code optimization is performed at the CVM level after code generation.

We sometimes summarize the roles of the front end and back end by saying that the primary focus of the front end is *analysis* of the source program and the primary focus of the back end is *synthesis* of the object program.

Now let's examine each of the components of a compiler in a little more detail.

2.1 Scanner

The lexical analyzer is often called the lexer or the scanner. We will use the term scanner primarily in the remainder of this book. The scanner identifies the basic lexical units of the language, which are called the tokens or symbols of the language. These lexical units are usually defined in terms of patterns called regular expressions. The scanner also usually removes extraneous white space and comments since they play no role in subsequent analysis or code generation, and it reports any errors encountered in the source code.

The diagram below illustrates the work of the scanner when it encounters a simple statement. Note that the scanner breaks the assignment statement into 5 lexical units and records the position (line number and column number) of each lexical unit.

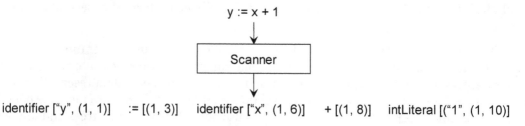

Chapter 5 provides a more complete explanation of the process of lexical analysis or scanning.

2.2 Parser

Using the lexical units produced by the scanner as input, the syntax analyzer or parser verifies that the grammatical rules of the language are satisfied. The grammar of a language is based on patterns called context-free grammars (a.k.a. BNF or Backus–Naur form). The parser also constructs an intermediate representation of the program that can be used for further analysis and code generation. The diagram below shows the parser constructing an abstract syntax tree (AST) for an assignment statement. The AST for an assignment statement consists of the left side, which in this case is an identifier, and the right side, which in this case is an adding expression.

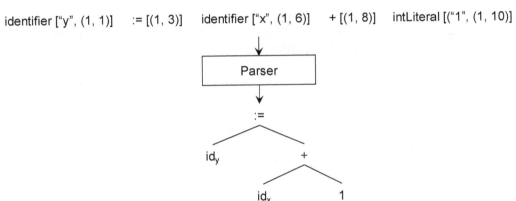

Chapter 6 provides a more complete explanation of the process of syntax analysis or parsing while Chapter 8 provides a more complete explanation of abstract syntax trees.

2.3 Constraint Analyzer

The grammatical rules of a programming language are expressed in a notation called a context-free grammar, and the parser verifies that a program conforms to those rules. However, there are some syntax-like features that can't be expressed in a context-free grammar. For example, suppose that we have a rule that states that a variable must be declared exactly once before it is used; e.g., in an assignment statement. Other rules involve scopes for identifiers or compatible types for an assignment statement. Many such rules can't be expressed (or can't be expressed succinctly) in context-free grammars. Most such rules involve scope or type analysis. Usually the constraint analyzer just checks for validity, with little or no modification of current representation.

Chapter 9 is devoted to the process of constraint analysis. Constraint analysis is sometimes referred to as analysis of static semantics, but constraint analysis seems to be a more appropriate term.

2.4 Code Generator

The role of the code generator is to translate intermediate code into machine code or assembly language for the target machine. The code generator encapsulates detailed knowledge of the target machine and is, therefore, highly machine dependent. The following diagram shows the code generator translating an abstract syntax tree for an assignment statement into assembly language for the CVM, a stack-based virtual machine. Code generation is simplified since the CVM is somewhat simpler than a real machine, and it is further simplified by allowing generation of assembly language rather than actual machine code.

Chapter 11 covers code generation in more detail, with emphasis on generating code for the CVM. Some of the exercises in Appendix B discuss alternative targets such as the JVM or assembly language for the Intel x86 architecture.

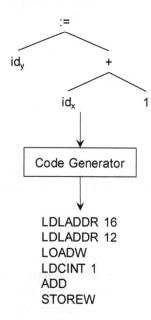

2.5 Optimizer

The optimizer is concerned with improving the run-time performance of the object code. As discussed in the previous chapter, performance can involve both the speed at which the object code runs and/or the amount of memory used by the program. Some optimizations can improve both, but more often there is a tradeoff between the two goals. Some compilers permit compiler directives or pragmas, where the programmer can provide guidance to the compiler as to how to resolve the tradeoffs.

The optimizer deals with issues such as allocation of machine registers, time/space performance of the code, moving invariant computations outside of a loop, and compile-time arithmetic. It is possible to perform optimization for different representations (e.g., intermediate versus object code optimizations) and at different levels (e.g., local versus global optimizations).

The diagram below shows the optimizer replacing instructions that "add 1" to an integer variable with instructions to "increment" the variable. Most target architectures would support an increment instruction, and using such an instruction would result in minor improvement in both time and space performance of the object code.

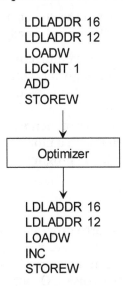

Chapter 12 provides additional details about code optimization.

2.6 Tables and Maps

Tables and maps are used in various places by compilers. Some parsing techniques use table-driven parsers, where tables drive the compilation process. The basic idea is that the grammar is used as input to a tool that generates the tables, and then the tables are used as input to the parser.

The approach described in this book does not use a table-driven parser, but we will use maps (a.k.a., associative arrays) to record information about identifiers such as whether the identifier represents an integer variable, the name of an array type, or the name of a procedure. Most compilers will use something similar, which is often referred to as an identifier table/map or a symbol table/map.

2.7 Error Handler

The error handler reports the nature and location of errors. Error messages can provide important feedback to the programs since most of the time, a compiler is used to compile incorrect programs. The error handler usually tries to perform some type of error recovery so that multiple errors can be detected and reported. But, as we will learn in Chapter 7, error recovery can be difficult, and sometimes a compiler will produce a misleading error message. Most software developers learn quickly that all errors reported after the first error are suspect and should be approached with caution.

Here is an example of an error message generated by the project compiler when testing it against one of the incorrect CPRL programs.

```
*** Syntax error detected near line 9, character 4:
    Expecting ";" but found "Reserved word: else" instead.
```

Some compilers dispense with error recovery altogether, stopping with the first error. First released in 1983, Turbo Pascal was a blazingly fast compiler that used this approach, stopping at the first error encountered and bringing up an editor with the cursor positioned at the point of error. It was convenient and quick to fix the first error and then recompile. Today, many Integrated Development Environments (IDEs) have built-in compilers (or at least syntax checkers) that accomplish this in a more integrated fashion. The Eclipse IDE will flag Java errors and warnings while the program is being typed.

2.8 Passes

A **pass** is a complete traversal of the source program or an equivalent intermediate representation. A pass can involve disk I/O (i.e., reading and/or writing a file to disk), but the intermediate representation can be in memory. Some authors restrict the definition of compiler pass to a traversal that involves disk I/O, but we will use a more general definition. Using our definition, code that traverses the in-memory AST representation for a program will be considered a pass.

A single-pass compiler makes only one traversal of the source program, whereas a multi-pass compiler makes several traversals. A language must be carefully crafted in order to permit a single-pass compiler. For example, if an identifier can be used before it is formally defined, then it can be very difficult to implement a single-pass compiler. The original definition of Pascal was designed for single-pass compilation, and some of the earlier Pascal compilers were implemented using a single pass. However, most modern languages are so complex as to preclude compilation using a single pass.

There are a number of advantages for using multiple passes in a compiler including increased modularity and improved ability to perform global analysis (optimization). Plus, multi-pass compilers often offer greater opportunity to exploit concurrency and multiprocessor architectures. And it is possible for a multi-pass compiler to use less memory at run time if the passes are overlaid, but this advantage has less significance for most modern computers with large physical memories and virtual memories.

Disadvantages of multi-pass compilers include slower compilation times, especially if extra disk I/O is involved, and they are usually larger (in terms of source lines of code) and more complex. In addition, a multi-pass compiler requires design of intermediate language(s)/representation(s).

The compiler project described in this book uses three passes as follows:

- Pass 1: Reads/analyzes source text and produces an intermediate representation (AST's)

- Pass 2: Performs constraint analysis on the intermediate representation

- Pass 3: Generates assembly language for the CVM

Technically the assembler is not part of the compiler project since it is provided with the book resources, but the assembler also makes several passes, including some passes to perform optimizations.

2.9 Compiler Design Goals

As with any substantial software or engineering project, designing a compiler involves tradeoffs among potentially conflicting goals. However, there is one goal for a compiler that can't be compromised – the goal of reliability.

Compiler Design Goal #1: A compiler must be error free.

Since writing a compiler is a large, human effort, this goal might not be fully achieved, but it should always be first and foremost. Software developers must be able to trust that the compiler will produce semantically equivalent object code.

Other possible goals for a compiler include the following:

- Modularity/maintainability. The goal is that the compiler will support future changes. Examples include new features or enhancements to the source language or changes in the compiler operating environment such as a new release of an operating system.

- Portability. The goal is to design the compiler in such a way as to minimize the amount of work needed to port from one environment to a different environment. This goal is closely related to the one above.

- Fast object programs.

- Small object programs. This goal is especially important for embedded systems, where the size of the object code and affect the cost or usability of the product containing the software.

- Fast compilation times. This is often a requirement during prototyping or in the early stages of software development. It is also a useful goal for compilers used in academic environments, where students are learning how to program for the first time.

- Small compiler size.

- Good error diagnostics and error recovery capabilities.
- Minimize compiler development time, so that the compiler is available as quickly as possible.

2.10 Essential Terms and Concepts

abstract syntax tree	back end (of a compiler)
code generator	constraint analyzer
error handler	front end (of a compiler)
identifier table	intermediate representation
optimizer	parser/syntax analyzer
pass (of a compiler)	scanner/lexical analyzer/lexer

2.11 Exercises

1. Name and describe the phases/components of a compiler.

2. What is the "front end" of a compiler? What is the "back end" of a compiler?

3. Discuss the relative advantages and disadvantages of a single-pass compiler versus a multi-pass compiler.

4. Which compiler goals from Section 2.9 might be more desirable for a compiler used in a teaching/learning environment such as academia? Which compiler goals might be more desirable in a production environment for commercial software?

Chapter 3
Context-Free Grammars

3.1 Specifying a Programming Language

The definition of a programming language must address the specification of three main characteristics of the language, which we will refer to as syntax, contextual constraints, and semantics (what actually happens at run time) of the language. The specification of these characteristics can be formal, using a precise notation similar to mathematics, or informal, using descriptions in English or some other natural language. The tradeoff is that a formal notation, while precise, requires an effort to learn and fully understand the notation itself independent of the programming language being defined. On the other hand, while an English description might seem easier to understand, it can be difficult to make such a description sufficiently precise. The approach used in this book follows a common practice of using a formal notation to specify syntax and informal specifications for contextual constraints and semantics.

The syntax of a language is a definition of the basic language symbols (or tokens) and the allowed structure of symbols to form programs. For example, what is the structure of an if statement, a variable declaration, a function definition, etc.? It is important for the syntax to be specified precisely, and for that purpose we will use a formal notation called a context-free grammar. Essentially all programming language definitions use context-free grammars to define the language syntax, and while there are some alternatives for the details of the notation, it is usually relatively straightforward to switch from one notation to the other.

While context-free grammars are powerful, they are, well, "context free," and there are language requirements that can't be expressed easily or can't be expressed at all in a context-free grammar. These language requirements essentially require some knowledge of the "context" in which they appear, and we call these requirements contextual constraints (a.k.a., static semantics). Contextual constraints consist primarily of type and scope rules, but they can include other miscellaneous rules that aren't directly related to types and scopes. An example of a contextual constraint would be that a loop's "while" expression must have type Boolean. Note that some languages allow numeric expressions in this context, for example, with zero corresponding to false and nonzero corresponding to true.

Finally, the semantics of a programming language address the meaning or behavior of programs when run on a real or virtual machine.

As illustrated in the diagram below, in general, each programming language is "approximated" by a context-free grammar. The outer cloud represents all possible programs that could be submitted to a compiler, including programs that are not valid according to the language definition. The outer circle inside the cloud represents all programs with valid syntax. As represented by the inner-most circle, contextual constraints further restrict the approximating language to coincide with the desired language. It is possible for a program to be valid with respect to syntax but not with respect to contextual constraints. In terms of the diagram, programs having valid syntax but failing to satisfy contextual constraints fall in the region between the two circles.

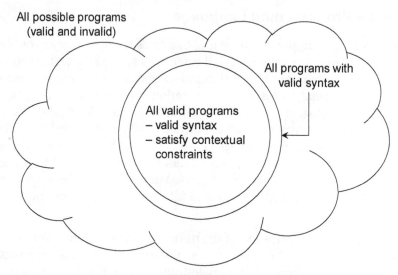

Here are two examples in CPRL that illustrate this point. Both examples are valid with respect to the context-free grammar that defines the CPRL syntax, but in the first example, the variable y has not been declared, which is required in CPRL.

```
var x : Integer;
begin
    y := 5;
end.
```

In this next example, an attempt is made to assign an integer value to a character variable, which is not permitted in CPRL.

```
var c : Char;
begin
    c := -3;
end.
```

3.2 Context-Free Grammars

A context-free grammar, also known as a Backus-Naur Form (BNF) grammar or simply BNF, provides a formal notation for specifying the syntax of a programming language. A context-free grammar is sometimes called a syntactic metalanguage since it uses a finite notation to formally define the syntax for a programming language. Context-free grammars show the structure of programs in the language, and they have been used extensively for almost every programming language since the definition of the programming language ALGOL 60. They also drive scanner and parser development. For example, in our compiler project, many of the rules in the grammar are converted systematically into methods in the parser. Other approaches to parser development use compiler tools (so called "compiler compilers") that read the grammar as input and produce various parts of the parts of the scanner and parser, essentially automating much of the work outlined in Chapters 5 and 6.

There are many different (but similar) notations for defining context-free grammars. The notation that we use to define CPRL is a variation of a form called an *extended* context-free grammar or EBNF.

A **context-free grammar** (CFG) consists of four major components:

1. A finite set T of terminal symbols (a.k.a. the vocabulary) that represent the symbols appearing in the language. Examples include 2, a, i, <, =, etc. These are the atoms of the language. Although these characters are not truly atomic since we can break them down into zeros and ones using a binary character code such as ASCII or Unicode, for the purposes of a context-free grammar we can consider them to be atomic. In addition, terminal symbols don't have to be single characters. For example, the keyword `while` or the operator `<=` could be considered terminal symbols.

2. A finite set N of nonterminal symbols that represent the syntactic classes in the language. Examples include `expression`, `statement`, `loopStmt`, etc.

3. A start symbol (a.k.a., goal symbol), which is one of one of the nonterminal symbols, often something like `program` or `compilationUnit`.

4. A finite set of rules that define how syntax phrases are structured from terminal and nonterminal symbols. These rules are often called "syntax equations," "production rules," or simply "productions." They characterize possible substitutions for nonterminal symbols.

Format of Grammar Rules

Rules have the following form:

- An equals symbol "=" separates the left side of the rule from the right side.

- The left side of a rule is a single nonterminal symbol. Furthermore, we require that every nonterminal symbol appear on the left side of exactly one rule.

- The right side of a rule is a sequence of terminal symbols, nonterminal symbols, and other special symbols as defined below.

- A period "." is used to terminate rules.

ASCII, Unicode, and Character Encodings

The following is a very brief and overly simplistic discussion of character encodings.

There have been several standard character encodings in widespread use over the years. One of the earliest was the American Standard Code for Information Interchange or simply ASCII, which used seven bits to encode the English alphabet, digits, punctuation characters, and a number of control characters such as newline. Since most computer memories and external storage devices were organized around 8-bit bytes, ASCII was later extended by the ISO/IEC 8859 series of standards for 8-bit character encodings, the most popular of which was ISO/IEC 8859-1. The ISO/IEC 8859 series have now been largely replaced by Unicode, which originally used a maximum of 16 bits (two bytes) to encode characters but can now use up to 32-bits (four bytes). Unicode is capable of representing essentially all of the characters used in different languages throughout the world as well as many historic scripts such as Egyptian Hieroglyphs.

The current Unicode standard defines more than 135,000 characters and several different ways to encode them. UTF-8 is a variable length encoding that uses a minimum of one byte to encode a character but can use up to four bytes for some characters. All characters in the ASCII subset are encoded in a single byte. UTF-8 is the most popular encoding for the Internet.

UCS-2, an older two byte encoding, was a popular encoding when Unicode was first developed and the number of Unicode characters was small enough that they could all be encoded using only 16 bits. UCS-2 is still in use today, but it has essentially been superseded by UTF-16, which encodes each character using either two bytes or four bytes. Both UCS-2 and UTF-16 use the same encodings for characters that are encoded in only two bytes. While file systems can use different encodings, internally Java uses UTF-16 at run time for characters and strings.

UTF-32 is a fixed length encoding that uses exactly 32 bits for each character. UTF-32 is not widely used since it requires significantly more space than other encodings.

All characters in the so-called Basic Multilingual Plane (BMP) of Unicode can be represented by 16 bits, and for simplicity CPRL, the source language defined in this book, restricts characters to this subset of Unicode. Each character in the Unicode BMP subset can be specified using four hexadecimal digits. The Unicode standard uses the notation U+xxxx to represent such a character, while Java and many other programming languages use the notation \uxxxx. For example, English capital "A" is represented as U+0041 or \u0041, and Greek capital sigma "Σ" is represented by U+03A3 or \u03A3. Characters in the range \u0000 to \u007F are the original ASCII characters.

Here is an example of the rule for assignment statements in the context-free grammar for CPRL.

```
assignmentStmt = variable ":=" expression ";" .
```

In this rule, `assignmentStmt` is the single nonterminal symbol on the left side of the rule, and the right side of the rule contains nonterminal symbols `variable` and `expression` plus terminal symbols `:=` (assignment operator) and `;` (semicolon).

Beyond terminal symbols and nonterminal symbols, the right side of a rule can make use of extra symbols to indicate notions of grouping, alternatives, repetition, and optional. It is the use of these additional symbols that makes the grammar *extended*. Our notation for context-free grammars adopts the following extra symbols:

- A vertical bar "|" for alternation (read "or" or "or alternatively").

- Parentheses "(" and ")" for grouping.

- An asterisk "*" as a postfix operator to indicate that a syntax expression may be repeated zero or more times.

- A plus sign "+" as a postfix operator to indicate that a syntax expression may be repeated one or more times. Since "one or more" is equivalent to "one" followed by "zero or more," we can write `(E)+` as `E(E)*`, and therefore technically we do not ever need to use a plus sign as a postfix operator. In general, it is probably the least used operator for context-free grammars. For the CPRL grammar, a plus sign is used in only one place – the definition of an integer literal, which is given as follows:

  ```
  intLiteral = ( digit )+ .
  ```

  We could have just as easily written this rule as

  ```
  intLiteral = digit ( digit )* .
  ```

- A question mark "?" as a postfix operator to indicate that a syntax expression is optional (i.e., it may be repeated zero or one times).

In addition to the above requirements, it is common to adopt certain conventions when writing grammar rules:

- Terminal symbols are quoted; i.e., we will use quotation marks to distinguish terminal symbols from nonterminal symbols.

- Set T consists of all terminal symbols appearing in the rules.

- Set N consists of all nonterminals appearing in the rules.

- The start symbol is the left-hand side of the first rule.

Following these conventions it is possible to specify a context-free grammar simply by specifying only the set of rules. We don't need to formally specify the set of terminal symbols, the set of nonterminal symbols, or the start symbols since that information can be derived by examining the set of rules.

> The CPRL grammar in Appendix D does not quite conform to these conventions since there
> are a few keywords that are reserved for possible use in the future. These keywords are
> essentially terminal symbols that do not appear in any rule.

Appendix D uses an extended grammar to specify the syntax for CPRL. Here are some of
the rules listed in this appendix.

```
program = declarativePart statementPart "." .
declarativePart = initialDecls subprogramDecls .
initialDecls = ( initialDecl )* .
initialDecl = constDecl | arrayTypeDecl | varDecl .
constDecl = "const" constId ":=" literal ";" .
literal = intLiteral | charLiteral | stringLiteral | booleanLiteral .
booleanLiteral = "true" | "false" .
arrayTypeDecl = "type" typeId "=" "array"
    "[" intConstValue "]" "of" typeName ";" .
varDecl = "var" identifiers ":" typeName ";" .
identifiers = identifier ( "," identifier )* .
... (See Appendix D)
```

The first rule says that a program consists of a declarative part (`declarativePart`) followed
by a statement part (`statementPart`) followed by a period. The nonterminal symbol
`program` is considered to be the start symbol since it appears on the left side of the first rule.
Both `declarativePart` and `statementPart` are nonterminal symbols and are further
defined by other rules in the grammar. The period in quotation marks is a terminal symbol
indicating that a period must appear at the end of a program, whereas the period not in
quotation marks at the end of the rule simply terminates the rule.

The second rule says that a declarative part (`declarativePart`) consists of initial
declarations (`initialDecls`) followed by subprogram declarations (`subprogramDecls`).
Reading further into the grammar we see that both the initial declarations and subprogram
declarations can be empty, which means that the declarative part is essentially optional.

The third rule says that the nonterminal symbol `initialDecls` (note the use of the plural
form) is simply a list of zero or more `initialDecl` (note the singular form) symbols, where
an initial declaration (`initialDecl`) is defined by the fourth rule as being either a constant
declaration (`constDecl`), an array type declaration (`arrayTypeDecl`), or a variable
declaration (`varDecl`).

The last rule listed above defines the nonterminal `identifiers` as a list of `identifier`
symbols, separated by commas. The list must include at least one identifier.

If N is a nonterminal symbol and E is an arbitrary syntax expression, then a rule of the form

```
N = E .
```

means that the syntax expression E on the right side of the rule is an allowable substitution for the nonterminal N on the left side of the rule, regardless of the context in which N appears – hence the name *context-free*.

Lexical Versus Structural Grammars

It is common practice to separate the context-free grammar for a programming language into two parts, a lexical grammar that will be handled by the scanner and a structural grammar that will be handled by the parser. In effect, we will build two recognizers, a scanner that recognizes basic language symbols and a parser that recognizes the more complex language structure. Doing this allows us to reduce the complexity of the parser by moving some processing to the scanner. The lexical grammar consists of simpler rules based on regular expressions. For a lexical grammar, it should be *possible* to define each nonterminal in a single rule using only terminal symbols and special symbols.

> Consider the following excerpt from the specification of the Java programming language, where it discusses the separation of the grammar into two parts as described in this section.
>
> **2.2. The Lexical Grammar**
>
> A lexical grammar for the Java programming language is given in §3. This grammar has as its terminal symbols the characters of the Unicode character set. It defines a set of productions, starting from the goal symbol Input (§3.5), that describe how sequences of Unicode characters (§3.1) are translated into a sequence of input elements (§3.5).
>
> These input elements, with white space (§3.6) and comments (§3.7) discarded, form the terminal symbols for the syntactic grammar for the Java programming language and are called tokens (§3.5). These tokens are the identifiers (§3.8), keywords (§3.9), literals (§3.10), separators (§3.11), and operators (§3.12) of the Java programming language.
>
> **2.3 The Syntactic Grammar**
>
> A syntactic grammar for the Java programming language is given in Chapters 4, 6-10, 14, and 15. This grammar has tokens defined by the lexical grammar as its terminal symbols. It defines a set of productions, starting from the goal symbol CompilationUnit (§7.3), that describe how sequences of tokens can form syntactically correct programs.
>
> Chapter 18 also gives a syntactic grammar for the Java programming language, better suited to implementation than exposition. The same language is accepted by both syntactic grammars.

Consider, for example, one possible definition of an identifier:

```
identifier = letter ( letter | digit )* .
letter = [A-Za-z] .
digit  = [0-9] .
```

Note that the last two rules use the notation of character classes from regular expressions, where the character class [A-Za-z] is simply shorthand notation for
'A' | 'B' | … | 'Z' |'a' |'b' | … |'z'.

Although we used three rules above, we could substitute the definition of letter and digit into the right side of the rule for an identifier to create a single rule as follows:

```
identifier = [A-Za-z] ( [A-Za-z] | [0-9] )* .
```

Typically the lexical grammar includes identifiers, reserved words, literals (e.g., integer literals, string literals, character literals, etc.), separators (e.g., parentheses, square brackets, commas, semicolons, etc.), and operators (e.g., +, -, <, <=, etc.). Note that the scanner will distinguish between a user-defined identifier (e.g., average) and a reserved word (e.g., while). The scanner will also recognize <= as a single symbol and not two separate single-character symbols. We will discuss these ideas in more detail in Chapter 5.

Regular expressions use a notation similar to our notation for context-free grammars, but they are more restrictive in that recursive rules are not allowed. Still, regular expressions are important enough that most modern programming languages and environments provide built-in support for regular expressions, usually as part of the standard library API. For example, Java support for regular expressions is provided by classes Pattern, Matcher, and PatternSyntaxException in package java.util.regex. The most common use of regular expressions is to define patterns that can be used in search or search/replace dialogs for applications such as text editors or text processing utilities. This book does not include a separate treatment of regular expressions, but many of the references and web sites listed at the end of the book provide additional information.

The syntax or structural grammar rules handled by the parser are more complex rules that describe the structure of the language. These rules typically use recursive definitions. For example, the rule for statements (plural) defines it as a list of zero or more statement symbols.

```
statements = ( statement )* .
```

The rule for a statement shows several alternatives, including a loop statement, as shown below.

```
statement = assignmentStmt | ifStmt | loopStmt | exitStmt | readStmt
          | writeStmt | writelnStmt | procedureCallStmt | returnStmt .
```

But nested within the body of a loop statement we can have other statements, which themselves could be loop statements.

```
loopStmt = ( "while" booleanExpr )? "loop" statements "end" "loop" ";" .
```

Hence we have used recursive definitions in the rules for statements. As we will see in Chapter 6, these recursive definitions give rise to recursive method calls in the parser.

Note that the parser treats the symbols returned by the scanner as terminal symbols. For example, consider the rule for a constant declaration.

```
constDecl = "const" constId ":=" literal ";" .
```

In this rule, `consDecl` is a nonterminal symbol, the symbol `constId` is simply an identifier and although it is not in quotes, the entire identifier is recognized and assembled by the scanner and is treated as a terminal symbol by the parser. The scanner handles all identifiers. The parser treats an identifier as if it were a terminal symbol in the part of the grammar that it handles.

As an analogy for the concepts of separating lexical and structural grammars, consider the progression that a child goes through in learning to read and write. The first step is to learn the alphabet, how the letters are put together to form words, and basic spelling. But the more complex part of learning to read and write is to master the structure of sentences in term of subjects and verbs, punctuation, and parts of speech (nouns, articles, adjective, adverbs, etc.). The lexical grammar, the part handled by the scanner, is analogous to the first step of learning the alphabet, forming words and spelling. The structural grammar, the part handled by the parser, is analogous to the more complex part of learning the structure of sentences, punctuation, and parts of speech. A similar analogy exists in mathematics, where the learning progression moves from numbers and counting to more complex mathematical expressions and formulas.

As specified in the first rule for CPRL, there should be a terminating period that signals the end of the program. But what if a "candidate" program submitted to a compiler contains other characters or symbols after the terminating period? Grammar rules often use an **augmenting rule** to ensure that all input is matched; i.e., that there is nothing following a valid program other than an end of file. The following is an example of an augmenting rule:

```
system = program <EOF> .
```

In this rule, `system` is now the start symbol instead of `program`, and `<EOF>` represents "end of file". With an augmenting, there can be nothing meaningful in the file other than whitespace after the terminating period of a program. The augmenting rule may be explicitly listed as the first rule, or it may be simply "understood". We adopt the convention that an augmenting rule is "understood" and is not explicitly written as a rule in the grammar.

3.3 Alternate Rule Notations

There are a number of common variations or alternate notations for expressing rules. Here are some examples.

- Use "→", "::=", or simply ":" instead of "=" to separate left and right sides of rules.

- Use end of line (instead of period) to terminate rules. For this variation it is common to provide some way of expressing the fact that a long rule is continued to the next line.

- Use curly braces "{" and "}" to enclose syntax expressions that can be repeated 0 or more times. Similarly, use square brackets "[" and "]" to enclose optional syntax expressions.

- Enclose nonterminal symbols in angle brackets "<" and ">" and omit quotes around terminal symbols.

- Use font highlights or changes such as bold instead of quotes to distinguish between terminal and nonterminal symbols.

Here are two examples of CPRL rules using an alternate notation.

```
<program> ::= <declarativePart> <statementPart> .
<initialDecls> ::= { <initialDecl> }
```

These example use ::= to separate the left and right sides of the rule, they enclose nonterminal symbols in angle brackets, and they use the end of the line to terminate the rule. Note that, for the first rule, the period at the end is a terminal symbol and not a rule terminator. Also, the second rule uses braces to enclose a syntax expression that can be repeated 0 or more times.

Additionally, some non-extended (a.k.a., simple) grammar notations do not use the special symbols for "alternation," "zero or more," "optional," etc. A rule in an extended grammar that uses alternation is expressed as multiple rules. For example, this rule in our extended grammar notation for CPRL

```
initialDecl = constDecl | arrayTypeDecl | varDecl .
```

becomes three rules in a simple or non-extended grammar.

```
initialDecl = constDecl .
initialDecl = arrayTypeDecl .
initialDecl = varDecl .
```

Also, for simple (non-extended) grammars, the right side of a rule may be empty string; e.g., "N = λ", where λ represents the empty string, and the concepts of "optional" or "zero or more" are expressed using recursion. So, for example, this rule in our extended grammar notation for CPRL

```
identifiers = identifier ( "," identifier )* .
```

could be represented as three rules in a non-extended grammar notation:

```
identifiers = identifier identifiersTail .
identifiersTail = "," identifiers .
identifiersTail = λ .
```

The last three rules use recursion to specify that "identifiers" is a sequence of one or more identifier symbols, separated by commas.

While an extended grammar notation is usually more compact and easier to read for humans, some compiler tools require that the grammar be in this simple or non-extended format.

Syntax Diagrams

Syntax diagrams (a.k.a., railroad diagrams) provide a graphical alternative to textual representations for a grammar. Textual representations for a grammar are more easily processed by compiler tools, but syntax diagrams are more easily understood by humans.

The basic idea is to use a directed graph, where each diagram has an entry point and an end point. Terminal symbols are represented by rounded boxes, while nonterminal symbols are represented by square boxes. The syntax diagram describes possible paths between these two points by going through other nonterminals and terminals.

Below are two examples of syntax diagrams representing the CPRL rules for loopStmt and statements.

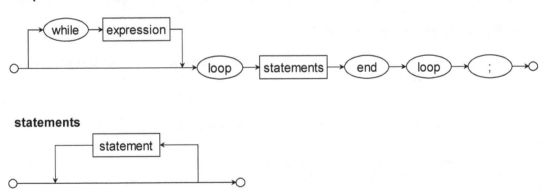

Use of Naming Conventions for Nonterminal Symbols

Many language designers use naming conventions for nonterminal symbols to convey contextual or semantic information in the grammar. This approach is illustrated by the following examples.

Example 1

```
functionCall = funcId ( actualParameters )? .
funcId = identifier .
```

This is equivalent to the following:

```
functionCall = identifier ( actualParameters )? .
```

From a language definition standpoint, there is no difference between the symbol `identifier` and the symbol `funcId`. The use of `funcId` is suggestive, but its use has no more effect on the language being defined than a comment has on source code.

Example 2

```
loopStmt = ( "while" booleanExpr )? "loop" statements "end" "loop" ";" .
booleanExpr = expression .
```

The name `booleanExpr` is chosen to indicate that the expression should have type `Boolean`, but as far as the grammar is concerned, there is no difference. A `booleanExpr` is just an `expression`. Again, the use of `booleanExpr` can be interpreted as being roughly equivalent to a comment for the reader.

3.4 Grammar Transformations

There are some grammar transformations that do not affect the language being compiled. That is, although the grammar could look different, any program considered valid by the original grammar would be considered valid by the transformed grammar, and vice versa.

Substitution of Nonterminal Symbols

One such transformation is the substitution of nonterminal symbols. For example, suppose we have a rule of the form

```
N = X .
```

where the rule is nonrecursive and is the only rule for the nonterminal N. Then we can substitute X (the right side of the rule) for every occurrence of N in the grammar, thereby eliminating the nonterminal N. But the language designer may elect to leave the rule in the grammar. Here is an example used earlier.

```
booleanExpr = expression .
```

The symbol `expression` can be substituted for `booleanExpr` everywhere `booleanExpr` occurs in the grammar without affecting the language defined by the grammar. We don't really need `booleanExpr`. It is used simply to convey information that cannot be expressed in the context-free grammar.

Left Factorization

Another grammar transformation is left factorization. Suppose that the right side of a rule has alternatives of the form

```
X Y | X Z
```

We can replace these alternatives by the following equivalent expression:

```
X ( Y | Z )
```

Elimination of Left Recursion

Suppose that a rule has the form

```
N = X | N Y .
```

where X and Y are arbitrary expressions. A rule of this form is said to be left-recursive since the nonterminal symbol on the left side of the rule is the first (left) symbol on one of the alternatives. We rewrite this rule to obtain an equivalent rule that is not left-recursive as follows:

```
N = X ( Y )* .
```

Example: Grammar Transformations

As a more concrete example, consider the following definition for identifier:

```
identifier = letter  | identifier letter | identifier digit .
```

If we left factor the last two terms, we get

```
identifier = letter | identifier ( letter | digit ) .
```

Now we can eliminate left recursion to obtain the rule as it appears in the definition of CPRL.

```
identifier = letter ( letter | digit )* .
```

Grammars versus Languages

Understand the distinction between a language and a grammar. As illustrated above, different grammars can generate (define) the same language.

Two grammars are said to be **equivalent** if they generate the same language; that is, if every program that is syntactically valid according to one grammar is also syntactically valid according to the other grammar. Applying the grammar transformations discussed above will result in an equivalent grammar, but the general problem of determining whether or not two grammars are equivalent is known to be undecidable, meaning that there does not exist an algorithm that can examine two different grammars and always determine if they are equivalent.

3.5 Derivations and Parse Trees

Using the rules of a context-free grammar, we should be able to demonstrate that a sequence of symbols conforms to the grammar by systematically applying the rules one at a time, beginning with the start symbol. For example, consider the following simple grammar.

```
expr = expr op expr  |  id  |  intLit .
op = "+"  |  "*" .
```

Here we treat id (identifier) and intLit (integer literal) as terminal symbols for the purpose of this discussion, and we assume that they have the obvious meaning.

Using this simple grammar, we want to show that the string "2 + 3 * x" is valid with respect to the grammar. Beginning with the start symbol expr, we choose a valid replacement from the alternatives on the right side of the rule for expr, with the goal of eventually matching
"2 + 3 * x". There are three alternatives on the right side of the rule for expr, but since neither of the last two can be expanded to match our desired target string, the only logical choice is the first alternative, "expr op expr". We write this as follows.

```
expr => expr op expr
```

The symbol => means "derives." It shows that we have replaced expr by an alternative allowed in the context-free grammar.

Now we choose one of the nonterminals in the replacement sequence of symbols, say the first (left) appearance of expr. Then choose the rule that has that nonterminal on the left side, and replace the nonterminal with an allowed alternative on the right side of the rule. Replacing expr by intLit we now have the following:

```
expr => expr op expr
     => intLit op expr
```

Notice that we have underlined the nonterminal symbol that gets replaced in the next line.

Repeat this process until no nonterminal symbols remain. In order to show that "2 + 3 * x" is valid, we want to "derive" the sequence "intLit + intLit * id". For the steps below, we will always elect to replace the left-most nonterminal, and we will comment to show its replacement used in the next line.

```
expr => expr op expr              // expr → intLit
     => intLit op expr            // op   → "+"
     => intLit + expr             // expr → expr op expr
     => intLit + expr op expr     // expr → intLit
     => intLit + intLit op expr   // op   → "*"
     => intLit + intLit * expr    // expr → id
     => intLit + intLit * id
```

The above series of replacements is called a **derivation**. At each step, the derivation simply replaced one nonterminal with one of its alternatives. Since we elected to always replace the left-most nonterminal symbol at each step of the above derivation, this is referred to as a **left-most derivation**. If we replaced the right-most nonterminal symbol at each step, we would have a **right-most derivation**.

We can view the derivation in a more graphical form using what is known as a parse tree. Instead of expanding the nonterminal using simply text, we put the replacement sequence of symbols below the nonterminal being replaced and draw a line from the nonterminal to each replacement symbol. So, for example, instead of writing the first step as

```
expr => expr op expr
```

we draw the first level of the parse tree as follows.

A **parse tree** (a.k.a. syntax tree) of a grammar G is a labeled tree with the following properties:

1. The leaves (terminal nodes) are labeled by terminal symbols.

2. The interior nodes (nonterminal nodes) are labeled by nonterminal symbols.

3. The children of an interior node N correspond in order to a rule for N.

Parse trees illustrate the rules used to recognize the input plus the terminal symbols. Below is the complete parse tree for the left-most derivation given above.

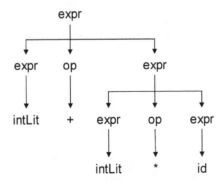

Note that the parse tree shows "2 + 3 * x" parsed with multiplication having a higher precedence than addition, which is what we want. But what if we were draw the parse tree corresponding to a right-most derivation? Would it look the same? Below we show both parse trees side by side.

Clearly we have a problem. An **ambiguous grammar** is one for which some legal phrase has more than one parse tree. The simple grammar defined at the beginning of this section is ambiguous.

Specifying Operator Precedence

Operator precedence refers to the relative priority of operators in that it defines the order in which "adjacent" operators of different precedence levels are evaluated. For example, multiplication is generally given higher precedence than addition, so that "2 + 3 * x" is evaluated unambiguously as "2 + (3 * x)".

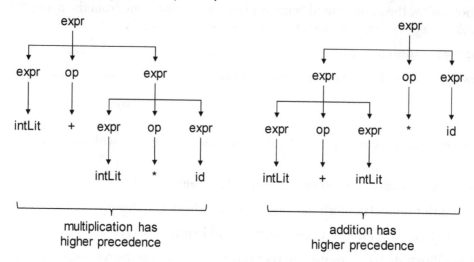

multiplication has
higher precedence

addition has
higher precedence

There are two general approaches to specifying operator precedence. We can define it within the grammar, or we can use an additional specification mechanism (e.g., a precedence table) separate from grammar. In this book we will use the first approach in our definition for CPRL, but the second approach results in a simpler grammar and is supported by some compiler tools (e.g., yacc).

Consider the following grammar:

```
expr = term ( "+" term )* .
term = factor ( "*" factor )* .
factor = id | intLit
```

The precedence of multiplication over addition is specified in the grammar itself. Below is a left derivation for "2 + (3 * x)" using this grammar. Note that some of the steps in the derivation allow choices for repetition.

```
expr => term ( "+" term )*              // replace term by factor
     => factor ( "+" term )*            // replace factor by intLit
     => intLit ( "+" term )*            // choose 1 repetition
     => intLit + term                   // replace term rule's right side
     => intLit + factor ( "*" factor)*  // choose 1 repetition
     => intLit + factor * factor        // replace factor by intLit
     => intLit + intLit * factor        // replace factor by id
     => intLit + intLit * id
```

We state without proof that, using the grammar above, the string "2 + 3 * x" can be parsed only one way. (Convince yourself that this statement is true by trying a different derivation, say a right derivation or one that is neither left nor right.) Below is the parse tree for "2 + 3 * x" using our non-ambiguous grammar.

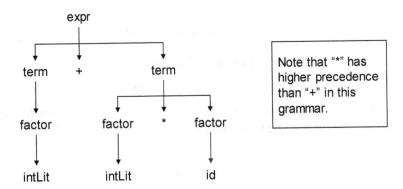

Note that "*" has higher precedence than "+" in this grammar.

Associativity

Closely related to the concept of operator precedence is that of associativity, which specifies the evaluation order of operators with the same precedence level when there are no parentheses. For example, in CPRL, the operators + and - are at the same precedence level and are *left associative*, meaning that 8 – 3 + 2 is evaluated as (8 - 3) + 2, which has the value 7. If they had been *right associative*, then 8 – 3 + 2 would have been evaluated as 8 - (3 + 2), which has the value 3. Since all operators in CPRL are left associative, we won't dwell on this topic except to point out a couple of examples of operators in other languages that are right associative.

Some languages support an exponentiation operator, and that operator is usually defined as right associative. So for example, if the exponentiation operator is ^, then 2^2^3 is evaluated as 2^(2^3), which is 2^8 or 256, and not (2^2)^3, which is 4^3 or 64.

As another example, the programming language C and some languages derived from C define assignment as an expression whose value is the value being assigned, and the assignment operator = is defined to be right associative, so that a = b = c is evaluated as a = (b = c).

3.6 Abstract Syntax Trees

An abstract syntax tree is similar to a parse tree but without extraneous nonterminal and terminal symbols. An abstract syntax tree retains the "essence" of a language construct without the details of how it was parsed. Abstract syntax trees are covered in detail in Chapter 8. In this section we illustrate with a couple of examples.

Example 1. For expressions, we could omit all the additional nonterminals introduced to define precedence (relation, simpleExpr, term, factor, etc.). Once they have been parsed, all binary expressions would retain only the operator and the left and right operands.

Example 2. Consider the following grammar for a `while` statement:

```
whileStmt = "while" expression "loop" statements "end" "loop" ";" .
```

Once a `while` statement has been parsed, we don't need to retain the terminal symbols. The abstract syntax tree for a while statement would contain only `booleanExpr` and `statements`.

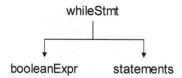

3.7 A Context-Free Grammar for Context-Free Grammars

We close this chapter by illustrating that the notation we use for defining a context-free grammar is powerful enough to specify its own syntax. Using the regular expression notation for character classes, here is one possible definition for the the syntax of context-free grammars defined in a itself:

```
grammar = ( rule )+ .

rule = identifier "=" syntaxExpr "." .

syntaxExpr = syntaxTerm ( "|" syntaxTerm )* .

syntaxTerm = ( syntaxFactor )+ .

syntaxFactor = identifier | terminalSym
             | "(" syntaxExpr ")" ( multChar )? .

multChar = "*" | "+" | "?" .

identifier = letter ( letter | digit )* .

terminalSym = "\"" ( terminalChar | escapedChar )* "\"" .

terminalChar = [ !#-\[\]-~] .

escapedChar = "\\" ("\"" | "\\") .

letter = [A-Za-z] .
    // equivalently, letter = "A" | "B" | ... | "Z" | "a" | "b"
                          | ... | "z" .
```

```
digit = [0-9] .
    // equivalently, digit = "0" | "1" | ... | "9" .
```

In the above rules, `terminalChar` is defined to be any graphic ASCII character except backslash (\) and double quote ("); i.e., `terminalChar` includes space, exclamation point, the range pound sign (a.k.a., hashtag) to left bracket, and the range right bracket to tilde ("~"). An alternate definition of `terminalChar` using Unicode escape notation would look as follows:

```
terminalChar = [\u0020\u0021\u0023-\u005B\u005D-\u007E] .
```

Similarly, `escapedChar` is defined to be a backslash (\) followed by either a double quote (") or another backslash.

For simplicity, the grammar in the above example restricts the character set to the ASCII subset of Unicode, but that restriction could be relaxed. See, for example, the context-free grammar for CPRL as defined in Appendix D. CPRL essentially allows a string literal to contain any graphic Unicode character that can be represented in 16 bits.

3.8 Essential Terms and Concepts

abstract syntax tree (AST)	alternate rule notations
ambiguous grammar	ASCII
associativity	augmenting rule
BNF/EBNF	CFG rules (productions)
context-free grammar (CFG)	contextual constraint
derivation	elimination of left recursion
extended grammar	equivalent grammars
grammars versus languages	grammar transformations
left associative	left factorization
left recursion	left-most derivation
lexical grammar	nonterminal symbol
non-extended (simple) grammar	parse tree
precedence	right-most derivation
right associative	semantics

start (goal) symbol   structural (syntactic) grammar

substitution of nonterminal symbols   symbol

syntax   syntax diagram

terminal symbol   Unicode

(E)*   (E)+

E | F   =>

λ (empty string)

3.9 Exercises

1. Is it possible for a program to be valid with respect to syntax and still not be a valid program? Explain.

2. Is it possible for two different grammars to generate (define) the same language. Explain.

3. Rewrite the CPRL rule for an if statement (ifStmt) (see Appendix D) using curly braces "{" and "}" to enclose syntax expressions that can be repeated 0 or more times and square brackets "[" and "]" to enclose optional syntax expressions.

4. Fill in the blanks.

    a. When developing a compiler, we usually divide the grammar into two parts, a lexical grammar that is handled by the _____, and a structural grammar handled by the _____.

    b. With respect to context-free grammars, the left-hand side of a rule must be a single, _____ symbol.

5. Consider the following simple (non-extended) grammar:

    ```
    S = "0" S "1" .
    S =    λ.
    ```

    Describe in words the language (i.e., the allowable sequence of symbols) defined by this grammar.

6. Consider the following simple (non-extended) grammar:

    ```
    S = "0" S "0" .
    S = "1" S "1" .
    S =    λ.
    ```

Describe in words the language (i.e., the allowable sequence of symbols) defined by this grammar. (Hint: What is a palindrome?)

7. Consider the following simple (non-extended) grammar:

```
S = A B .
A = "a" A1 .
A1 = "a" .
A1 = λ .
B = "b" B .
B = λ .
```

a. Describe in words the language (i.e., the allowable sequence of symbols) defined by this grammar.

b. Give an equivalent extended grammar definition.

8. Consider the following extended grammar:

```
S = ( A )* ( B )? .
A = "a" .
B = "b" .
```

Give an equivalent simple (non-extended) grammar definition.

9. Consider the following grammar for expressions:

```
expr = expr + term | term .
term = expr * id | id .
id = "a" | "b" | "c" .
```

Using this grammar, show a leftmost derivation for the following: a + b * c

10. In CPRL, an integer literal is defined of a sequence of 1 or more digits.

```
intLiteral = ( digit )+ .
digit   = [0-9] .
```

This definition allows a sequence of zeros at the beginning, as in 0000 and 0000095. Rewrite the definition of an integer literal so that a sequence of zeros at the beginning is not allowed, but a single zero by itself should still be allowed.

Hint: Start by defining nonZeroDigit as follows:

```
nonZeroDigit = [1-9] .
```

11. Look up the definition of the context-free grammar for a programming language that you are familiar with and compare the notation used to express rules to the notation used in this book.

12. *Dangling else.* Many languages, especially C-based languages, define an *if-statement* in a manner equivalent to the following:

```
ifStmt = "if" "(" expression ")" statement ( "else" statement )? .
```

Essentially this rule says that an *if-statement* can have an optional *else* clause. The problem with this rule as defined above is that it is ambiguous. Show that this rule is ambiguous by showing that a statement of the form

```
if (expression₁) if (expression₂) statement₁; else statement₂
```

can parsed in two different ways as shown below:

```
if (expression₁)                          if (expression₁)
  {                                          {
     if (expression₂)                           if (expression₂)
         statement₁;                                statement₁;
     else                                      }
         statement₂;                        else
  }                                             statement²;
```

Hint: For one derivation/parse tree, substitute an `ifStmt` without an `else` clause as the first statement in the above rule, and for a second derivation/parse tree, substitute an `ifStmt` without an `else` clause as the second statement in the above rule. Make reasonable assumptions about other language rules not shown above (e.g., about the use of semicolons).

This ambiguity is known as the *dangling else* problem. While it is possible to define the rules for an *if-statement* to avoid the ambiguity, doing so complicates the grammar. Language definitions that have a *dangling-else* problem usually just specify that, in the absence of braces, an *else* clause is associated with the nearest *if-statement* without an else clause; that is, the first option (the option on the left) above is the one to be chosen. Most compiler tools will choose this option by default even if they complain about the ambiguity. Note that CPRL does not have this problem since each *if-statement* is explicitly closed with an "end if".

Chapter 4
The Programming Language CPRL

This chapter provides an overview of CPRL, the source language for our compiler. Appendices C and D contain additional details of the language definition.

The name CPRL is an acronym for Compiler PRoject Language. Originally it was called simply CPL, but it turned out that a different programming language had been defined with that acronym in the early 1960's. Plus, Microsoft Windows used the extension ".cpl" for Control Panel files in the Windows system folder, so the name of the project language was changed to CPRL to avoid any confusion or conflicts.

CPRL is a small but complete programming language with statement-level constructs similar to those found in Ada, Java, C++, and Pascal. It was designed to be suitable for use as a project language in an undergraduate or beginning graduate course on compiler design and construction. CPRL features illustrate many of the basic techniques and problems associated with language translation.

4.1 General Lexical Considerations

Identifiers in CPRL are case sensitive. Upper-case letters and lower-case letters are considered to be distinct in all tokens, including reserved words. Spaces may not appear in any token except character and string literals. In general white space characters are used to separate tokens; otherwise they are ignored. No token can extend past an end-of-line. Similar to Java and C++, a comment begins with two forward slashes (//) and extends to the end of the line. Multiline comments are not available in CPRL, but it is not difficult to add them. In fact, that is one of the exercises described in Appendix B.

Identifiers

Identifiers start with a letter and contain letters and digits.

```
identifier = letter ( letter | digit )* .
letter = [A-Za-z] .
digit  = [0-9] .
```

There are 41 predefined identifiers that serve as keywords in CPRL – examples include begin, end, const, if, else, loop, and while. All such keywords are reserved; i.e., a programmer is not permitted to use them as names for program entities such as variables, types, subprograms, etc.

Literals

Literal values for various types are described and illustrated as follows:

- Literal values for type Integer consists of 1 or more digits. Examples include 0, 1, 1842, etc. Technically -1 is not an integer literal but an expression – the unary negation symbol followed by the integer literal 1.

- Type Boolean has only two literal values, true and false.

- As with Java and C++, a character literal is simply a single character enclosed by a pair of apostrophes (sometimes called single quotes). Note that a character literal is distinct from a string literal with length one. Examples of character literals include 'A', 'x', and '$'. The backslash character (\) denotes escape sequences within character and string literals; e.g., \t for the tab character, \n for a newline character, \" for a quote character within a string, and \\ for the backslash itself.

- A string literal consists of zero or more printable characters enclosed by a pair of quotation marks (double quotes). Although string literals are permitted in certain contexts such as in write and writeln statements, for language simplicity the type String is not fully supported in CPRL. One of the exercises in Appendix B is to implement String as a full-fledged type in CPRL.

Other Tokens

The following tokens serve as delimiters and operators in CPRL:

```
:    ;    ,    .    (    )    [    ]        // one character
+    -    *    /    <    =    >
:=   !=   >=   <=                          // two characters
```

4.2 Typing in CPRL

CPRL is a statically typed language. This means that every variable or constant in the language belongs to exactly one type, and that type is a static property and can be determined by the compiler.

Types

There are three standard (predefined) scalar types in CPRL – Boolean, Integer, and Char. In addition, CPRL has one structured data type – array. Technically CPRL supports only one dimensional arrays, but arrays of arrays can be declared. An array type is defined by the number of elements in the array and component type.

Examples

```
type T1 = array[10] of Boolean;
type T2 = array[10] of Integer;
type T3 = array[10] of T2;
```

Array indices are integers ranging from 0 to n-1, where n is the number of elements in the array.

Constants and Variables

A constant is simply an identifier (name) associated with a literal value. As one would expect, the value for the constant cannot be changed at run time. The type of the constant identifier is inferred to be the type of the literal. For example,

```
const maxIndex := 100;
```

declares a constant name maxIndex initialized to an integer value 100.

As with many other programming languages, variables associate an identifier (name) with a type. The value of the variable is allowed to change as the program is running. Here are some examples.

```
var x1, x2 : Integer;
var found : Boolean;
type IntArray = array[100] of Integer;
var table : IntArray;
```

In CPRL, constants and variables must be declared before they can be referenced.

Operators and Expressions

CPRL has a standard set of operators with common precedence. Here we point out a few differences between CPRL operators and those of Java and C++.

- In CPRL the boolean negation operator is the reserved word not instead of the exclamation point (!) used in Java and C++, but the relational operator for "not equal" is still !=.

- The modulo operator in CPRL is the reserved word mod, not the percent sign (%) as used in Java and C++.

- The logical operators in CPRL are the reserved words "and" and "or" instead of the Java/C++ operators && and ||.

For expressions with binary operators, both operands must be of the same type. Similarly, for assignment compatibility, both the left and right sides must have the same type. CPRL uses name type equivalence in that variables are considered to have the same type if only if they are declared with the same type name. Consider the following illustrative example using arrays.

```
type T1 = array[10] of Integer;
type T2 = array[10] of Integer;
var x : T1;
var y : T1;
```

```
var z : T2;
```

In this example, x and y have the same type, but x and z do not even though both x and z are both arrays of 10 integers.

As with Java, expressions involving logical operators and/or use short-circuit evaluation.

4.3 Statements

Assignment Statement

The assignment operator is ":=". An assignment statement has the following form:

```
variable := expression;
```

Example

```
i := 2*i + 5;
```

If Statement

An if statement starts with the keyword "if" and ends with the keywords "end if". It may contain zero or more elsif clauses (note spelling of "elsif") and an optional else clause.

Examples

```
if x > 0 then
    sign := 1;
elsif x < 0 then
    sign := -1;
else
    sign = 0;
end if;

if a[i] = searchValue then
    found := true;
end if;
```

Loop and Exit Statements

A loop statement may be preceded by an optional "while" clause, but the body of the loop statement is bracketed by the keywords "loop" and "end loop". An exit statement can be used to exit the inner most loop that contains it.

Examples

```
while i < n loop
    sum := sum + a[i];
    i := i + 1;
end loop;

loop
    read x;
    exit when x = SIGNAL;
    process(x);
end loop;
```

Input/Output Statements

CPRL defines only sequential text I/O for two basic character streams – standard input and standard output. The write and writeln statements can have multiple expressions separated by commas. Input is supported only for integers and characters.

Examples

```
read x;
writeln "The answer is ", 2*x + 1;
```

4.4 Programs

A program has a declarative part followed by a statement part. The declarative consists of a (possibly empty) list of initial declarations followed by a (possibly empty) list of subprogram declarations. The statement part is bracketed by reserved words "begin" and "end". A period (".") terminates the program.

Examples

```
begin
    writeln "Hello, world.";
end.

var x : Integer;
begin
    read x;
    writeln "x = ", x;
end.
```

4.5 Subprograms

CPRL provides two separate forms of subprograms – procedures and functions. Procedures are similar to void functions in C or C++ in that a procedure does not return a value. Procedures are invoked through a procedure call statement. Functions must return a value and are invoked as part of an expression.

Recursive invocations of subprograms are allowed. All subprograms must be declared before they are called, and all subprogram names must be distinct. The name of a subprogram must be repeated at the closing "end" of the subprogram declaration.

Subprograms can have parameters. There are two parameter modes in CPRL – value parameters and variable parameters. Value parameters are passed by value (a.k.a. copy-in) and are the default. Variable parameters are passed by reference and must be explicitly declared using the var keyword. Functions cannot have variable parameters, only value parameters.

Procedures

Procedures are similar to those in Pascal except that explicit return statements are allowed within the statement part – the return must not be followed by an expression. Procedures are called by simply giving their name followed by actual parameters (if any) enclosed in parentheses followed by a semicolon. Procedure calls are statements.

Procedure Example

```
procedure inc(var x : Integer) is
begin
   x := x + 1;
end inc;
```

Functions

Functions are similar to procedures except that functions can (and must) return values. Function calls are expressions. A function returns a value by executing a return statement of the form

```
return <expression>;
```

Function Example

```
function max(x : Integer, y : Integer) return Integer is
begin
   if x >= y then
      return x;
   else
      return y;
   end if;
```

```
    end max;
```

Assuming that we have two integer variables a and b, then the following would call this function and write out its value.

```
    writeln max(a, b);
```

Return Statements

A return statement terminates execution of a subprogram and returns control back to the point where the subprogram was called.

A return statement within a function must be followed by an expression whose value is returned by the function. The type of the expression must be assignment compatible with the return type of the function.

A return statement within a procedure must not be followed by an expression – it simply returns control to the statement following the procedure call statement.

A procedure has an implied return statement as its last statement, and therefore most procedures will not have an explicit return statement. A function requires one or more return statements to return the function value. There is no implicit return statement at the end of a function.

The CPRL/0 Subset of CPRL

To simplify the discussion and implementation of constraint analysis and code generation in later chapters, we find it convenient to focus initially on a subset of the full CPRL language. The "zero" subset of CPRL, denoted CPRL/0, is defined to be that part of the language **not** related to subprograms and arrays. CPRL/0 includes programs, constant declarations, variable declarations, predefined types such as Integer and Boolean, and most statements. Excluded are array type declarations, subprogram declarations, procedure call statements, function call expressions, and return statements. The sample CPRL programs used to test various parts of your compiler are organized into separate directories to clearly indicate which examples are based only on the CPRL/0 subset.

4.6 Essential Terms and Concepts

array	Boolean
constant	Character
CPRL comment	expression
function	identifier
Integer	literal (integer, boolean, character, string)

operators   operator precedence

pass by value   pass by reference

parameter (value versus variable)   procedure

reserved word/keyword   statements (assignment, if, loop, etc.)

subprogram   variable

//

4.7 Exercises

1. **Project Assignment.** Implement **Project 0: Getting Started** as described in Appendix A.

2. Consider the following procedure:

    ```
    procedure inc(x : Integer) is
    begin
        x := x + 1;
    end inc;
    ```

    If n has the value 5, then what value does n have after a call to the procedure of the form inc(n)? (Hint: How is the parameter passed for this procedure?)

3. Explain what it means for a programming language to be statically typed.

4. Fill in the blanks.

    a. CPRL provides two separate forms of subprograms:
        _____ and _____ .

    b. In CPRL, value parameters are passed by _____ .

    c. In CPRL, variable parameters are passed by _____ .

5. True or false.

    a. CPRL is case sensitive.

    b. CPRL defines certain reserved words that are not currently used within the language.

    c. CPRL is a statically typed language.

    d. CPRL uses the operator "%" to denote modulus operator; i.e., the remainder when one integer is divided by another.

    e. CPRL uses "=" as the assignment operator.

6. Consider the following declarations:

   ```
   type T1 = array[10] of Integer;
   type T2 = array[10] of Integer;
   var x : T1;
   var y : T1;
   var z : T2;
   ```

   True or false.

   a. In the above declarations, variables x and y are considered to have the same type.

   b. In the above declarations, variables x and z are considered to have the same type.

7. Write a CPRL function that implements integer exponentiation. The function should take two integer parameters and return the result of the first integer raised to the power of the second integer. The declaration for the function should look something like the following:

   ```
   function pow(n : Integer, exp : Integer) return Integer is ...
   ```

   Calling pow(5, 3) should return the value 125.

8. Write a CPRL function that uses integer arithmetic to compute the average of the first n integers in an array. Both the array and the value for n should be passed as parameters. The declarations for the array type and function should look something like the following:

   ```
   type IntArray = array[100] of Integer;
   ...
   function average(a : IntArray, n : Integer) return Integer is ...
   ```

   Note that the array is passed by value. Discuss the performance implications of passing the array by value versus passing it by reference. Can the array be passed by reference?

9. Write a CPRL procedure that merges two sorted integer arrays. The two arrays and the number of items in each array should be passed as parameters, and the resulting merged array should be returned via a reference parameter. The declarations for the array type and procedure should look something like the following:

   ```
   type IntArray = array[100] of Integer;
   ...
   procedure merge(var a1 : IntArray, n1 : Integer,
                   var a2 : IntArray, n2 : Integer,
                   var result : IntArray) is ...
   ```

Chapter 5
Lexical Analysis (a.k.a. Scanning)

We are now at a place where we can (finally!) start to implement a compiler for CPRL. For most students, this is where the fun begins. We start with the scanner.

The role of lexical analysis or scanning is to identify the basic lexical units of the language, which are called the symbols or tokens of the language. The scanner also usually removes extraneous white space and comments since they play no role in subsequent analysis or code generation, and it reports any errors encountered in the source code. The scanner makes use of several helper classes, primarily `Position`, `Source`, `Symbol`, and `Token`.

5.1 Class `Position`

Class `Position` encapsulates the concept of a position in a source file, where a position is characterized by ordered pair of integers representing the line number relative to the source file and the character number relative to that line. `Position` objects are used primarily for error reporting. Note that class `Position` is immutable; i.e., objects of class `Position` can't be modified after they have been created and initialized by a constructor.

Key constructor and methods for class `Position` are as follows:

```
/**
 * Construct a position with the given line number and character number.
 */
public Position(int lineNumber, int charNumber)

/**
 * Returns the current line number of the position.
 */
public int getLineNumber()

/**
 * Returns the current character number of the position.
 */
public int getCharNumber() Class Source
```

5.2 Class `Source`

Class `Source` is essentially an iterator that steps through the characters in a source file one character at a time. At any point during the iteration you can examine the current character and its position within the source file before advancing to the next character. Class `Source` encapsulates a source file reader and maintains the position of each character in the source file. The input to class source is a Reader (usually a `FileReader`), and the output is the sequence of individual characters and their positions within the file.

Key constructor and methods for class `Source` are as follows:

```
/**
 * Initialize Source with a Reader and advance to the first character.
 */
public Source(Reader sourceReader) throws IOException

/**
 * Returns the current character (as an int) in the source
 * file.  Returns EOF if the end of file has been reached.
 */
public int getChar()

/**
 * Returns the position (line number, char number) of the
 * current character in the source file.
 */
public Position getCharPosition()

/**
 * Advance to the next character in the source file.
 */
public void advance() throws IOException
```

Class `TestSource` is used to test classes `Position` and `Source` before integrating them into the scanner. The main logic of `TestSource` is as follows:

```
String fileName = args[0];
FileReader fileReader = new FileReader(fileName);
Source source = new Source(fileReader);

while (source.getChar() != Source.EOF)
  {
    int c = source.getChar();
    if (c == '\n')
        System.out.print("\\n");
    else if (c != '\r')
        System.out.print((char) c);

    System.out.println("\t" + source.getCharPosition());

    source.advance();
  }
```

We can test class Source by running the test program on its own source file Source.java. The results of testing class Source are as follows (read the first character vertically):

```
p    Line 1, Character 1
a    Line 1, Character 2
c    Line 1, Character 3
k    Line 1, Character 4
a    Line 1, Character 5
g    Line 1, Character 6
e    Line 1, Character 7
     Line 1, Character 8
e    Line 1, Character 9
d    Line 1, Character 10
u    Line 1, Character 11
.    Line 1, Character 12
c    Line 1, Character 13
i    Line 1, Character 14
t    Line 1, Character 15
a    Line 1, Character 16
...
```

5.3 Class Symbol

The term **symbol** will be used to refer to the a basic lexical unit returned by the scanner. Another common name for symbol is "token type." From the perspective of the parser, these are the terminal symbols.

Symbols include reserved words ("while", "if", "procedure", ...), operators and punctuation (":=", "+", ";", ...), identifiers, integer literals, and special scanning symbols EOF and unknown. To prevent name clashes with Java reserved words, class Symbol adopts the naming convention that all reserved words end with the "RW" suffix; e.g., ifRW, whileRW, etc. Symbols are defined using a Java enum class as follows:

```java
public enum Symbol
  {
    // reserved words
    BooleanRW("Boolean"),
    IntegerRW("Integer"),
    ...
    whileRW("while"),
    writeRW("write"),
    writelnRW("writeln"),

    // arithmetic operator symbols
    plus("+"),
```

```
        minus("-"),
        times("*"),
        divide("/"),
        ...

        // literal values and identifier symbols
        intLiteral("Integer Literal"),
        charLiteral("Character Literal"),
        stringLiteral("String Literal"),
        identifier("Identifier"),

        // special scanning symbols
        EOF("End-of-File"),
        unknown("Unknown");
        ...
    }
```

In addition to the enum constants, class Symbol also contains several boolean methods that will be useful later on for implementing the parser. Examples include isStmtStarter(), which returns true if the symbol can appear at the start of a CPRL statement, and isRelationalOperator(), which returns true if the symbol is one of the six relational operators such as Symbol.equals or Symbol.lessThan. The role of these methods will be discussed in more detail in the next chapter.

5.4 Class Token

The term **token** will be used to refer to a symbol together with additional information including the position (line number and character number) of the symbol in the source file and the text associated with the symbol. The additional information provided by a token is used for error reporting and code generation, but it is not used to determine if the program is syntactically correct.

Examples of the text associated with symbols are as follows:

- "average" for an identifier
- "100" for an integer literal
- ""Hello, world."" for a string literal
- "while" for the reserved word while
- "<=" for the operator "<="

The text associated with a symbol is most meaningful for identifiers, integer literals, character literals, and string literals since, in all other cases, the text can be inferred directly from the symbol itself.

Class Token is actually implemented in two separate classes as follows:

- An abstract, generic class that can be instantiated with any Symbol enum class

  ```
  public abstract class AbstractToken<Symbol extends Enum<Symbol>>
  ```

  This class is contained in package edu.citadel.compiler since it is independent of the programming language being compiled. Most of the logic for class Token is contained in this abstract class.

- A concrete class that instantiates the generic class using the Symbol enum class for CPRL

  ```
  public class Token extends AbstractToken<Symbol>
  ```

  This class is contained in package edu.citadel.cprl since it is implemented specifically for the CPRL programming language.

Key constructor and methods for class AbstractToken are as follows:

```
/**
 * Constructs a new Token with the given symbol, position, and text.
 */
public AbstractToken(Symbol symbol, Position position, String text)

/**
 * Returns the token's symbol.
 */
public Symbol getSymbol()

/**
 * Returns the token's position within the source file.
 */
public Position getPosition()

/**
 * Returns the string representation for the token.
 */
public String getText()
```

5.5 Class Scanner

Class Scanner is essentially an iterator that steps through the tokens in a source file one token at a time. At any point during the iteration you can examine the current token, its text, and its position within the source file before advancing to the next token.

Class `Scanner`

- − Consumes characters from the source code file as it constructs the tokens.
- − Removes extraneous white space and comments.
- − Reports any errors.
- − Gets individual characters from class Source as input.
- − Produces Tokens (to be consumed by the parser) as output.

The following diagram illustrates the interaction between classes `Source` and `Scanner` to produce the tokens for a simple assignment statement. Note that the positions of the individual characters have been omitted from the diagram to save space, but they are shown as part of the output of the scanner.

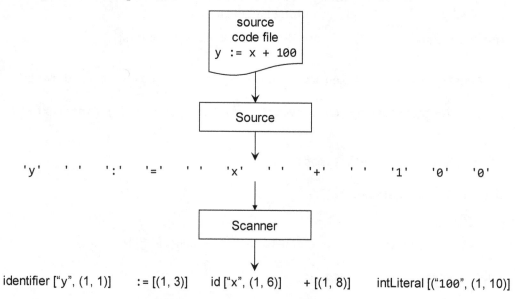

Key constructor and methods for class `Scanner` are as follows:

```
/**
 * Initialize scanner with its associated source and advance to the
 * first token.
 */
public Scanner(Source source) throws IOException

/**
 * Returns a copy of the current token in the source file.
 */
public Token getToken()
```

```
/**
 * Returns a reference to the current symbol in the source file.
 */
public Symbol getSymbol()

/**
 * Returns a reference to the position of the current symbol in the
 * source file.
 */
public Position getPosition()

/**
 * Advance to the next token in the source file.
 */
public void advance() throws IOException
```

Much of the work of the parser can be performed by simply using the symbol returned from the scanner's getSymbol() method, but sometimes the parser needs to save the entire token. At those times the parser calls the scanner's getToken() method, which returns a reference to a new token.

Method advance() is the most complicated method in class Scanner since it is responsible for combining characters into tokens. Plus, it is also responsible for skipping extraneous whitespace and comments. Here is an outline of the logic for method advance().

```
public void advance() throws IOException
  {
    try
      {
        skipWhiteSpace();

        // currently at starting character of next token
        position = source.getCharPosition();
        text = null;

        if (source.getChar() == Source.EOF)
          {
            // set symbol but don't advance
            symbol = Symbol.EOF;
          }
        else if (Character.isLetter((char) source.getChar()))
          {
            String idString = scanIdentifier();
            symbol = getIdentifierSymbol(idString);
```

```
        if (symbol == Symbol.identifier)
            text = idString;
    }
    else if (Character.isDigit((char) source.getChar()))
      {
        text    = scanIntegerLiteral();
        symbol = Symbol.intLiteral;
      }
    else
      {
        switch((char) source.getChar())
          {
            case '+':
                symbol = Symbol.plus;
                source.advance();
                break;
            case '-':
                symbol = Symbol.minus;
                source.advance();
                break;

                ...

        case '>':
                source.advance();
                if ((char) source.getChar() == '=')
                  {
                    symbol = Symbol.greaterOrEqual;
                    source.advance();
                  }
                else
                    symbol = Symbol.greaterThan;
                break;

        ...
```

Note that the one- and two-character symbols are handled by a large switch statement. When the scanner sees a "+" character as the next character in the input stream, it immediately recognizes a plus symbol. When the scanner sees a ">" character in the input stream, it needs to look at the next character in order to recognize the symbol. If the next character is "=", then the scanner recognizes a greaterOrEqual symbol. If the next character is anything other than "=", then the scanner recognizes a greaterThan symbol, and the character following ">" is not consumed; i.e., it remains in the input stream.

In addition to one- and two-character symbols, the switch statement also recognizes a single quote (apostrophe) as the start of a character literal and a double quote as the start of a string literal. In both cases it calls helper methods as described below to complete the scanning of these two types of symbols.

> **Important observation:** The scanner always advances the source object whenever a symbol has been recognized, so that the Source object remains one character ahead of the characters that have been consumed by the scanner.

There are four symbols that require special attention when scanning – identifiers, integer literals, string literals, and character literals. The bulk of the work in recognizing these four symbols is performed in separate methods, two of which are described below. Since the text for these four symbols needs to be retained as part of the token, and since the text can be several characters long, these methods use a StringBuilder object named scanBuffer to accumulate the token text. Additionally, there is a simple helper method named clearScanBuffer() that reinitializes scanBuffer; i.e., makes it empty.

Additionally, there are several other helper methods in class Scanner such as skipComment(), which skips over a comment and then recursively calls the advance() to move the scanner to the next token.

Scanning an Integer Literal

Recall that an integer literal is defined by the grammar as a sequence of one or more digits.

```
intLiteral = ( digit )+ .
```

This suggests that we scan an integer literal using a loop. Below is an example method for scanning an integer literal. Note how the logic of the code parallels the grammar definition. When method advance() encounters a digit, it calls this method to complete the scanning process.

```
protected String scanIntegerLiteral() throws IOException
  {
     // assumes that source.getChar() is the first digit
     // of the integer literal

     clearScanBuffer();

     do
       {
          scanBuffer.append((char) source.getChar());
          source.advance();
       }
     while (Character.isDigit((char) source.getChar()));

     return scanBuffer.toString();
  }
```

Scanning an Identifier

Recall that an identifier is defined by the grammar as a letter followed by zero or more letters or digits.

```
identifier = letter ( letter | digit )* .
```

The scanning of an identifier starts out simply enough. When method `advance()` encounters a letter, it calls method `scanIdentifier()` to complete the scanning process, similar to the way that `scanIntegerLiteral()` is called when `advance()` encounters a digit. The problem is that user-defined identifiers and reserved words "look" alike, and so after scanning an identifier, we still need to distinguish between CPRL reserved words and user-defined identifiers such as variable or procedure names. Here is one approach for making the distinction.

First, use a single method named `scanIdentifier()` to scan all identifiers, including reserved words. In other words, initially we don't make a distinction between user-defined identifiers and reserved words. This method returns a string.

```
/**
 * Scans characters in the source file for a valid identifier.
 */
protected String scanIdentifier() throws IOException
```

Then, after calling `scanIdentifier()`, use an "efficient" search routine to determine if the string returned by `scanIdentifier()` is a user-defined identifier or a reserved word. The search will "look up" the string assembled by the above method to determine what type of symbol it is. If the string is "while," then the method will return `Symbol.while` indicating the `while` reserved word. If the string is something like "averageGrade," then the method will return `Symbol.identifier` indicating a user-defined identifier, and the string "averageGrade" will be stored as the token's text.

```
/**
 * Returns the symbol associated with an identifier
 * (Symbol.arrayRW, Symbol.ifRW, Symbol.identifier, etc.)
 */
protected Symbol getIdentifierSymbol(String idString)
```

One **very inefficient** way to implement `getIdentifierSymbol()` is to perform a sequential search (a.k.a., linear search) of all the reserved words, comparing the string parameter to see if there is a match. If so, you would return the appropriate reserved word symbol. If the entire list of reserved words is searched without a match, you would return `Symbol.identifier`.

Here is one way to implement the logic for `getIdentifierSymbol()` as just described.

```
/**
 * Returns the symbol associated with an identifier
 * (Symbol.arrayRW, Symbol.ifRW, Symbol.identifier, etc.)
 */
private Symbol getIdentifierSymbol(String idString)
  {
    if (idString.equals("and"))
        return Symbol.andRW;
    else if (idString.equals("array"))
        return Symbol.arrayRW;
    ...

    else if (idString.equals("writeln"))
        return Symbol.writelnRW;
    else
        // if you get this far, it must be a plain old identifier
        return Symbol.identifier;
  }
```

An alternative (and equally inefficient) way to implement a sequential search is to create a class called ReservedWord that contains a pair consisting of the string for a reserved word and the symbol for the reserved word. A constructor could look something like the following:

```
public ReservedWord(String rwString, Symbol rwSymbol)
```

Then create code to initialize an array of ReservedWord objects containing entries for all CPRL reserved words. To determine if a string represents a reserved word, you could loop through the array comparing the string parameter of getIdentifierSymbol() to the first (String) component of each ReservedWord in the array to see if there is a match. If so, you would return the second (Symbol) component. If the entire array is searched without a match, you would return Symbol.identifier.

Here is the logic for getIdentifierSymbol() using this second approach.

```
private Symbol getIdentifierSymbol (String idString)
    {
      for (int i = 0;  i < reservedWords;  ++i)
        {
          if (idString.equals(reservedWords[i].rwString))
              return reservedWords[i].rwSymbol;
        }

        return Symbol.identifier;
    }
```

While the programming logic used in the second approach above is shorter and simpler, it is not more efficient.

We want method `getIdentiferSymbol()` to be as efficient as possible since it will be called many times, so the above implementations are too inefficient to be acceptable. One obvious performance improvement is put the reserved words in the array alphabetically and the use a binary search instead of a sequential search. Students are encouraged to explore other, possibly more efficient alternatives. (See Exercise 7 at the end of this chapter.)

5.6 Handling Lexical Errors

There are several kinds of errors that can be detected by the scanner when processing a source file. Examples include failure to properly close a character or string literal (e.g., encountering an end-of-line before a closing quote), encountering a character that does not start a valid symbol (e.g., '#' or '@'), etc. As outlined in Chapters 7 and 9, a lot of error handling is performed by the parser and within the abstract syntax tree classes, but the scanner needs to take action when encountering lexical errors.

In general, our compiler will use Java's exception handling mechanism to signal and report all errors. Lexical errors are encapsulated by class `ScannerException`, which is defined in package `edu.citadel.compiler`. When any of the scanning methods detect an error, they call a private scanner method named `error()` with an appropriate error message. Method `error()` simply creates and returns a new `ScannerException` with that error message and the current token position, and the exception is then thrown by the method that detected the lexical error. Method `error()` is defined as follows:

```
private ScannerException error(String message)
  {
    return new ScannerException(getPosition(), message);
  }
```

Most lexical errors are handled in the scanner method `advance()`, which, as shown earlier, has its processing logic enclosed in `try/catch` blocks. The `catch` block uses class `ErrorHandler` from package `edu.citadel.compiler` to report the error, and then it sets the token's symbol to either `Symbol.EOF` (if end-of-file has been reached) or `Symbol.unknown`, so that the parser can handle it appropriately. The `catch` block at the end of method `advance()` is written as follows:

```
catch (ScannerException e)
  {
    ErrorHandler.getInstance().reportError(e);

    // set token to either EOF or unknown
    if (source.getChar() == Source.EOF)
      {
        if (getSymbol() != Symbol.EOF)
```

```
            currentToken.setSymbol(Symbol.EOF);
      }
   else
        currentToken.setSymbol(Symbol.unknown);
}
```

Class ErrorHandler is used throughout the compiler to report errors, and it implements the singleton pattern; i.e., there is only one instance of this class, and that instance is obtained by calling the static method getInstance().

Beyond the scanner exceptions handled in method advance(), both scanCharLiteral() and scanStringLiteral() contain special logic to handle an invalid escaped character. Recall that, like Java, certain characters can be escaped by prepending a backslash character ('\'). Escape sequences like '\t' and '\n' are valid, but not something like '\x'. Upon encountering an invalid escape sequence, these methods report the error and then attempt a weak form of error recovery so as to continue processing the string or character literal.

In addition to detecting and reporting on errors in a CPRL source file, there are several checks for internal consistency throughout the compiler. Most internal checks within the compiler make use of Java's assert statement with a boolean expression and a string. Assuming that assertions are enabled, if the boolean expression evaluates to true, then the statement takes no action. But if the boolean expression evaluates to false, then assert throws an AssertionError with the specified string used as an error message. AssertionError is an unchecked exception and therefore does not need to be handled or declared in a throws clause.

For example, the scanner method scanIdentifier() assumes that source.getChar() is the first letter of the identifier to be scanned, and so a check is performed to ensure that the character is, in fact, a letter. This is illustrated in the following excerpt from method scanIdentifier() in class Scanner:

```
// assumes that source.getChar() is the first letter of the identifier
assert Character.isLetter((char) source.getChar()) :
    "scanIdentifier(): check identifier start for letter at position "
    + getPosition();
```

The above code simply checks that this condition is satisfied and that the compiler has not made an erroneous call to scanIdentifier(). Internal compiler assertions represent problems with the implementation of the compiler and should never occur if the compiler is implemented correctly. By default, Java assertions are disabled at run time, but they can be enabled using a command-line switch. A normal scenario is to enable assertion checking when developing a compiler and to turn it off when the compiler goes into production. Even when they aren't enabled, assertions serve to document assumptions serve to document assumptions and inner workings of your compiler.

Most IDEs have a way to enable or disable Java assertions. For example, Eclipse creates a "run configuration" when you run a Java program, and you can enable assertions for a specific run configuration as follows: From the menu select **Run** and then **Run Configurations...** Select the run configuration for the application you want to edit, and then click on the **Arguments** tab. In the text area for **VM Arguments**, simply type -ea or -enableassertions. It is also possible to enable assertions globally for all Eclipse run configurations, but those details will not be covered here.

Assertions in Java

By default, Java assertions are disabled at run time. They are enabled using a switch (either -enableassertions or -ea) to the java command, allowing the use of assertion checking during development and easy removal of assertion checking for production code or when efficiency concerns dominate. For example, the following command enables assertions checking for an application.

```
java -ea MyApplication
```

Note that source code does not need to be recompiled to enable or disable assertions in Java. Enabling or disabling assertions is a function of the class loader. Even when assertion checking is disabled, the assertions remain as useful comments in the code to document run-time assumptions.

5.7 Testing Class Scanner

It is important that we fully test the scanner before trying to integrate it with the parser. The book resources include a test program TestScanner.java that can be used for this purpose. Omitting error handling, the basic logic of class TestScanner is as follows:

```
String fileName = args[0];
FileReader fileReader = new FileReader(fileName);

Source  source  = new Source(fileReader);
Scanner scanner = new Scanner(source);
Token   token;

do
  {
    token = scanner.getToken();
    printToken(token);
    scanner.advance();
  }
while (token.getSymbol() != Symbol.EOF);
```

As shown below, method printToken() is used to print out the text associated with each token, using special logic to print the text for identifiers, integer literals, string literals, and character literals.

```
public static void printToken(Token token)
  {
    System.out.printf("line: %2d    char: %2d    token: ",
        token.getPosition().getLineNumber(),
        token.getPosition().getCharNumber());
    if (    token.getSymbol() == Symbol.identifier
        || token.getSymbol() == Symbol.intLiteral
        || token.getSymbol() == Symbol.stringLiteral
        || token.getSymbol() == Symbol.charLiteral)
        System.out.print(token.getSymbol().toString() + " -> ");
    System.out.println(token.getText());
```

The book resources contain a directory named ScannerTests with subdirectories Correct and Incorrect containing several CPRL scanner test examples (not necessarily complete CPRL programs). In addition, there are a Windows command script and a Bash shell script that can be used to invoke TestScanner from the command line. Below are the results of testing the scanner with file Correct01.cprl as input.

```
line:  2    char:  1    token: and
line:  2    char: 11    token: array
line:  2    char: 21    token: begin
line:  2    char: 31    token: Boolean
...
line:  9    char: 31    token: while
line:  9    char: 41    token: write
line: 10    char:  1    token: writeln
line: 13    char:  1    token: +
line: 13    char:  6    token: -
line: 13    char: 11    token: *
line: 13    char: 16    token: /
line: 16    char:  1    token: =
line: 16    char:  5    token: !=
line: 16    char: 10    token: <
line: 16    char: 14    token: <=
...
```

5.8 Essential Terms and Concepts

AbstractToken (class)   character literal

immutable class   integer literal

keyword/reserved word   Position (class)

Scanner (class)   Source (class)

Symbol (enum class)   string literal

symbol   token

Token (class)

5.9 Exercises

1. **Project Assignment.** Implement **Project 1: Scanner** as described in Appendix A.

2. Explain the difference between the terms "symbol" and "token" as used in this book.

3. True or false.

    The scanner typically removes extraneous white space and comments from the source file.

4. Consider the **first two lines** of the following CPRL source code:

    ```
    while x1 <= 2*y loop
        writeln("less than");
        ...
    end loop;
    ```

    List the symbols that will be identified by the scanner. Just list the text part of the symbols.
    (Hint: In the first two lines there are 12 symbols, and the first symbol is `while`.)

5. As described in Section 5.1, a class is said to be **immutable** if instances (objects) of that class can't be modified after they have been created and initialized by a constructor. Class Position is immutable. Name several classes defined in Java that are immutable. (Hint: You can find several in package java.lang.)

6. Many programming languages allow the use of an underscore character (_) as part of an identifier. Rewrite the definition of an identifier to allow underscores after the first initial letter (i.e., the first character must still be a letter). Rewrite the scanner method scanIdentifier() to accommodate this change.

7. One of the tasks of a scanner is to scan identifiers and then determine if the identifiers are reserved words or user-defined identifiers. Part of this task involves searching through the list of reserved words to see if an identifier matches any of them. Section 5.5 illustrates an approach using two different implementations of a sequential search (a.k.a., linear search).

    a. List and briefly describe two additional approaches for searching through the list of reserved words. (Hint 1: One such approach is mentioned in Section 5.5) (Hint 2: HashMap)

    b. Including the two approaches outlined in Section 5.5, which of the four approaches would you use? Why?

8. The scanner described in this chapter provides one token lookahead for the parser. That is, the parser can see only the next token in the input stream of tokens, and it can use that one token to make parsing decisions. Once you have the scanner working as described in Project 1: Scanner (see Exercise 1 above), extend the scanner so that it provides two tokens lookahead, and extend the test program for the scanner to test your implementation. One way to extend your scanner would be to implement scanner methods peekToken() and peekSymbol(). Method peekToken() would return the token in the input stream after the current one (i.e., the second lookahead token), and peekSymbol() would return the symbol for peekToken().

9. Building on Exercise 8 above, extend the scanner so that it provides an arbitrary number of lookahead tokens. One way to do this is to add an integer parameter to the peek methods. For example, peekSymbol(3) would allow you to peek three symbols ahead in the input stream. A call to peekSymbol(0) would be equivalent to calling getSymbol(), and a call to peekSymbol(1) would be equivalent to the method peekSymbol() described in Exercise 8 above.

Chapter 6
Syntax Analysis (a.k.a. Parsing)

This is the longest and arguably the most challenging chapter in the book. Students should read every word, parse every sentence, and try to fully understand each paragraph, example, section, etc., before continuing. (Note how I managed to sneak the word "parse" into the previous sentence. ☺)

First and foremost, the role of a parser is to verify that the grammatical rules defined by the context-free grammar are satisfied. Additionally, a parser should implement some form of error handling and recovery, and it should create an intermediate representation of the source code suitable for additional analysis and code generation.

The overall structure of the parser is based on the context-free grammar for the language. Using the approach outlined in this book, most rules in the grammar translate directly into methods in class Parser. The input to the parser is the stream of tokens from the scanner. From the perspective of the parser, each token is treated as a terminal symbol. The output of the parser is an intermediate representation of the source code. For our project we will create abstract syntax trees. We can visualize the work of the parser as follows:

Sequence of tokens returned by the scanner

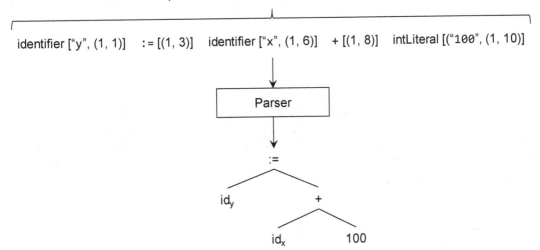

As outlined in Appendix A, we will build a parser in three separate projects. Version 1 of the parser will only check for valid syntax. If a program is not syntactically valid, then version 1 of the parser will print an error message and exit, stopping at the first error it encounters. Version 2 of the parser will add error recovery so that multiple errors can be detected and reported. Version 3 of the parser will generate abstract syntax trees, which will be used as the basis for additional analysis and code generation.

The primary focus of this chapter is language recognition; i.e., verification that the program submitted to the compiler conforms to the context-free grammar. The two following chapters will cover error recovery and generation of abstract syntax trees.

6.1 Example: Implementing method `parseLoopStmt()`

The parsing technique used in this course is called recursive descent with a single symbol lookahead. Most rules in the grammar will be implemented directly as methods in the parser. When implementing a method for a rule, if the right side of a rule references another nonterminal symbol, we simply call the method corresponding to its rule. Since the rules contain recursive references to nonterminal symbols, the parser methods contain recursive calls to other parser methods. All decisions made by the parser about what to do next are based on looking at only the next (single) symbol in the input stream.

While there are a lot of details to be covered, a brief example should illustrate recursive descent parsing and provide an overview of where we are headed in this chapter. Don't worry if you don't initially understand every detail of this example. Just try to focus on the big picture. We will cover the details later in this chapter.

Consider the grammar rule for `loopStmt`.

```
loopStmt = ( "while" booleanExpr )? "loop" statements "end" "loop" ";" .
```

We will continue to refer back to this rule as we implement its corresponding parse method named `parseLoopStmt()`.

```
public void parseLoopStmt()
   {
     . . .
   }
```

The right side of the rule starts with an optional syntax expression that begins with the reserved word `while`. Since this part of the rule is optional, that suggests that we use an `if` statement. But what should we use for the condition? This is where we look ahead at the next symbol in the input stream. If the next symbol is `while`, we know that we want to parse the optional part. So now we have the following:

```
public void parseLoopStmt()
   {
     if (scanner.getSymbol() == Symbol.whileRW)
        {
          . . .
        }
     . . .
   }
```

At this point we need to stop and explain two "helper" parsing methods named match() and matchCurrentSymbol() that we will use to recognize terminal symbols. Implementations for methods match() and matchCurrentSymbol() are shown in the next section.

Method match() has a single parameter of type Symbol. It simply verifies that the next symbol in the input stream has the same value as its parameter, and if so, it advances the scanner. If the next symbol in the input stream does not match the parameter, it signals an error by throwing an exception, specifically, an instance of ParserException.

Method matchCurrentSymbol() is used when we already know that the next symbol in the input stream is the one we want. This method takes no parameters and doesn't throw an exception. It simply advances the scanner. We could use match() for this purpose, but matchCurrentSymbol() is slightly more efficient.

Methods match() and matchCurrentSymbol() are the only two parser methods that advance the scanner to the next token. All other parser methods use these two methods when recognizing terminal symbols.

Now back to the implementation of parsing method parseLoopStmt(). Since the if condition at the beginning of the method has already checked that the next symbol in the input stream is the reserved word while, we can use the more efficient matchCurrentSymbol() to handle this symbol. Method parseLoopStmt() now becomes the following:

```
public void parseLoopStmt()
  {
    if (scanner.getSymbol() == Symbol.whileRW)
      {
        matchCurrentSymbol();
        ...
      }
    ...
  }
```

Looking back at the grammar rule for whileStmt, we see that the reserved word while must be followed by a boolean expression. Since a boolean expression is just an expression, parsing the boolean expression is handled by calling another parsing method parseExpression(). So now we have the following:

```
public void parseLoopStmt()
  {
    if (scanner.getSymbol() == Symbol.whileRW)
      {
        matchCurrentSymbol();
        parseExpression();
      }
    ...
```

```
        }
```

We will have to wait until a later chapter to see how to check that the expression does, in fact, have type `Boolean`. For now the best we can do is to call `parseExpression()`.

Continuing with our implementation of method `parseLoopStmt()`, let's return to the grammar rule. Note that the next five symbols after the boolean expression are the terminal symbol `loop`, the nonterminal symbol `statements`, and the three terminal symbols `end`, `loop`, and `semicolon` (";"). We can call method `match()` to handle the nonterminal symbols, and we will call another parsing method `parseStatements()` to parse the nonterminal symbol `statements`. Ignoring exceptions that correspond to invalid syntax for the CPRL program being parsed, the basic flow of our method for parsing loop statements now becomes the following:

```java
public void parseLoopStmt()
   {
     if (scanner.getSymbol() == Symbol.whileRW)
       {
         matchCurrentSymbol();
         parseExpression();
       }

     match(Symbol.loopRW);
     parseStatements();
     match(Symbol.endRW);
     match(Symbol.loopRW);
     match(Symbol.semicolon);
   }
```

But, of course, we don't really want to ignore syntax errors, so we enclose our parsing logic in a `try/catch` block that reports the error and then calls a helper method `exit()` to terminate. Error reporting will be handled by another class named `ErrorHandler`. Our final version of `parseLoopStmt()` is as follows:

```java
public void parseLoopStmt() throws IOException
   {
     try
       {
         if (scanner.getSymbol() == Symbol.whileRW)
           {
             matchCurrentSymbol();
             parseExpression();
           }

         match(Symbol.loopRW);
         parseStatements();
         match(Symbol.endRW);
```

```
            match(Symbol.loopRW);
            match(Symbol.semicolon);
        }
    catch (ParserException e)
        {
            ErrorHandler.getInstance().reportError(e);
            exit();
        }
    }
```

Note how the basic parsing logic inside the `try` block corresponds directly to the terminal and nonterminal symbols of the rule in the context-free grammar. Terminal symbols are handled by calling either `match()` or `matchCurrentSymbol()`, while nonterminal symbols are handled by calling a corresponding `parseN()` method. This approach is easy to comprehend, and it is easy to implement if the context-free grammar meets certain criteria. The grammar for CPRL as defined in Appendix D does not quite meet all of the criteria needed for recursive descent parsing with one symbol lookahead, but it is close. We will need to develop workarounds in a couple of places.

6.2 Recursive Descent Parsing

Recursive descent parsing uses recursive methods to "descend" through the parse tree (top-down parsing) as it parses a program. The parser is constructed systematically from the grammar using a set of programming refinements.

In general, a grammar needs to have certain "nice" properties if it is to be used for recursive descent parsing. Not all grammars are suitable for this purpose, but sometimes we can perform certain grammar transformations to make the grammar more suitable without changing the language being defined. That is, as discussed in Chapter 3, even though the two grammars appear to be different, any program considered syntactically valid by the first grammar will also be considered syntactically valid by the second grammar, and vice-versa.

Let's assume that we start with an unambiguous grammar. The first step is to separate lexical grammar rules from structural rules. We will let the scanner handle simple rules based on regular expressions such as reserved words, operators, identifiers, integer literals, etc. Symbols composed by the scanner are treated as terminal symbols in the grammar for the parser.

Additionally, we would want to simplify the grammar by substituting nonterminals where appropriate. So, for example, since syntactically a `booleanExpr` is simply an `expression` and a `varId` is simply an `identifier`, we could substitute `expression` for `booleanExpr` and `identifier` for `varId` within the rules, thereby eliminating nonterminals `booleanExpr` and `varId`. The CPRL grammar defined in Appendix D does not make the substitutions, but we will mentally make them as we implement our parser.

Here are a few of the properties that we want our grammar to have if we are going to use it to implement a recursive descent parser. First, we want to use a single rule for each nonterminal; i.e., each nonterminal appears on the left side of only one rule. Second, we want to eliminate left recursion. Some approaches to parsing can handle rules with left recursion, but left recursion is problematic for recursive descent parsers since it leads to infinite recursion within the method calls. And third, we want to left factor the grammar wherever possible. Other grammar restrictions will be discussed in more detail later on in this chapter.

We will learn how to build a recursive descent parser systematically based on the context-free grammar by providing a set of refinements or guidelines.

Recursive Descent Parsing: Refinement 1

For (almost) every rule in the grammar

```
N = ...  .
```

we define a parsing method with the name

```
parseN()
```

As an example, for the rule

```
assignmentStmt = variable ":=" expression ";" .
```

we define a parsing method named `parseAssignmentStmt()`.

The caveat "almost" for Refinement 1 refers to the fact that some very simple rules in the grammar are not implemented as parsing methods. For example, as previously discussed, the rules

```
booleanExpr = expression .
```

and

```
varId = identifier .
```

have no corresponding parsing methods. We simply make a mental substitution for these symbols as we write the parsing methods.

Similarly, the rules

```
addingOp = "+" | "-" .
```

and

```
multiplyingOp = "*" | "/" | "mod" .
```

have no corresponding parsing methods, but there are helper methods in class `Symbol` that check whether or not a symbol has one of these properties; e.g., methods `isAddingOperator()` and `isMultiplyingOperator()`.

In general, the `parseN()` methods of the parser function as follows:

- The scanner method `getSymbol()` provides one symbol "lookahead" for the parsing methods.

- On entry into the method `parseN()`, the symbol returned from the scanner should contain a symbol that could start on the right side of the rule `N = ...` .

- On exit from the method `parseN()`, the symbol returned from the scanner should contain a symbol that could follow a syntactic expression corresponding to `N`. (We will use this idea to implement error recovery in the next chapter.)

- If the production rules contain recursive references, the parsing methods will also contain recursive calls.

Parsing the "Right" Side of a Rule

We now turn our attention to refinement of the method `parseN()` associated with a grammar rule by examining the form of the grammatical expression on the right side of the rule. As an example, for the rule

```
assignmentStmt = variable ":=" expression ";" .
```

we have defined a parsing method named `parseAssignmentStmt()`. We now focus on systematic implementation of this method by examining the right side of the rule.

Recursive Descent Parsing: Refinement 2

A sequence of syntax factors F_1 F_2 F_3 ... is recognized by parsing the individual factors one at a time in order. In other words, the algorithm for parsing F_1 F_2 F_3 ... is simply

- the algorithm for parsing F_1 followed by

- the algorithm for parsing F_2 followed by

- the algorithm for parsing F_3 followed by

- ...

For example, the algorithm used to parse

```
variable ":=" expression ";"
```

is simply

- the algorithm used to parse `variable` followed by

- the algorithm used to parse `":="` followed by

- the algorithm used to parse `expression` followed by

- the algorithm used to parse `";"`.

Recursive Descent Parsing: Refinement 3

A single terminal symbol t on the right side of a rule is recognized by calling the "helper" parsing method match(t), where method match() is defined as follows:

```
private void match(Symbol expectedSymbol)
    throws IOException, ParserException
  {
    if (scanner.getSymbol() == expectedSymbol)
        scanner.advance();
    else
      {
        String errorMsg = "Expecting \"" + expectedSymbol
            + "\" but found \"" + scanner.getSymbol() + "\" instead.";
        throw error(errorMsg);
      }
  }
```

As an example, the algorithm for recognizing the assignment operator ":=" is simply the method call

```
match(Symbol.assign);
```

Note that match() calls method error() to create the exception. Actually there are two overloaded methods named error(). One takes a single string parameter for the error message and returns a ParserException using the current scanner position. The second version takes two parameters, both an error message and an explicit position to be used in creating the ParserException. The latter version is useful for reporting the position of an error associated with a previously recognized token. There is a third similar method named internalError() that can be used to create an InternalCompilerException. Similar to the use of assertions, internal compiler exceptions are used to represent problems detected within the implementation of the compiler and should never occur if the compiler is implemented correctly.

As mentioned in the previous section, in addition to match() there is another helper method named matchCurrentSymbol() that can used when we already know that the next symbol in the input stream is the one we are expecting. Method matchCurrentSymbol() is slightly more efficient in that it takes no parameters and doesn't throw an exception. It simply advances the scanner. Method matchCurrentSymbol() is implemented as follows:

```
private void matchCurrentSymbol() throws IOException
  {
     scanner.advance();
  }
```

In order to simplify explanation of the parsing methods, we will temporarily ignore exceptions thrown by the helper parsing method match(). Just assume that, instead of throwing an exception, the helper method simply prints an error message and then exits. We will return to the handling of exceptions near the end of this chapter.

Recursive Descent Parsing: Refinement 4

A nonterminal symbol N on the right side of a rule is recognized by calling the method corresponding to the rule for N; i.e., the algorithm for recognizing nonterminal N is simply a call to the method parseN().

For example, the algorithm for recognizing the nonterminal symbol expression on the right side of the rule for assignmentStmt is simply a call to the method parseExpression().

Let's consider applying all of these refinements for the rule

```
assignmentStmt = variable ":=" expression ";" .
```

The complete parsing method for recognizing an assignment statement can be implemented as follows:

```
public void parseAssignmentStmt()
  {
    parseVariable();
    match(Symbol.assign);
    parseExpression();
    match(Symbol.semicolon);
  }
```

6.3 First and Follow Sets

First Sets

The set of all terminal symbols that can appear at the start of a syntax expression E is called the first set of E and is denoted First(E). First sets provide important information that can be used to guide decisions during parser development. Let's consider some relatively straightforward examples from CPRL.

constDecl:
```
    constDecl = "const" constId ":=" literal ";" .
```
First(constDecl) = { "const" }

varDecl:
```
    varDecl = "var" identifiers ":" typeName ";" .
```
First(varDecl) = { "var" }

arrayTypeDecl:
```
    arrayTypeDecl = "type" typeId "=" "array" ... ";" .
```

First(arrayTypeDecl) = { "type" }

initialDecl:
    initialDecl = constDecl | arrayTypeDecl | varDecl .

First(initialDecl) = { "const", "var", "type" }

statementPart:
    statementPart = "begin" statements "end" .

First(statementPart) = { "begin" }

loopStmt:
    loopStmt = ("while" booleanExpr)? "loop" ... ";" .

This one requires a little more explanation. A loopStmt can begin with the terminal symbol "while, but since the while part is optional, a loopStmt can also begin with the terminal symbol "loop". Therefore, First(loopStmt) = { "while", "loop" }.

At this point we give a slightly more formal presentation of the rules used to compute first sets. While the presentation might seem a little daunting at first, the actual application of these ideas is usually a little more straightforward, as evidenced by the examples above. Using the set notation of mathematics and assuming that E and F are arbitrary syntax expressions, here are some basic rules for computing first sets.

- If t is a terminal symbol, First(t) = { t }.

- If all strings derived from E are nonempty (that is, if E is not optional), then First(E F) = First(E) .

- If some strings derived from E can be empty (that is, if E is optional or can occur zero times), then First(E F) = First(E) ∪ First(F).

- First(E | F) = First(E) ∪ First(F) .

The following rules can be derived as special cases of the previous rules:

- First((E)*) includes all terminal symbols in First(E); mathematically we write First(E) ⊆ First((E)*). As an example from CPRL, First((initialDecl)*) includes First(initialDecl), which is the set { "const", "var", "type" }.

- First((E)?) includes all terminal symbols in First(E); equivalently, First(E) ⊆ First((E)?).

- Since (E)* can occur zero times, First((E)* F) includes all terminal symbols in First(E) and all terminal symbols in First(F); equivalently First(E) ∪ First(F) ⊆ First((E)* F).

- Since (E)? can occur zero times, First((E)? F) includes all terminal symbols in First(E) and all terminal symbols in First(F); equivalently

  First(E) ∪ First(F) ⊆ First((E)? F).

For simplification, the above discussion does not address cases where the postfix operator plus ("+") is used in a syntax expression, but similar ideas apply. Recall that (E)+ is equivalent to
E (E)* (i.e., E followed by (E)*). When forming similar rules about first sets involving the (E)+, we need to consider the case whether or not strings derived from E can be empty.

As a general strategy for computing first sets, we recommend using a bottom-up approach; i.e., start with simplest rules and work toward more complicated (composite) rules.

Follow Sets

The set of all terminal symbols that can follow immediately after a syntax expression E is called the follow set of E and is denoted Follow(E). Understanding follow sets is important not only for parser development but also for error recovery. If N is a nonterminal, we will use Follow(N) during error recovery when trying to parse N. To compute Follow(N) for a nonterminal N, you must analyze all rules that reference N. Computation of follow sets can be a bit more involved than computation of first sets. Let's start with some follow set examples from CPRL.

As an example, let's consider what can follow an initialDecl. From the rule

```
initialDecls = ( initialDecl )* .
```

we know that another initialDecl can follow an initialDecl, so the follow set for initialDecl includes the first set of initialDecl; i.e., "const", "var", and "type".

From the rules

```
declarativePart = initialDecls subprogramDecls .
subprogramDecls = ( subprogramDecl )* .
subprogramDecl = procedureDecl | functionDecl .
```

we know that a procedureDecl or functionDecl can follow an initialDecl, so the follow set for initialDecl also includes "procedure" and "function".

But what if there are no subprogram declarations? After all, the rule says that there could be zero. Then from the rules

```
program = declarativePart statementPart "." .
statementPart = "begin" statements "end" .
```

we know that statementPart can follow an initialDecl, so the follow set for initialDecl includes "begin".

Conclusion:

> Follow(initialDecl) = { "const", "var", "type", "procedure", "function",
>   "begin" }

Let's consider another example. What can follow a loopStmt?

... (This one is left as an exercise, but here are a couple of hints. First, any statement can follow a loop statement, and therefore Follow(loopStmt) can include any terminal symbol that can start another statement. Second, a loop statement could appear as the last statement at the end of a program. Here is the answer — see if you can analyze the grammar to get this result.)

Conclusion:

> Follow(loopStmt) = { identifier, "return", "end", "if", "elsif",
>   "else", "while", "loop", "exit", "read", "write",
>   "writeln" }

Assuming that N is a nonterminal and S, T, and U are arbitrary syntax expressions, here are some basic rules for computing follow sets for T:

- Consider all production rules similar to the following, where T is followed by U in a rule:

  N = S T U .   N = S (T)* U .   N = S (T)? U .

  In all of these cases, Follow(T) includes all terminal symbols in First(U); equivalently, First(U) ⊆ Follow(T). Additionally, if U can be empty, then Follow(T) also includes Follow(N); equivalently, Follow(N) ⊆ Follow(T).

- Now consider all production rules similar to the following, where T is at the end of a rule:

  N = S T .   N = S (T)* .   N = S (T)? .

  In all these cases, Follow(T) includes all terminal symbols in Follow(N); equivalently Follow(N) ⊆ Follow(T).

- If T occurs in the form (T)* or (T)+, then Follow(T) includes all terminal symbols in First(T); equivalently, First(T) ⊆ Follow(T).

As a general strategy for computing follow sets, we recommend using a top-down approach; i.e., start with first rule (the one containing the start symbol) and work toward the simpler rules.

Recursive Descent Parsing: Refinement 5

This refinement handles the case where a syntax expression can be repeated zero or more times. Repetition zero or more times suggests that we need a loop. Therefore, a syntax expression of the form (E)* is recognized by the following algorithm:

```
while current symbol is in First(E) loop
    apply the algorithm for recognizing E
end loop
```

But what if a terminal symbol in First(E) could also follow (E)*? In that case we would not know whether to continue looping or to exit the loop and parse the input following (E)*. This leads us to our first of several grammar restrictions.

Grammar Restriction 1: First(E) and Follow((E)*) must be disjoint in this context.

In mathematical terms, First(E) ∩ Follow((E)*) = ∅. (Why?)

Example: Recursive Descent Parsing Refinement 5

Consider the rule for initialDecls as follows:

```
initialDecls = ( initialDecl )* .
```

The first set for initialDecl is the set of three reserved words constRW, varRW, and typeRW. Therefore, the CPRL method for parsing initialDecls can be implemented as follows:

```
public void parseInitialDecls()
  {
    while (scanner.getSymbol() == Symbol.constRW ||
           scanner.getSymbol() == Symbol.varRW   ||
           scanner.getSymbol() == Symbol.typeRW)
      {
        parseInitialDecl();
      }
  }
```

In CPRL, the symbols constRW, varRW, and typeRW cannot follow initialDecls (plural form), and therefore the loop will exit appropriately whenever all initial declarations have been parsed. (Exercise: Which symbols can follow initialDecls?)

Class Symbol provides several helper methods for testing properties of symbols. Examples include the following:

```
public boolean isReservedWord()
public boolean isInitialDeclStarter()
public boolean isStmtStarter()
public boolean isRelationalOperator()
public boolean isLiteral()
```

For example, method isInitialDeclStarter() is implemented as follows:

```
/**
 * Returns true if this symbol can start an initial declaration.
 */
public boolean isInitialDeclStarter()
   {
      return this == constRW || this == varRW || this == typeRW;
   }
```

Using the helper methods in class Symbol, we can rewrite the method for
parseInitialDecls() as follows:

```
public void parseInitialDecls()
   {
      while (scanner.getSymbol().isInitialDeclStarter())
         parseInitialDecl();
   }
```

Recursive Descent Parsing: Refinement 6

Since a syntax expression of the form (E)+ is equivalent to E (E)* since "one or more" is
equivalent to "one" followed by "zero or more." A syntax expression of the form (E)+ is
recognized by the following algorithm:

```
apply the algorithm for recognizing E
while current symbol is in First(E) loop
     apply the algorithm for recognizing E
end loop
```

Equivalently, the algorithm for recognizing (E)+ can be written using a loop that tests at the
bottom.

```
loop
     apply the algorithm for recognizing E
     exit when current symbol is not in First(E)
end loop
```

In Java, the loop structure that tests at the bottom is called a do-while loop, so the
algorithm implemented in Java would more closely resemble the following:

```
do
     apply the algorithm for recognizing E
while current symbol is in First(E)
```

As an aside, note that none of the *structural* grammar rules for CPRL actually use the
postfix + syntax to indicate "one or more." The postfix + is used only in the rule for an
integer literal, and that rule is part of the lexical grammar and is handled by the scanner,
not the parser.

Grammar Restriction 2: If E can generate the empty string, then `First(E)` and `Follow((E)+)` must be disjoint in this context; i.e., `First(E) ∩ Follow((E+)) = Ø`. (Why?)

Recursive Descent Parsing: Refinement 7

This refinement handles the case where a syntax expression can be optional, which suggests that we need an if statement. A syntax factor of the form `(E)?` is recognized by the following algorithm:

```
if current symbol is in First(E) then
      apply the algorithm for recognizing E
end if
```

As before this leads to another grammar restriction.

Grammar Restriction 3: `First(E)` and `Follow((E)?)` must be disjoint in this context; i.e., `First(E) ∩ Follow((E)?) = Ø`. (Why?)

Example: Recursive Descent Parsing Refinement 7

Consider the rule for an exit statement:

```
exitStmt = "exit" ( "when" booleanExpr )? ";" .
```

The method for parsing an exit statement is as follows:

```
public void parseExitStmt()
  {
    match(Symbol.exitRW);
    if (scanner.getSymbol() == Symbol.whenRW)
      {
        matchCurrentSymbol();
        parseExpression();
      }

    match(Symbol.semicolon);
  }
```

Note that the first set for the optional when clause is simply { "when" }, so we use the reserved word when to tell us whether or not to parse a when clause.

Questions: What is the follow set for the optional when clause? What problem would we have if it contained the reserved word "when"?

Recursive Descent Parsing: Refinement 8

This refinement applies when we have alternatives and need to decide which alternative to choose for parsing. A syntax factor of the form E | F is recognized by the following algorithm:

```
if current symbol is in First(E) then
      apply the algorithm for recognizing E
elsif current symbol is in First(F) then
      apply the algorithm for recognizing F
else
      syntax error
end if
```

Grammar Restriction 4: First(E) and First(F) must be disjoint in this context; i.e., First(E) ∩ First(F) = ∅. (Why?)

Example: Recursive Descent Parsing Refinement 8

Consider the rule in CPRL for initialDecl:

```
initialDecl = constDecl | varDecl | arrayTypeDecl .
```

The method for parsing an initialDecl in CPRL is implemented similar to the following:

```java
public void parseInitialDecl()
  {
    if (scanner.getSymbol() == Symbol.constRW)
        parseConstDecl();
    else if (scanner.getSymbol() == Symbol.varRW)
        parseVarDecl();
    else if (scanner.getSymbol() == Symbol.typeRW)
        parseArrayTypeDecl();
    else
        throw internalError("Invalid initial declaration.");
  }
```

6.4 LL(1) Grammars

If a grammar satisfies the restrictions imposed by the previous parsing rules, then the grammar is called an **LL(1)** grammar. Recursive descent parsing using one symbol lookahead can be used only if the grammar is LL(1). The interpretation of the characters in LL(1) is as follows:

- First 'L': read the source file from left to right.

- Second 'L': descend into the parse tree from left to right.

- Number '1': one symbol lookahead.

The phrase "recursive descent" refers to the fact that we descend (top-down) the parse tree using recursive method/function calls.

Not all grammars are LL(1); e.g., any grammar that has left recursion is not LL(1). In practice, the syntax of most programming languages can be defined, or at least closely approximated, by an LL(1) grammar; e.g., by using grammar transformations such as eliminating left recursion.

Developing a Parser

As outlined in Appendix A, we divide the parser implementation into three major projects as follows:

1. Parser version 1 (Project 2): Language recognition based on a context-free grammar (with minor checking of language constraints).

2. Parser version 2 (Project 3): Add error-recovery.

3. Parser version 3 (Project 4): Add generation of abstract syntax trees.

Based on this chapter, version 1 of the parser focuses on language recognition. Using the parsing refinements discussed earlier, we need to verify that the grammar restrictions in terms of first and follow sets are satisfied by the grammar for CPRL. This means that we will need to analyze the grammar to compute first and follow sets.

6.5 Variables versus Named Values

From the perspective of the grammar, there is no real distinction between a variable and a named value. Consider the two grammar rules.

```
variable = ( varId | paramId ) ( "[" expression "]" )* .
namedValue = variable .
```

Both are parsed similarly, but we make a distinction based on the context. For example, consider the assignment statement below.

```
x := y;
```

The identifier "x" represents a variable, and the identifier "y" represents a named value. Loosely speaking, it's a variable if it appears on the left side of an assignment statement, and it's a named value if it is used as an expression. The distinction between a variable and a named value will become important later when we consider the topics of error recovery and code generation. The error recovery and code generation are different for a variable than for a named value.

6.6 Handling Grammar Limitations

As given, the grammar for CPRL is "not quite" LL(1). For example, consider the rule for a statement.

```
statement = assignmentStmt | ifStmt | loopStmt | exitStmt | readStmt
          | writeStmt | writelnStmt | procedureCallStmt | returnStmt .
```

When we write the method `parseStatement()`, we want to use the lookahead symbol to select the parsing method to call.

- If the lookahead symbol is "`if`", we know that we want to call `parseIfStmt()`.

- If the lookahead symbol is "`while`" or "`loop`", we know that we want to call `parseLoopStmt()`.

- If the lookahead symbol is "`return`", we know that we want to call `parseReturnStmt()`.

- If the lookahead symbol is "`identifier`", we know that we want to call either `parseAssignmentStmt()` or `parseProcedureCallStmt()`, but which one? An identifier is in the first set of both an assignment statement and a procedure call statement.

A similar problem exists when parsing a factor.

```
factor = "not" factor | constValue | namedValue
       | functionCall | "(" expression ")" .
```

An identifier is in the first set of `constValue`, `namedValue`, and `functionCall`.

There are several possible approaches to solving these kinds of dilemmas. Below we describe three such approaches.

Approach 1: Use an Additional Lookahead Symbol

In some cases, using an additional lookahead symbol might resolve the problem. For example, when trying to decide whether or not to call `parseAssignmentStmt()` or `parseProcedureCallStmt()`, suppose that we could peek at the symbol following the identifier.

- If the symbol following the identifier were "`[`" or "`:=`", we would know to call `parseAssignmentStmt()`.

- If the symbol following the identifier were "`(`" or "`;`", we would know to call `parseProcedureCallStmt()`.

- If the symbol following the identifier were anything else, we would know that the program is not valid according to the rules of the context-free grammar.

If a grammar meets all of our restrictions for parsing except that it requires 2 symbols of lookahead, then the grammar is said to be LL(2).

Approach 2: Rewrite/Factor the Grammar

A second possible solution to our problem is to use factoring to rewrite the grammar. For example, since both an assignment statement and a procedure call statement start with an identifier, let's factor out the identifier part and create a different kind of statement called `idStmt` that encompasses both, so that the rule for `statement` becomes the following:

```
statement = idStmt | ifStmt | loopStmt | exitStmt | readStmt
          | writeStmt | writelnStmt | returnStmt .
```

Now when parsing a statement, if the lookahead symbol is an identifier, we would know to call parseIdStmt().

We could define idStmt as

```
idStmt = identifier ( assignCompletion | procCallCompletion ) .
```

where assignCompletion and procCallCompletion are defined as follows:

```
assignCompletion = ( "[" expression "]" )* ":=" expression ";" .
procCallCompletion = ( actualParameters )? ";" .
```

Approach 3: Use an Identifier Table

A third approach to solving our parsing problem is to use an identifier table to store information about how the identifier was declared; e.g., if the identifier was declared as a constant, a variable, a procedure name, etc. Using this approach, when trying to decide whether to call parseAssignmentStmt() or parseProcedureCallStmt(), we could extract the text contained in the lookahead token for the identifier, look up the text in the identifier table, and then use information about how it was declared to determine which parsing method to call. This is the approach we will use in this book, and this approach is explained in more detail in the next section.

6.7 Class IdTable

For now we will create a preliminary version of class IdTable to help track the types of identifiers that have been declared. This class will be extended in subsequent chapters to contain more information, and it will allow us to perform a more complete analysis of CPRL scope and type rules.

We start by defining a simple enum class IdType as follows:

```
enum IdType
   {
     constantId, variableId, arrayTypeId, procedureId, functionId;
   }
```

For our current purposes, we don't need to distinguish between subprogram parameters and variables; all will be assigned an IdType value of variableId.

The implementation of class IdTable needs to address the issue of scope since it is possible to have more than one identifier with the same name. Consider the following example where variable x is declared in two different scopes.

```
var x : Integer;
var y : Integer;

procedure p is
   var x : Integer;
   var n : Integer;
begin
    x := 5;    // which x?
    n := y;    // which y?
end p;

begin
   x := 8;        // which x?
end.
```

In the assignment statement

```
x := 5;
```

the name x refers to the integer variable declared in procedure p.

In the assignment statement

```
n := y;
```

the name n refers to the integer variable declared in procedure p, but the name y refers to the integer variable declared in the enclosing program scope.

In the assignment statement

```
x := 8;
```

near the end of the above program, the name x refers to the integer variable declared in the program scope, not the one declared in procedure p.

Handling Scopes within Class `IdTable`

Variables and constants can be declared at the program level or at the subprogram level, introducing the concept of scope. Class `IdTable` will need to search for names both within the current scope and possibly in an enclosing scope. Therefore, we implement class `IdTable` as a stack of maps, where the map is from identifier strings to their `IdType`. Since CPRL subprograms can't be nested, we will never use more than two levels of the stack, one for program scope and one for subprogram scope. But note that the flexibility exists for having more than two levels of scope, and this flexibility can be used for some of the project exercises that extend the CPRL programming language.

When a new scope is opened, a new map is pushed onto the stack. Searching for a declaration involves searching within the current level (top map in the stack) and then, if necessary, within enclosing scopes (maps under the top).

Key methods in class `IdTable` are as follows:

```
/**
 * Opens a new scope for identifiers.
 */
public void openScope()

/**
 * Closes the outermost scope.
 */
public void closeScope()

/**
 * Add a token and its type at the current scope level.
 *
 * @throws ParserException if the identifier token is already defined in
 *                         in the current scope.
 */
public void add(Token idToken, IdType idType) throws ParserException

/**
 * Returns the id type associated with the identifier token's text.
 * Returns null if no such declaration is found.  Searches enclosing
 * scopes if necessary.
 */
public IdType get(Token idToken)
```

Adding Declarations to `IdTable`

During parsing, when an identifier is declared, the parser will attempt to add its token and `IdType` to the table within the current scope. If an identifier with the same name (same token text) has been previously declared in the current scope, then an exception will be thrown indicating that the program being compiled has an error since all identifiers declared in the same scope must have unique names.

As an example, consider the following excerpt from method `parseConstDecl()`:

```
Token constId = scanner.getToken();
match(Symbol.identifier);
...
idTable.add(constId, IdType.constantId);
```

Calling `idTable.add()` will throw a `ParserException` if the identifier token is already defined in the current scope.

Using `IdTable` to Check Applied Occurrences of Identifiers

When an identifier is encountered in the statement part of the program or a subprogram, the parser will check that the identifier has been declared and then use the information about how the identifier was declared to facilitate correct parsing; e.g., you can't assign a value to an identifier that was declared as a constant.

As an example of using the table to check applied occurrence of identifiers, consider the following excerpt from method `parseFactor()`, where we use the type of the identifier to determine whether to parse a constant value, a named value or a function call.

```
else if (scanner.getSymbol() == Symbol.identifier)
  {
    // Handle identifiers based on whether they are
    // declared as variables, constants, or functions.
    Token idToken = scanner.getToken();
    IdType idType = idTable.get(idToken);

    if (idType != null)
      {
        if (idType == IdType.constantId)
            parseConstValue();
        else if (idType == IdType.variableId)
            parseNamedValue();
        else if (idType == IdType.functionId)
            parseFunctionCall();
        else
            throw error("Identifier \"" + scanner.getToken()
                    + "\" is not valid as an expression.");
      }
    else
        throw error("Identifier \"" + scanner.getToken()
                + "\" has not been declared.");
  }
```

Additional Examples Using IdTable

The following example shows the use of `IdTable` in parsing a procedure declaration.

```
// procedureDecl = "procedure" procId ( formalParameters )?
//      "is" initialDecls statementPart procId ";" .
match(Symbol.procedureRW);
Token procId = scanner.getToken();
match(Symbol.identifier);
idTable.add(procId, IdType.procedureId);
idTable.openScope();
```

```
if (scanner.getSymbol() == Symbol.leftParen)
    parseFormalParameters();

match(Symbol.isRW);
parseInitialDecls();
parseStatementPart();
idTable.closeScope();

Token procId2 = scanner.getToken();
match(Symbol.identifier);

if (!procId.getText().equals(procId2.getText()))
    throw error(procId2.getPosition(), "Procedure name mismatch.");

match(Symbol.semicolon);
...
```

Note that the procedure name is defined in the outer (program) scope, but its parameters and initial declarations are defined within the scope of the procedure. Also, note the check that the procedure names (procId and procId2) match. Technically, ensuring that the procedure names match goes beyond simple syntax analysis and represents more of a constraint check. As far as the context-free grammar is concerned, they are both just identifiers.

The following example in method parseStatement() shows the use of IdTable to help decide whether to parse an assignment statement or a procedure call statement based on the type of an identifier.

```
public void parseStatement() throws IOException
  {
    Symbol symbol = scanner.getSymbol();

    if (symbol == Symbol.identifier)
      {
        IdType idType = idTable.get(scanner.getToken());
        if (idType != null)
          {
            if (idType == IdType.variableId)
                parseAssignmentStmt();
            else if (idType == IdType.procedureId)
                parseProcedureCallStmt();
            else
                throw error(...);
          }
```

```
        else
            throw error(...);
    }
    else if (symbol == Symbol.ifRW)
        parseIfStmt();
    else if (symbol == Symbol.loopRW || symbol == Symbol.whileRW)
        parseLoopStmt();
    else if (symbol == Symbol.exitRW)
        parseExitStmt();
    ...
}
```

Class `ErrorHandler`

For consistency in error reporting, we implement a class named `ErrorHandler`. This class implements the singleton pattern in that there is only one instance, which can be obtained by calling the static method `ErrorHandler.getInstance()`.

Here are several key methods in class `ErrorHandler`.

```
/**
 * Reports the error.  Stops compilation if the maximum
 * number of errors have been reported.
 */
public void reportError(CompilerException e)


/**
 * Reports the error and exits compilation.
 */
public void reportFatalError(Exception e)


/**
 * Reports a warning and continues compilation.
 */
public void reportWarning(String warningMessage)
```

Version 1 of the parser does not implement error recovery. When an error is encountered, the parser will print an error message and then exit. In order to ease the transition to error recovery in the next version of the parser, most parsing methods will wrap the basic parsing methods in a try/catch block. Any parsing method that calls `match()` or the `add()` method of `IdTable` will need to have a try/catch block. Error reporting will be implemented within the catch clause of the try/catch block.

For example, the complete implementation of method `parseAssignmentStmt()` for version 1 of the parser is as follows:

```java
public void parseAssignmentStmt() throws IOException
  {
    try
      {
        parseVariable();
        match(Symbol.assign);
        parseExpression();
        match(Symbol.semicolon);
      }
    catch (ParserException e)
      {
        ErrorHandler.getInstance().reportError(e);
        exit();
      }
  }
```

The call to method `exit()` at the end of the `catch` block simply writes out a message that errors have been detected and that compilation is being terminated.

Parsing Variables and Named Values

Recall that variables and named values are equivalent with respect to the context-free grammar, but we make a distinction since error recovery and code generation are different for a variable than for a named value. However, with respect to language recognition, the basic logic for parsing a variable is identical to the logic for parsing a named value.

To implement methods `parseVariable()` and `parseNamedValue()` we use a helper method to provide common logic for both methods. The helper method does not handle any parser exceptions but instead throws them back to the calling method where they can be handled appropriately. An outline of the helper method, `parseVariableExpr()`, is shown below. Both `parseVariable()` and `parseNamedValue()` call the helper method to parse the grammar rule for variable.

```java
/**
 * Parse the following grammar rule:<br>
 * <code>variable = ( varId | paramId ) ( "[" expression "]" )* .</code>
 */
public void parseVariableExpr() throws IOException, ParserException
  {
    Token idToken = scanner.getToken();
    match(Symbol.identifier);
    IdType idType = idTable.get(idToken);

    if (idType == null)
      {
        String errorMsg = "Identifier \"" + idToken
```

```
                         + "\" has not been declared.";
             throw error(idToken.getPosition(), errorMsg);
          }
       else if (idType != IdType.variableId)
          {
             String errorMsg = "Identifier \"" + idToken
                            + "\" is not a variable.";
             throw error(idToken.getPosition(), errorMsg);
          }

       while (scanner.getSymbol() == Symbol.leftBracket)
          {
             matchCurrentSymbol();
             parseExpression();
             match(Symbol.rightBracket);
          }
    }
```

As shown below, method `parseVariable()` simply calls the helper method to parse its grammar rule.

```
    public void parseVariable() throws IOException
       {
          try
             {
                parseVariableExpr();
             }
          catch (ParserException e)
             {
                ErrorHandler.getInstance().reportError(e);
                exit();
             }
       }
```

Method `parseNamedValue()` is implemented similarly.

We are now ready to implement version 1 of the parser, as described in Project 2 of Appendix A. Start with the skeletal code provided on the book web site and fill in the missing parts to implement the parser.

6.8 Essential Terms and Concepts

ErrorHandler (class)	first set
follow set	IdTable (class)
LL(1)	LL(1) grammar restrictions
LL(2)	match(Symbol expectedSymbol) (method)
matchCurrentSymbol() (method)	named value
parseN() (where N is a nonterminal)	Parser (class)
recursive descent	variable

6.9 Exercises

1. **Project Assignment.** Implement **Project 2: Language Recognition** as described in Appendix A.

2. True or false.

    a. All context-free grammars are LL(1).

    b. The context-free grammar for CPRL is LL(1).

3. What is the primary programming language construct used to parse a syntax expression of the form:

    a. (E)*

    b. (E)+

    c. (E)?

    d. E | F | ...

    > Hint: Your answers should be something like "while loop," "if statement without an else part," etc.

4. What is the primary role of a parser that is addressed in this chapter?

5. Describe the three alternative approaches outlined in Section 6.5 for handling the issue where both nonterminals assignmentStmt and procedureCallStmt start with an identifier, and therefore the grammar for CPRL is not LL(1).

6. Explain the difference between the terms "variable" and "named value" as used in this book.

7. Explain the role of methods openScope() and closeScope() in class IdTable.

8. Assuming that the scanner provides two tokens lookahead (see Exercise 8 at the end of Chapter 5), implement method `parseStatement()` as described in Approach 1 of Section 6.5. Use the extra token lookahead to decide whether to call `parseAssignmentStmt()` or `parseProcedureCallStmt()`.

9. For this exercise, treat symbols recognized by the scanner as terminal symbols with respect to the parser. For example, in addition to operators and reserved words quoted in the CPRL grammar, the following are all terminal symbols with respect to the parser: `identifier`, `intLiteral`, `charLiteral`, `stringLiteral`, and `EOF`.

   Using the grammar for CPRL, compute the following:

   a. `First(program)`

   b. `First(initialDecl)`

   c. `First(loopStmt)`

   d. `First(simpleExpr)` (Hint: There are 10 terminal symbols in the answer.)

   e. `First(statement)`

   f. `Follow(statement)` (Hint: There are 12 terminal symbols in the answer.)

   g. `Follow(formalParameters)`

   h. `Follow(constDecls)`

   i. `Follow(factor)` (Hint: There are 19 terminal symbols in the answer.)

Chapter 7
Error Handling/Recovery

Using the concepts explained in the previous chapter, we were able to build version 1 of the parser. The primary purpose of version 1 is to check that a CPRL program is valid according to the rules expressed in the context-free grammar. In addition, using class IdTable, version 1 of the parser can also detect certain scope errors. For example, it detects an attempt to declare two different identifiers with the same name within the same scope.

If a program fails to satisfy the CPRL rules checked by version 1 of the parser, the parser stops at the first error and prints an error message. In this chapter we implement version 2 of class Parser by adding error recovery to version 1, so that multiple syntax errors can be detected and reported. When a compiler is integrated with an editor or as part of integrated development environment (IDE), it might be acceptable to stop compilation after detecting the first error and pass control to the editor. But in general, even if integrated with an editor, a compiler should try to detect and report as many errors as possible.

7.1 Types of Compilation Errors

When defining the CPRL language, we can categorize compilation errors into four general groups as follows:

- Syntax errors – violation of the language syntax as defined by a context-free grammar; e.g., invalid or missing tokens such as missing semicolons or using "=" instead of ":=" for assignment.

- Scope errors – violation of language scope rules; e.g., declaring two identifiers with the same name within the same scope.

- Type errors – violation of language type rules; e.g., the expression following an "if" does not have type Boolean.

- Miscellaneous errors – other errors not categorized above; e.g. trying to use a var parameter in a function.

Version 1 of our parser was able to detect syntax errors and scope errors. While version 1 could reject many invalid CPRL programs, it did not check for all possible errors. Detection of type errors and miscellaneous errors will wait until Chapter 9 where we cover constraint analysis.

As an alternative to categorizing errors based on the general type of error as described above, we can also categorize errors based on when and where they are detected during the compilation process. So, for example, some syntax errors will be detected by the scanner and some by the parser. As outlined in Chapters 5 and 6, we will use exception classes to assist with error handling. Following is a diagram of the inheritance hierarchy for the exceptions used by the CPRL compiler.

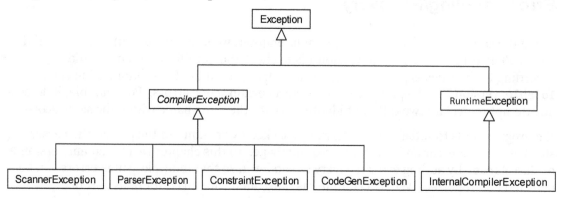

Class `CompilerException` is an abstract class whose functionality is inherited by four classes `ScannerException`, `ParserException`, `ConstraintException`, and `CodeGenException`. All four subclasses of `CompilerException` are checked exceptions in Java.

As indicated by their names, `ScannerException` is used to encapsulate errors detected by the scanner, `ParserException` is used to encapsulate errors detected by the parser, `ConstraintException` is used to encapsulate errors detected during constraint analysis, and `CodeGenException` is used to encapsulate errors detected during code generation. Instances of `CodeGenException` should be rare compared to the other three types of exceptions.

Checked versus Unchecked Exceptions

Java makes a distinction between checked and unchecked exceptions. Any exception that derives from class `Error` or class `RuntimeException` is called an *unchecked* exception. All other exceptions are called *checked* exceptions. In the above diagram, `InternalCompilerException` is an unchecked exception.

There are two special situations involving checked exceptions. If a call is made to a method that throws a checked exception or if a checked exception is explicitly thrown, then an enclosing block must either handle the exception locally or else the enclosing method must declare the exception as part of its exception specification list. Unchecked exceptions may be declared in the exception specification list or handled, but doing so is not required.

Instances of `InternalCompilerException` represent problems with the implementation of the compiler and should never get thrown if the compiler is implemented correctly. As outlined in Section 5.6, we will continue to use Java's `assert` statement to signal most of the internal errors within the compiler.

7.2 Handling Errors

The phrase **error handling** means finding errors and reporting them to the user. The phrase **error recovery** means that the compiler attempts to resynchronize its state and possibly the state of the input token stream so that compilation can continue normally. The purpose of error recovery is to find as many errors as possible in a single compilation, with the goal of reporting every error exactly one time.

Effective error recovery is extremely difficult. Any attempt to resynchronize the state of the compiler and/or the input token stream means that we are trying to make an educated guess as to what the programmer was trying to do at the point the error was detected. Therefore, programmers learn early in their careers that any error reported by a compiler after the first error should be considered suspect. Correcting the first reported error could reveal new errors that were not detected before, or it could eliminate "false" errors reported by the compiler.

Recall that version 1 of the parser used class ErrorHandler to report errors. When an error was detected, we threw an exception, reported the error in a catch block, and then exited the program. For version 1 of the parser our catch blocks looked like the following:

```
catch (ParserException e)
  {
    ErrorHandler.getInstance().reportError(e);
    exit();
  }
```

Note that class ErrorHandler implements the singleton pattern; i.e., there is only one ErrorHandler object, and it is accessed solely through the static getInstance() method. With error recovery we don't want to exit after encountering an error. Instead, we try to *recover* in order to detect/report additional errors. But what if we encounter many compilation errors? We don't want to overwhelm the programmer with an excessive number of error messages. Therefore, class ErrorHandler keeps track of the number of errors reported, and it exits compilation after a fixed number of errors have been reported.

Here are three key methods in class ErrorHandler:

```
/**
 * Returns true if errors have been reported.
 */
public boolean errorsExist()

/**
 * Reports the error.  Exits compilation if more than a fixed number
 * of errors have been reported.
 */
public void reportError(CompilerException e)
```

```
/**
 * Reports the error and exits compilation.
 */
public void reportFatalError(Exception e)
```

7.3 Error Recovery

Here is our general approach to error handling and recovery. As with version 1 of the parser, we will enclose the parsing code for each rule with a `try/catch` block, and when errors are detected, we will throw an exception so that control transfers to the `catch` block. The `catch` block will report the error by calling appropriate methods in class `ErrorHandler`. But here is the main change for error recovery. Instead of exiting the program after reporting an error, the `catch` block will skip tokens until it finds one whose symbol is in the follow set of the nonterminal of the rule being parsed. The catch block will then return from the parsing method for that rule, so that the next symbol in the input stream will be valid as if no errors had been detected.

For example, consider the grammar rule for a `varDecl`.

```
varDecl = "var" identifiers ":" typeName ";" .
```

The corresponding parser method is `parseVarDecl()`. Based on the context-free grammar, a `varDecl` can be followed by a `constDecl`, another `varDecl`, a `typeDecl`, a `procedureDecl`, a `functionDecl`, or a `statementPart`. Therefore, the follow set for a `varDecl` is the following set of reserved words:

```
{ const, var, type, procedure, function, begin }
```

If there are no compilation errors in the program being compiled, then when `parseVarDecl()` returns, the next symbol in the input stream **should** be one of those reserved words. If there are compilation errors, then we skip over all tokens until we encounter one of those reserved words. So when `parseVarDecl()` returns, the next symbol in the input stream is valid just as though `parseVarDecl()` had not detected any errors.

Method recover()

Method `recover()` implements error recovery by skipping tokens until it finds one in the follow set of the nonterminal defined by the rule. The follow set is implemented by an array of symbols, which is passed as a parameter to method `recover()`. Here is the complete implementation for method `recover()`.

```
/**
 * Advance the scanner until the current symbol is one of
 * the symbols in the specified array of follows.
 */
private void recover(Symbol[] followers) throws IOException
  {
```

```
      scanner.advanceTo(followers);
   }
```

Using these ideas, a possible implementation of `parseVarDecl()` **with error recovery** is as follows:

```
   public void parseVarDecl() throws IOException
   {
     try
       {
         match(Symbol.varRW);
         parseIdentifiers();
         match(Symbol.colon);
         parseTypeName();
         match(Symbol.semicolon);
       }
     catch (ParserException e)
       {
         ErrorHandler.getInstance().reportError(e);
         Symbol[] followers =
           {
             Symbol.constRW,     Symbol.varRW,      Symbol.typeRW,
             Symbol.procedureRW, Symbol.functionRW, Symbol.beginRW
           };
         recover(followers);
       }
   }
```

Shared Follow Sets

When several nonterminals have the same follow set, it is convenient to declare the array of "followers" once as a static final field and then reference it as needed, rather than repeat the declaration in all catch blocks. For example, all initial declarations have the same follow set. Rather than repeat the array of six symbols in the three methods `parseConstDecl()`, `parseVarDecl()`, and `parseArrayTypeDecl()`, we declare it once in the parser as follows:

```
   /** Symbols that can follow an initial declaration. */
   private static final Symbol[] initialDeclFollowers =
     {
       Symbol.constRW,     Symbol.varRW,      Symbol.typeRW,
       Symbol.procedureRW, Symbol.functionRW, Symbol.beginRW
     };
```

The array `initialDeclFollowers` can be used for error recovery in all three parsing methods for initial declarations; i.e., in `parseConstDecl()`, `parseVarDecl()`, and `parseArrayTypeDecl()`.

Using the idea of shared follow sets, the implementation for parseVarDecl() now becomes the following:

```
public void parseVarDecl() throws IOException
  {
    try
      {
        ...
      }
    catch (ParserException e)
      {
        ErrorHandler.getInstance().reportError(e);
        recover(initialDeclFollowers);
      }
  }
```

Error Recovery for parseStatement()

Method parseStatement() handles the following rule:

```
statement = assignmentStmt | ifStmt | loopStmt | exitStmt | readStmt
          | writeStmt | writelnStmt | procedureCallStmt | returnStmt .
```

Error recovery for parseStatement() requires special care when the symbol is an identifier since an identifier can not only start a statement but can also appear elsewhere in the statement such as in an expression. Consider, for example, an assignment statement or a procedure call statement. If, during error recovery, we advance to an identifier, we could be in the middle of a statement rather than at the start of the next statement.

Since the most common identifier-related error is to declare or reference an identifier incorrectly, we will assume that this is the case and advance to the next semicolon before implementing error recovery. The goal is that by advancing to the next semicolon, we hopefully move the scanner to the end of the erroneous statement.

Assuming that stmtFollowers is the name of the shared follow set for statements, we implement error recovery in parseStatement() as follows:

```
try
  {
    ...
  }
catch (ParserException e)
  {
    ErrorHandler.getInstance().reportError(e);
    scanner.advanceTo(Symbol.semicolon);
    recover(stmtFollowers);
  }
```

Implementing Error Recovery

Not all parsing methods will need a `try`/`catch` block for error recovery at this stage of parser development. For example, method `parseInitialDecls()` does not need a `try`/`catch` block.

```
public void parseInitialDecls() throws IOException
  {
    while (scanner.getSymbol().isInitialDeclStarter())
        parseInitialDecl();
  }
```

Similarly, method `parseStatements()` will not need a `try`/`catch` block.

Method `match()` throws a `ParserException` when an error is detected. This method does not implement error recovery, but any parsing method that calls `match()` will need a `try`/`catch` block for error recovery. Similarly, any method that calls the `add()` method of `IdTable` will need to have a `try`/`catch` block.

7.4 Additional Error Recovery Strategies

Here we briefly describe a couple of additional possible error recovery strategies.

One common strategy is to first report the error and then replace the token that caused the error with one that might be allowed at that point in the parsing process. Specific examples include:

- Replace "=" by ":=" when parsing an assignment statement in a CPRL compiler. The assumption here is that the programmer might have experience with other languages that use "=" as the assignment operator.

- Replace "=" by "==" when expecting a relational operator in a C++ or Java compiler. Every programmer who first learns a C-like languages misuses "=" to mean equality at some point, and therefore this error recovery strategy would be appropriate most of the time.

The following code shows how to replace "=" by ":=" in method `parseAssignmentStmt()` for CPRL by enclosing the call to `match(Symbol.assign)` in its own `try`/`catch` block.

```
try
  {
    match(Symbol.assign);
  }
catch (ParserException e)
  {
    if (scanner.getSymbol() == Symbol.equals)
      {
        ErrorHandler.getInstance().reportError(e);
```

```
        matchCurrentSymbol();    // treat "=" as ":=" in this context
    }
  else
      throw e;
}
```

Instead of simply calling `match(Symbol.assign)`, we use a nested `try/catch` block that treats "=" as ":=".

Another common strategy is to first report the error and then insert a new token in front of the one that generated the error. Specific examples include:

- When parsing an `exit` statement, after matching "`exit`", if a symbol encountered is in the first set of an expression, then report the error, insert "`when`", and continue parsing. The assumption here is that the programmer forgot the "`when`".

- When parsing an expression, if a right parenthesis ")" is expected but a semicolon ";" is encountered as the next symbol, report the error and then insert a right parenthesis with the expectation that the semicolon will likely terminate a statement. The assumption here is that the programmer forgot the closing parenthesis.

Of the four specific examples described above, the only one actually implemented in the compiler project is the replacement of "=" by ":=" in method `parseAssignmentStmt()`.

7.5 Essential Terms and Concepts

checked exception

CompilerException (class)

ErrorHandler (class)

error recovery

ParserException (class)

ScannerException (class)

syntax errors

unchecked exception

CodeGenException (class)

ConstraintException (class)

error handling

miscellaneous errors

recover() (method)

scope errors

type errors

7.6 Exercises

1. **Project Assignment.** Implement **Project 3: Error Recovery** as described in Appendix A.

2. Name, describe, and give examples for the four general types of compilation errors as discussed in this chapter.

3. Fill in the blank.
   Given a grammar rule for a nonterminal N, our general approach to error handling involves enclosing the basic parsing code of `parseN()` in a `try/catch` block. When errors are detected, control transfers to the `catch` block, which will report the error and then skip tokens in the input stream until it finds a token in the _____ of N.

4. True or false.

   a. All parsing methods should have a `try/catch` block for error recovery

   b. All parsing methods that calls `match()` should have a `try/catch` block for error recovery.

   c. All parsing methods that call the `add()` method of `IdTable` will need to have a `try/catch` block.

5. Explain the concept of shared follow sets and their roll in error recovery.

6. Explain why we need to take a slightly different approach to error recovery for the method `parseStatement()`. (Why didn't the general approach used in other parsing methods work very well in this case?)

7. Describe the *special* error recovery strategy used when trying to match the assignment operator (`:=`) as part of parsing an assignment statement in CPRL.

Chapter 8
Abstract Syntax Trees

In this chapter we will describe the final modification to class Parser so that, as it parses the source code, it will also generate an intermediate representation of the program known as abstract syntax trees (ASTs). Once the parser is successfully generating abstract syntax trees, work on the parser will be complete. All remaining work for the compiler will take place in the AST objects, which provide the framework for performing constraint analysis and code generation.

8.1 Overview of Abstract Syntax Trees

An abstract syntax tree is similar to a parse tree but without extraneous nonterminal and terminal symbols. Abstract syntax trees provide an explicit representation of the structure of the source code that can be used for additional constraint analysis (e.g., for analysis of type constraints), some optimizations (tree transformations), and code generation. We will use different classes to represent different node types in our abstract syntax trees. Most AST classes correspond to a rule in the grammar, and the name of the class is often the name of the nonterminal symbol for the rule. Examples of AST classes that we will develop include AssignmentStmt, LoopStmt, Variable, and Expression. Each AST class has named instance variables (fields) to reference its children. These instance variables provide the "tree" structure. Occasionally we also include additional fields to support error handling and code generation.

> In his book *Language Implementation Patterns* [Parr 2010], Terence Parr refers to this type of AST structure as an irregular (named child fields) heterogeneous (different node types) AST.

Abstract Syntax Trees: Example 1

Consider the grammar for an assignment statement.

```
assignmentStmt = variable ":=" expression ";" .
```

The important parts of an assignment statement are the variable (the left side of the assignment) and the expression (the right side of the assignment). We create an AST node for an assignment statement with the following structure:

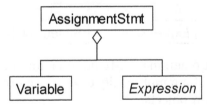

Here is an outline for the implementation of class `AssignmentStmt`.

```
public class AssignmentStmt extends Statement
  {
    private Variable   variable;
    private Expression expr;

    // position of assignment operator (for error reporting)
    private Position assignPosition;

    public AssignmentStmt(Variable   variable,
                          Expression expr,
                          Position   assignPosition)
      {
        this.variable = variable;
        this.expr = expr;
        this.assignPosition = assignPosition;
      }
    ...
  }
```

Note that parameter position in the above constructor is the position of the assignment operator (`:=`), which is not actually part of the "tree" structure but is used in error reporting.

Abstract Syntax Trees: Example 2

Consider the following grammar for a loop statement:

```
loopStmt = ( "while" booleanExpr )?
           "loop" statements "end" "loop" ";" .
```

Once a loop statement has been parsed, we don't need to retain the nonterminal symbols. The AST for a loop statement would contain only the statements in the body of the loop and the optional boolean expression. We can visualize the AST for a loop statement as follows:

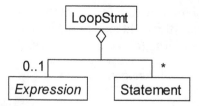

The notation 0..1 in the above diagram is UML notation for optional (0 or 1), and the asterisk ("*") is UML notation for a multiplicity of zero or more; i.e., a `LoopStmt` can contain a list of zero or more `Statement` objects.

Here is an outline for the implementation of class `LoopStmt`:

```
public class LoopStmt extends Statement
   {
     private Expression whileExpr;
     private List<Statement> statements;

     public LoopStmt(Expression whileExpr, List<Statement> statements)
        {
          this.whileExpr  = whileExpr;
          this.statements = statements;
          ...
        }
     ...
   }
```

Note that `whileExpr` can be null to indicate that the optional boolean expression is not present.

Abstract Syntax Trees: Example 3

For binary expressions, part of the grammar exists simply to define operator precedence. Once an expression has been parsed, we do not need to preserve additional information about nonterminals that were introduced to define precedence (relation, simpleExpr, term, factor, etc.). A binary expression AST would contain only the operator and the left and right operands. The parsing algorithm would build the AST so as to preserve operator precedence. We can visualize the AST for a binary expression as follows:

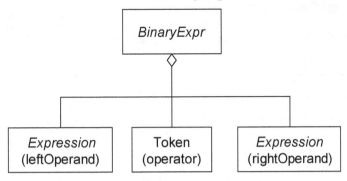

Here is an outline for the implementation of class `BinaryExpr`:

```
public abstract class BinaryExpr extends Expression
   {
     private Expression leftOperand;
     private Token operator;
     private Expression rightOperand;
```

```
    public BinaryExpr(Expression leftOperand, Token operator,
                      Expression rightOperand)
      {
        this.leftOperand  = leftOperand;
        this.operator     = operator;
        this.rightOperand = rightOperand;
        ...
      }
    ...
  }
```

Note that `BinaryExpr` is an abstract class. Concrete subclasses include `AddingExpr`, `LogicalExpr`, `MultiplyingExpr`, and `RelationalExpr`.

> Caution: The word "abstract" is used in two different ways in this chapter. It is used as part of the name for the intermediate representation known as abstract syntax trees, but it is also used in the Java/object-oriented sense of an abstract class; i.e., a class for which instances cannot be created. The meaning should be clear from the context of the term.

8.2 Structure of Abstract Syntax Trees

There is an abstract class `AST` that serves as the superclass for all other abstract syntax tree classes. Class `AST` contains implementations of methods common to all subclasses plus declarations of abstract methods required by all concrete subclasses. All AST classes will be defined in an "`...ast`" subpackage.

> Note the use of AST (in monospaced font) for the specific class and AST (in normal font) as an abbreviation for "abstract syntax tree".

Here is an outline of class `AST`:

```
  public abstract class AST
    {
      ...

      /** Check semantic/contextual constraints. */
      public abstract void checkConstraints();

      /** Emit the object code for the AST. */
      public abstract void emit() throws CodeGenException, IOException;
    }
```

Methods checkConstraints() and emit() "walk" the tree structure using recursive calls to subordinate tree nodes. These methods are used in constraint analysis and code generation, respectively, and will be covered in more detail in subsequent chapters.

We will create a hierarchy of classes, some of which are abstract. All classes in the hierarchy are direct or indirect subclasses of AST. Each node in the abstract syntax tree constructed by the parser will be an object of a class in the AST hierarchy. Most classes in the hierarchy will correspond to and have names similar to the nonterminal symbols in the grammar, but not all abstract syntax trees have this property. See, for example, the earlier discussion about binary expressions. We do not need abstract syntax tree classes corresponding to nonterminals simpleExpr, term, factor, etc.

In addition, some parsing methods simply return lists of AST objects. Examples include:

```
public List<InitialDecl> parseInitialDecls() throws IOException
public List<SubprogramDecl> parseSubprogramDecls() throws IOException
public List<Token> parseIdentifiers() throws IOException
public List<Statement> parseStatements() throws IOException
public List<ParameterDecl> parseFormalParameters() throws IOException
public List<Expression> parseExpressions() throws IOException
public List<Expression> parseActualParameters() throws IOException
```

Our AST classes adopt the following naming conventions:

- Most AST classes have names similar to nonterminals in the grammar.

- The parsing method for that nonterminal will create the corresponding AST object.

- Parsing methods with plural names will return lists of AST objects. (Note that we wrote the grammar so that related nonterminals have this property.)

As examples, we will create classes Statement and LoopStmt as follows:

```
public abstract class Statement extends AST ...
public class LoopStmt extends Statement ...
```

The parsing method parseLoopStmt() would be responsible for creating the AST node for LoopStmt. Instead of returning void as we did in the previous chapters, method parseLoopStmt() will return an object of class LoopStmt.

Similarly, the parsing method parseStatements() will return a list of Statement objects, where each Statement object is either an AssignmentStmt, a LoopStmt, an IfStmt, etc.

Method parseLiteral() is a special case. The grammar rules define literal to be one of the following: intLiteral, charLiteral, stringLiteral, "true", or "false". Since all of these literals are tokens returned from the scanner, method parseLiteral() simply returns a Token. There is no AST class named Literal.

```
public Token parseLiteral() throws IOException
```

A partial inheritance diagram for the AST hierarchy is shown below. Names for abstract classes are shown in italics.

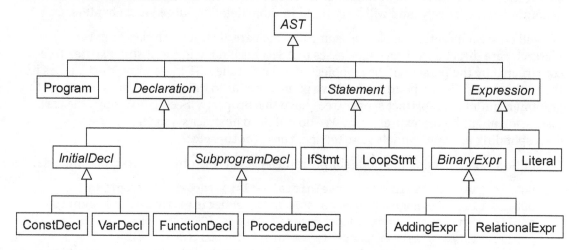

8.3 Extending Class `IdTable` with References to Declarations

There are a number of CPRL language constraints associated with identifiers that are not expressed in the context-free grammar for CPRL, and a parser built using only the set of grammar-related parsing rules will not reject programs that violate these language constraints. Examples of such constraints include rules such as the following:

- An identifier must be declared exactly once in the current scope before it is used.

- For an assignment statement, the variable on the left side of the assignment operator and the expression on the right side must have the same type.

So, for example, the following programs would be valid with respect to syntax but not valid with respect to contextual constraints.

Example 1

```
var x : Integer;
begin
   y := 5;    // y has not been declared
end.
```

Example 2

```
var c : Char;
begin
   c := -3;    // can't assign an integer value to a character
end.
```

We will extend class IdTable to help track not only the types of identifiers that have been declared but also their complete declarations. Class IdTable will now map type String (identifier name) to type Declaration, not String to IdType as done previously. We no longer need class IdType; it was simply a bridge to simplify the implementation of earlier versions of the parser. While the original version of IdTable allowed us to catch the error in Example 1 above, the new version will put us in a position to catch type errors as shown in Example 2. Details of the approach to catching type errors will be covered in the next chapter, where we discuss constraint analysis in more detail.

Class Declaration is part of the AST hierarchy. A declaration object contains a reference to the identifier token and information about its type. We will use different subclasses of Declaration for kinds of declarations; e.g., ConstDecl, VarDecl, ProcedureDecl, etc. Here are a few selected methods in the modified version of class IdTable.

```
/**
 * Opens a new scope for identifiers.
 */
public void openScope()

/**
 * Closes the outermost scope.
 */
public void closeScope()

/**
 * Add a declaration at the current scope level.
 * @throws ParserException if the identifier token associated with the
 *                 declaration is already defined in the current scope.
 */
public void add(Declaration decl) throws ParserException

/**
 * Returns the Declaration associated with the identifier token.
 * Searches enclosing scopes if necessary.
 */
public Declaration get(Token idToken)

/**
 * Returns the current scope level.
 */
public ScopeLevel getCurrentLevel()
```

ScopeLevel is defined as an enum class with two constants, PROGRAM and SUBPROGRAM. Additional details of the scope level of a declaration are discussed in the next section and in subsequent chapters on code generation for variables. As illustrated in Section 13.6, within a subprogram, different code is generated for variables declared at PROGRAM (global) scope than for variables declared at SUBPROGRAM (local) scope.

Adding Declarations to `IdTable`

During parsing, when an identifier is declared, the parser will attempt to add the declaration to the table within the current scope. Note that the declaration already contains the identifier token, so we do not need to pass it as a separate parameter. The identifier table can extract the identifier name from the declaration when adding it to the map. As before, if an identifier with the same name (same token text) has been previously declared in the current scope, then an exception will be thrown indicating that the program being compiled has an error.

As an example, consider the following excerpt from method `parseConstDecl()`:

```
Token constId = scanner.getToken();
match(Symbol.identifier);
...
ConstDecl constDecl = new ConstDecl(constId, constType, literal);
idTable.add(constDecl);
```

Interface `NamedDecl`

Recall the grammar rule for `variable`.

```
variable = ( varId | paramId ) ( "[" expression "]" )* .
```

Since `varId` and `paramId` are just identifiers, we could have written the rule more simply as follows:

```
variable = identifier ( "[" expression "]" )* .
```

The reason for writing the rule using different types of identifiers was to *suggest* that the variable could have been declared using a `VarDecl` (which we convert to a `SingleVarDecl`) or a `ParameterDecl`.

As an example, consider the assignment statement:

```
x := y;
```

The variable x could have been declared in a variable declaration or a parameter declaration. Similarly, the named value y on the right side of the assignment statement could have been declared as a variable or a subprogram parameter.

Even though variables (and therefore named values) could have different types of declarations associated with them, there is a need to treat both types of declarations uniformly at several points during parsing. We achieve this uniformity by creating interface `NamedDecl` and specifying that AST classes `SingleVarDecl` and `ParameterDecl` implement this interface. Interface `NamedDecl` contains five methods common to both AST classes as follows:

```
public Type getType();
public int getSize();
public ScopeLevel getScopeLevel();
public void setRelAddr(int relAddr);
public int getRelAddr();
```

As an example of where `NamedDecl` is used during parsing, consider the following excerpt from `parseStatement()`:

```
if (symbol == Symbol.identifier)
  {
    Declaration decl = idTable.get(scanner.getToken());

    if (decl != null)
      {
        if (decl instanceof NamedDecl)
            stmt = parseAssignmentStmt();
        ...
      }
  }
...
```

Using `IdTable` to Check Applied Occurrences of Identifiers

When an identifier is encountered in the statement part of the program or a subprogram (e.g., as part of an expression or subprogram call), the parser will check that the identifier has been declared. The parser will then use the information about how the identifier was declared to facilitate correct parsing (e.g., you can't assign a value to an identifier that was declared as a constant).

As an example, consider the following excerpt from method `parseVariableExpr()`:

```
Token idToken = scanner.getToken();
match(Symbol.identifier);
Declaration decl = idTable.get(idToken);

if (decl == null)
    throw error("Identifier \"" + idToken + "\" has not been declared.");
else if (!(decl instanceof NamedDecl))
    throw error("Identifier \"" + idToken + "\" is not a variable.");
```

8.4 Types and Declarations

The compiler uses two classes to provide support for CPRL types.

1. Class Type encapsulates the language types and their sizes.

2. Class ArrayType extends Type to provide additional support for arrays.

Class Type encapsulates the language types and sizes (number of bytes) for the programming language CPRL. Type sizes are initialized to values appropriate for the CPRL virtual machine; e.g., 4 for Integer, 2 for Character, 1 for Boolean, etc.

Class type is defined as follows:

```
public class Type
   {
     private String name;
     private int    size;


     ...

   }
```

Predefined types are declared as static constants within the class.

```
public static final Type Boolean = new Type(...);
public static final Type Integer = new Type(...);
public static final Type Char    = new Type(...);
public static final Type String  = new Type(...);
public static final Type Address = new Type(...);
public static final Type UNKNOWN = new Type(...);
```

Class Type also contains a static method that returns the type of a literal symbol.

```
public static Type getTypeOf(Symbol literal)
```

Class ArrayType extends class Type, and therefore array types are also types. In addition to the total size of the array, class ArrayType also keeps track of the number of elements in the array and the element type.

```
/**
 * Construct an array type with the specified name, number of
 * elements, and the type of elements contained in the array.
 */
public ArrayType(String typeName, int numElements, Type elementType)
```

When the parser parses an array type declaration, the constructor for AST class ArrayTypeDecl creates an ArrayType object.

Parsing ConstDecl

As an example of using class Type, consider the following code for parsing a ConstDecl:

```
/**
 * Parse the following grammar rule:<br>
 * <code>constDecl = "const" constId ":=" literal ";" .</code>
 *
 * @return the parsed ConstDecl.  Returns null if parsing fails.
 */
public ConstDecl parseConstDecl() throws IOException
  {
    try
      {
        match(Symbol.constRW);
        Token constId = scanner.getToken();
        match(Symbol.identifier);
        match(Symbol.assign);
        Token literal = parseLiteral();
        match(Symbol.semicolon);

        Type constType = Type.UNKNOWN;
        if (literal != null)
            constType = Type.getTypeOf(literal.getSymbol());

        ConstDecl constDecl = new ConstDecl(constId, constType, literal);
        idTable.add(constDecl);
        return constDecl;
      }
    catch (ParserException e)
      {
        ErrorHandler.getInstance().reportError(e);
        recover(initialDeclFollowers);
        return null;
      }
  }
```

The Scope Level of a Variable Declaration

During code generation, when a variable or named value is referenced in the statement part of a program or subprogram, we need to be able to determine where the variable was declared. Class IdTable contains a method getCurrentLevel() that returns the block nesting level for the current scope; i.e., it returns PROGRAM for objects declared at the outermost (program) scope, and it returns SUBPROGRAM for objects declared within a subprogram.

When a variable is declared, the declaration is initialized with the current level.

```
ScopeLevel scopeLevel = idTable.getCurrentLevel();
varDecl = new VarDecl(identifiers, varType, scopeLevel);
```

CPRL scope levels are illustrated in the following example:

```
var x : Integer;   // scope level of declaration is PROGRAM
var y : Integer;   // scope level of declaration is PROGRAM

procedure p is     // scope level of declaration is PROGRAM
   var x : Integer;  // scope level of declaration is SUBPROGRAM
   var b : Integer;  // scope level of declaration is SUBPROGRAM
begin
   ... x ...    // x was declared at SUBPROGRAM scope
   ... b ...    // b was declared at SUBPROGRAM scope
   ... y ...    // y was declared at PROGRAM scope
end p;

begin
   ... x ...    // x was declared at PROGRAM scope
   ... y ...    // y was declared at PROGRAM scope
   ... p ...    // p was declared at PROGRAM scope
end.
```

VarDecl versus SingleVarDecl

Recall that a variable declaration can declare several identifiers, all with the same type.

```
var x, y, z : Integer;
```

This declaration is logically equivalent to declaring each variable separately.

```
var x : Integer;
var y : Integer;
var z : Integer;
```

To simplify constraint checking and code generation, within the AST we will view a variable declaration as a collection of single variable declarations.

We will use a class `SingleVarDecl` that contains a variable declaration for only one identifier. Here is an outline for the implementation of this class:

```
public class SingleVarDecl extends InitialDecl implements NamedDecl
  {
    private ScopeLevel scopeLevel;
    ...

    public SingleVarDecl(Token identifier, Type varType,
                         ScopeLevel scopeLevel)
      {
        super(identifier, varType);
        this.scopeLevel = scopeLevel;
```

```
        }

    ...
    }
```

Class VarDecl contains a list of SingleVarDecl objects, as illustrated below:

```
public class VarDecl extends InitialDecl
    {
      // the list of SingleVarDecls for the variable declaration
      private List<SingleVarDecl> singleVarDecls;

      public VarDecl(List<Token> identifiers, Type varType,
                     ScopeLevel scopeLevel)
        {
          super(null, varType);
          singleVarDecls = new ArrayList<>(identifiers.size());
          for (Token id : identifiers)
              singleVarDecls.add(new SingleVarDecl(id,
                                 varType, scopeLevel));
        }
      ...
    }
```

Method parseInitialDecls() constructs/returns a list of initial declarations. For constant and array type declarations, this method simply adds them to the list. For variable declarations (VarDecls), this method extracts the list of single variable declarations (SingleVarDecls) and adds them to the list. The original VarDecl is no longer used after this point.

Here is an excerpt from method parseInitialDecls() illustrating these ideas.

```
InitialDecl decl = parseInitialDecl();

if (decl instanceof VarDecl)
    {
      // add the single variable declarations
      VarDecl varDecl = (VarDecl) decl;
      for (SingleVarDecl singleVarDecl : varDecl.getSingleVarDecls())
          initialDecls.add(singleVarDecl);
    }
else
    initialDecls.add(decl);
```

Example: Abstract Syntax Tree

Consider the following small CPRL program:

```
var x : Integer;
begin
    x := 5;
    writeln x;
end.
```

We can visualize the associated abstract syntax tree as shown in the diagram as follows. This diagram uses solid lines to indicate the structural links for the tree and dotted lines to indicate back references to declarations.

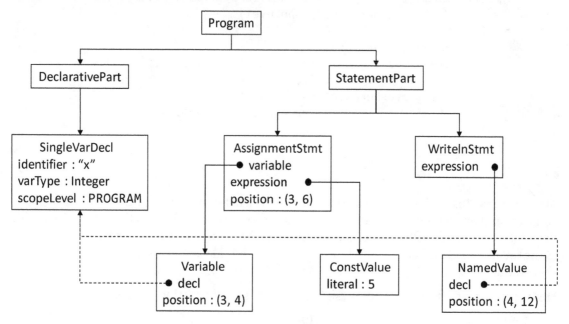

8.5 Maintaining Context During Parsing

Certain CPRL statements need access to an enclosing context for constraint checking and proper code generation. Consider, for example, the following exit statement:

```
exit when n > 10;
```

An exit statement has meaning only when nested inside a loop. Correct code generation for an exit statement requires knowledge of which loop encloses it. Similarly, a return statement requires knowledge of its enclosing subprogram. Classes LoopContext and SubprogramContext will be used to maintain contextual information in these cases.

Following are several key methods from class LoopContext.

```
/**
 * Returns the loop statement currently being parsed.
 * Returns null if no such loop statement exists.
 */
public LoopStmt getLoopStmt()

/**
 * Called when starting to parse a loop statement.
 */
public void beginLoop(LoopStmt stmt)

/**
 * Called when finished parsing a loop statement.
 */
public void endLoop()
```

Similarly, here are several key methods from class SubprogramContext.

```
/**
 * Returns the subprogram declaration currently being parsed.
 * Returns null if no such procedure exists.
 */
public SubprogramDecl getSubprogramDecl()

/**
 * Called when starting to parse a subprogram declaration.
 */
public void beginSubprogramDecl(SubprogramDecl subprogDecl)

/**
 * Called when finished parsing a procedure declaration.
 */
public void endSubprogramDecl()
```

As an example using context, consider the following code for parsing a loop statement:

```
LoopStmt stmt = new LoopStmt();
...
loopContext.beginLoop(stmt);
stmt.setStatements(parseStatements());
loopContext.endLoop();
```

Then when parsing an exit statement as one of the statements inside the loop, we gain access to the enclosing loop by doing the following:

```
ExitStmt stmt = null;
...
LoopStmt loopStmt = loopContext.getLoopStmt();
if (loopStmt == null)
    throw error(exitPosition,
            "Exit statement is not nested within a loop");
match(Symbol.semicolon);
return new ExitStmt(expr, loopStmt);
```

8.6 Essential Terms and Concepts

abstract syntax tree (AST)	AST (class)
binary expression	checkConstraints() (method)
emit() (method)	IdTable (class)
LoopContext (class)	NamedDecl (class)
parsing method return values	PROGRAM scope
scope level	SingleVarDecl (class)
SUBPROGRAM (scope)	SubprogramContext (class)
VarDecl (class)	

8.7 Exercises

1. **Project Assignment.** Implement **Project 4: Abstract Syntax Trees** as described in Appendix A.

2. Describe the structure defined by the fields (instance variables) of the following AST classes:
    a. AssignmentStmt
    b. LoopStmt
    c. BinaryExpr

3. The AST class BinaryExpr is an abstract Java class. What are some of the concrete classes that extend BinaryExpr?

4. Explain the terms VarDecl and SingleVarDecl as used in this chapter. Give examples to illustrate the distinction.

5. Describe the role of class LoopContext in parsing loops and exit statements.

6. Describe the role of class SubprogramContext in parsing subprograms and return statements.

7. If you study the implementation of classes LoopContext and SubprogramContext, you will notice that class SubprogramContext maintains a reference to only one subprogram, but LoopContext has a stack of loop statements. Why is it necessary for LoopContext to maintain references to more than one loop statement? (Hint: What can be nested?)

8. Explain what is meant by the "scope level" of a variable declaration.

Chapter 9
Constraint Analysis

9.1 Overview of Constraint Analysis

Recall that the definition of a programming language involves the specification of its syntax, contextual constraints, and semantics. Syntax involves defining the basic language symbols (or tokens) and the allowed structure of symbols to form programs. Syntax is almost always specified by a context-free grammar, and that is the approach we have taken in defining CPRL.

Contextual constraints are program rules and restrictions that cannot be specified (or cannot be easily specified) in a context-free grammar. For CPRL these constraints consist primarily of type and scope rules. Note that what we are calling "constraint analysis" is sometimes referred to as "contextual analysis" or "analysis of static semantics." For CPRL, contextual constraints are specified informally using English descriptions.

The semantics of a programming language is its meaning; i.e., its behavior of program when it is run on a machine. Semantics is often specified using informal descriptions in a natural language.

Syntax Analysis versus Constraint Analysis

Syntax analysis verifies that a program conforms to the formal syntax of the language as defined by a context-free grammar. Syntax analysis is performed by the parser. Constraint analysis verifies that a program conforms to the additional language rules and requirements that are not expressed in a context-free grammar. While there exist formalisms for expressing these additional rules, these formalisms are much more complex than context-free grammars, and therefore the additional rules that go beyond context-free grammars are often expressed informally in a natural language such as English.

As implemented in the compiler project for CPRL, constraint analysis is performed partly by the parser using helper classes IdTable, LoopContext, and SubprogramContext, and partly by the abstract syntax trees using methods named checkConstraints().

Our constraint rules fall into three general categories as follows:

- Scope rules: Rules associated with declarations and applied occurrences of identifiers.

- Type rules: Rules associated with the types of expressions and their uses in certain contexts.

- Miscellaneous rules: Language constraints that do not fall into either of the above categories. Some of these rules represent internal errors within the compiler that might have occurred during parsing.

Scope Rules in CPRL

CPRL has what is known as a flat block structure in that there are only two scope levels. Declarations are either global in scope or local to a subprogram. The scope rules for CPRL are fairly simple. There are essentially only two scope rules.

First, every user-defined identifier (constant, variable, type name, subprogram name, etc.) must be declared. When we encounter an applied occurrence of an identifier, we must be able to discover its declaration and associate the declaration with the identifier.

And second, all identifiers appearing in declarations must be unique within their scope. In other words, the same identifier must not be used in two different declarations within the same scope.

Scope analysis (a.k.a., identification) is the process of verifying the scope rules. For CPRL, scope analysis is implemented within the parser using class `IdTable`. Class `IdTable` is capable of handling nested scopes of two levels as required by CPRL, but it could easily be extended to handle arbitrary nesting of scopes.

We implemented a version of scope analysis in Chapter 6 and enhanced it in Chapter 8, where we associated an identifier with a reference to its actual declaration. Having a reference to the complete declaration will allow us to check additional constraints as outlined in this chapter. For example, having a reference to an identifier's declaration lets us know not only that the identifier was declared as a variable but also that it was declared to have type `Integer`.

Scope analysis using class `IdTable` is summarized below.

- When an identifier is declared, the parser will attempt to add a reference to its declaration to `IdTable` within the current scope. If a declaration with the same name (same token text) has been previously added in the current scope, then an exception will be thrown indicating that the program being compiled has a scope error.

- When an applied occurrence of an identifier is encountered (e.g., in a statement), the parser will check that the identifier has been declared. If not, then a scope error has occurred. If the identifier has been declared, then the parser will store a reference to the identifier's declaration as part of the AST where the identifier is used. This reference will be used during constraint analysis to help verify that the additional constraints are satisfied by the program.

Type Rules in CPRL

CPRL is a statically-typed language, which means that every variable and expression has a type and that type compatibility is a static property; i.e., it can be determined by the compiler. Type rules for CPRL define how and where certain types can be used. We define type rules in any context where a variable or expression can appear. Here are a couple of examples.

For an assignment statement, the type of the variable on the left side of the assignment symbol must be the same as the type of the expression on the right side. So for CPRL, we can assign an integer expression to an integer variable and a boolean expression to a boolean variable, but we can't assign a character expression to an integer variable. Note that some languages do not require type equality here; they require only that the types be assignment compatible. For example, in C it is perfectly acceptable to assign a character to an integer.

As a second example of a type rule, consider that for a negation expression, the operand must have type Integer, and the result of a negation expression has type Integer.

Implementing Constraint Analysis

Constraint analysis is the process of verifying that all constraint rules have been satisfied. For CPRL, most type and miscellaneous rules are verified using the method checkConstraints() in the AST classes. Even AST classes that do not have associated constraints will implement the method checkConstraints() if they contain references to objects of other AST classes since they will need to call checkConstraints() on those other AST objects.

We illustrate with a couple of examples. Here is the code for constraint checking in class Program, which has references to the declarative part and the statement part.

```
@Override
public void checkConstraints()
  {
    if (declPart != null)
        declPart.checkConstraints();

    stmtPart.checkConstraints();
  }
```

Similarly, here is the code for constraint checking in class StatementPart, which is essentially a list of Statement objects.

```
@Override
public void checkConstraints()
  {
    for (Statement stmt : statements)
        stmt.checkConstraints();
  }
```

9.2 Constraint Rules for CPRL

This section lists the additional type and miscellaneous rules for CPRL organized in terms of the AST classes whose checkConstraints() methods will be responsible for implementing the rules. The constraint rules for CPRL/0 are listed first, followed by the rules for subprograms and then arrays. The constraint rules for subprograms and arrays will be revisited in Chapters 13 and 14, respectively.

Constraint Rules for CPRL/0

- **Adding Expression and Multiplying Expression**
  - Type Rule: Both operands must have type `Integer`.
  - Miscellaneous Rule: The result has type `Integer`

- **Assignment Statement**
  - Type Rule: The variable (on the left side of the assignment) and the expression (on the right side) must have the same type.

- **Exit Statement**
  - Type Rule: If a "when" expression exists, it must have type `Boolean`.
  - Miscellaneous Rule: The exit statement must be nested within a loop statement. (This constraint will be handled by the parser using class `LoopContext`.)

- **If Statement**
  - Type Rule: The expression must have type `Boolean`.
  - Type Rule: The expression for any "elsif" clauses must have type `Boolean`.

- **Read Statement**
  - Type Rule: The variable must have either type `Integer` or type `Char`.

- **Logical Expression**
  - Type Rule: Both operands must have type `Boolean`.
  - Miscellaneous Rule: The result has type `Boolean`.

- **Loop Statement**
  - Type Rule: If a "while" expression exists, it must have type `Boolean`.

- **Negation Expression**
  - Type Rule: The operand must have type `Integer`.
  - Miscellaneous Rule: The result has type `Integer`.

- **Not Expression**
  - Type Rule: The operand must have type `Boolean`.
  - Miscellaneous Rule: The result has type `Boolean`.

- **Relational Expression**
  - Type Rule: Both operands must have the same type.
  - Type Rule: Only scalar types (Integer, Char, or Boolean) are allowed for operands. (For example, in CPRL, you can't have a relational expression where both operands are arrays or string literals.)
  - Miscellaneous Rule: The result has type Boolean.

- **Variable Declaration and Single Variable Declaration**
  - Type Rule: The type should be Integer, Boolean, Char, or a user-defined array type.

- **Constant Declaration and Constant Value**
  - Miscellaneous Rule: If the literal value has type Integer, then it must be able to be converted to an integer value on the CPRL virtual machine. (In other words, check that Integer.parseInt() will not fail.) If the check fails for a constant declaration, then set the literal's value to a valid value for Integer in order to prevent additional error messages every time that the constant declaration is used.

- **Write Statement**
  - Miscellaneous Rule: For a "write" statement (but not "writeln"), there should be at least one expression.

Constraint Rules for Subprograms

- **Return Statement**
  - Type Rule: If the statement returns a value for a function, then the type of expression being returned must be the same as the function return type.
  - Miscellaneous Rule: If the return statement returns a value, then the return statement must be nested within a function declaration.
  - Miscellaneous Rule: If the return statement is nested within a function, then it must return a value.
  - Miscellaneous Rule: The return statement must be nested within a subprogram. (This rule is already handled by the parser using class SubprogramContext.)

- **Function Declaration**
  - Miscellaneous Rule: There should be no var parameters.
  - Miscellaneous Rule: There should be at least one return statement.

- **Subprogram Call (for both procedures and functions)**
  - Type Rule: The number of actual parameters should be the same as the number of formal parameters, and each corresponding pair of parameter types should match.

- **Procedure Call**
  - Miscellaneous Rule: If the formal parameter is a var parameter, then the actual parameter must be a named value (not an arbitrary expression).

Constraint Rules for Arrays

- **Array Type Declaration**
  - Type Rule: The constant value specifying the number of items in the array must have type Integer, and the associated value must be a positive number.

- **Variable (and therefore also for Named Value)**
  - Type Rule: Each index expression must have type Integer.
  - Miscellaneous Rule: Index expressions are permitted only for variables with an array type.

9.3 Examples of Constraint Analysis

Example. Constraint checking for class AssignmentStmt

```
@Override
public void checkConstraints()
  {
    try
      {
        expr.checkConstraints();
        var.checkConstraints();

        if (!matchTypes(var.getType(), expr.getType()))
          {
            String errorMsg = "Type mismatch for ...";
            throw error(assignPosition, errorMsg);
          }
      }
    catch (ConstraintException e)
      {
        ErrorHandler.getInstance().reportError(e);
      }
  }
```

Example. Constraint checking for class `NegationExpr`

```java
@Override
public void checkConstraints()
  {
    try
      {
        Expression operand = getOperand();
        operand.checkConstraints();

        // unary +/- can only be applied to an integer expression
        if (operand.getType() != Type.Integer)
          {
            String errorMsg = "Expression ...";
            throw error(operand.getPosition(), errorMsg);
          }
      }
    catch (ConstraintException e)
      {
        ErrorHandler.getInstance().reportError(e);
      }

    setType(Type.Integer);
  }
```

9.5 Essential Terms and Concepts

`checkConstraints()` (method)	contextual constraint
flat block structure	`IdTable` (class)
miscellaneous rule	scope rule
statically typed	type rule

9.6 Exercises

1. **Project Assignment.** Implement **Project 5: Constraint Analysis** as described in Appendix A.

2. Describe the two scope rules for CPRL.

3. Describe and give several examples of type rules for CPRL

4. Describe and give several examples of miscellaneous rules for CPRL

5. Fill in the blanks.
   Constraint analysis is performed in two separate places within the CPRL compiler,
   _____ and

   _____.
   (Hints: Where are scope rules verified? Where are type rules verified?)

6. In Chapter 6 we implemented a form of scope analysis using classes `IdTable` and
   `IdType`. Describe the changes to scope analysis as implemented in this chapter. (Hint:
   Class `IdType` is no longer used.)

7. Select several type and miscellaneous rules for CPRL/0, and for each such rule, write
   two test programs in CPRL, one correct program that satisfies the rule and one
   incorrect program that does not satisfy the rule. The incorrect program should be valid
   CPRL except for the single rule violation. After completing Project 5 (Appendix A), use
   the test programs to check if your compiler correctly implements the rules.

Chapter 10
The CPRL Virtual Machine

This chapter presents an overview of the CVM (CPRL Virtual Machine), a hypothetical computer designed to simplify the code generation phase of a compiler for CPRL. Additional details of the CVM are provided in subsequent chapters as part of code generation, and Appendix E contains a detailed definition of the CVM, including complete descriptions of every instruction.

10.1 Overview of the CVM

CVM uses a stack architecture; i.e., most instructions either expect values on the run-time stack, place results on the run-time stack, or both. Memory is organized into 8-bit bytes, and each byte is directly addressable. A word is a logical grouping of 4 consecutive bytes in memory. The address of a word is the address of its first (low) byte.

Boolean values are represented in a single byte, where a zero value means false and any nonzero value is interpreted as true. Character values use 2 bytes based on Unicode Basic Multilingual Plane (Plane 0). Character code points range from U+0000 to U+FFFF. Integer values use a word and are represented using 32-bit 2's complement.

Each CVM instruction operation code (opcode) occupies one byte of memory. Some instructions take one or two immediate operands, which are always located immediately following the instruction in memory. Depending on the opcode, an immediate operand can be a single byte, two bytes (e.g., for a char), four bytes (e.g. for an integer or a memory address), or multiple bytes (e.g., for a string literal). Most instructions get their operands from the run-time stack. In general, the operands are removed from the stack whenever the instruction is executed, and any results are left on the top of the stack.

Here are some examples of CVM instructions:

- ADD: Remove two integers from the top of the stack and push their sum back onto the stack.

- INC: Add 1 to the integer at the top of the stack.

- CMP (compare): Remove two integers from the top of the stack and compare them. Push a byte representing -1, 0, or 1 back onto the stack depending on whether the first integer is less than, equal to, or greater than the first integer, respectively. Note that CMP compares only integers. Comparison of smaller operands such as bytes and characters requires that they be promoted to integers by left-padding with zeros to fill out four bytes.

- BGE (Branch if Greater or Equal): Remove one byte from the top of the stack. If it is greater than or equal to zero, then branch according to displacement operand immediately following the opcode; otherwise continue with the next instruction. Note that the immediate operand for the displacement can be positive or negative representing forward or backward branching.

- LOADW (load word): Load (push) a word onto the stack. A word is four consecutive bytes. The address of the first byte of the word is obtained by popping it off the top of the stack.

- LDCINT (load constant integer): Fetch the integer immediately following the opcode and push it onto the top of the stack; e.g., LDCINT 500.

- LDCINT0 (load constant integer zero): Optimized replacement for LDCINT 0. LDCINT0 occupies only one byte in memory for the opcode, whereas LDCINT 0 occupies five bytes, one for the opcode and four for the integer 0. Also LDCINT0 executes slightly faster since there is no need to fetch the immediate operand. (Note: This instruction is similar to the JVM instruction iconst_0.)

Appendix E describes seven functional groupings of the CPRL opcodes as follows:

- Arithmetic Opcodes. Examples include ADD, SUB (subtract), MUL (multiply), INC (increment), etc.

- Logical Opcodes. There is only one opcode in this grouping, NOT (logical not).

- Shift Opcodes. There are only two opcodes in this grouping, SHL (shift left) and SHR (shift right).

- Compare/Branch Opcodes. Examples include CMP (compare), BR (unconditional branch), BZ (branch if zero), BG (branch if greater), BGE (branch if greater or equal), etc.

- Load/Store Opcodes. Examples include LOADW (load word), LDCINT (load constant integer), LDGADDR (load global address), STOREB (store byte), STOREW (store word), etc.

- Program/Procedure Opcodes. Examples include PROGRAM, PROC (procedure), CALL, RET (return), etc.

- I/O Opcodes. Examples include GETINT (get integer), GETCH (get character), PUTINT (put integer), PUTSTR (put string), etc.

CVM does not have any general-purpose registers, but it has four 32-bit internal registers as follows:

- PC (program counter, a.k.a. instruction pointer): holds the address of the next instruction to be executed.

- SP (stack pointer): holds the address of the top of the stack. The stack grows from low-numbered memory addresses to high-numbered memory addresses.

- SB (stack base): holds the address of the bottom of the stack. When a program is loaded, SB is initialized to the address of the first free byte in memory.

- BP (base pointer): holds the base address of the subprogram currently being executed. BP and SB have the same value (i.e., the both reference the same memory location) if there are no currently active subprograms

10.2. CVM Uses Relative Addressing

At this point we need a basic understanding of how variables are addressed. All addressing in CVM is relative to an address contained in a register. Variables declared at program scope are addressed relative to the SB register, while variables declared at subprogram scope are addressed relative to the BP register. For example, suppose that we have a program scoped variable named x with relative address 8. If SB has the value 112, then the actual memory address of x is [SB] + relAddr(x) or 120, but rarely will we need to know the actual memory address. Simply knowing the relative address is sufficient for understanding the CVM architecture and for code generation.

Let's work through a relative addressing example. Suppose a program contains the following declarations:

```
var m, n : Integer;
var c : Char;
var a, b : Boolean;
```

Based on the sizes (number of bytes) for types Integer, Char, and Boolean, the relative addresses of the variables are computed as follows:

- m has relative address 0.

- n has relative address 4.

- c has relative address 8.

- a has relative address 10.

- b has relative address 11.

The total variable length for the program is 12.

The layout of the variables in memory is illustrated by the diagram on the right.

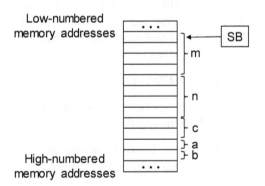

10.3 Loading a Program into Memory

When a program is run, the object code is loaded into the beginning of memory starting at byte 0. Register PC is initialized to 0, the address of the first instruction. Registers SB and BP are initialized to the address following the last instruction, and register SP is initialized to BP - 1. The value in SB does not change while the program is running, but BP will change based on calls to subprograms.

If variables are declared at program scope, the first instruction has the form "program n". When executed, it allocates n bytes on the top of the stack for global variables. The following diagram depicts the layout for a program loaded in memory after a number of instructions have been executed:

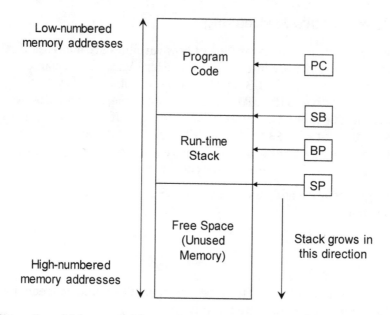

As stated earlier, all variables are addressed using the SB and BP Registers. When preparing for code generation, the compiler needs to determine the relative address of every variable. For programs that don't have subprograms, both SB and BP will always point to the same memory location.

Opcodes LDGADDR and LDLADDR are used to push the address of a variable onto the stack.

- LDGADDR n: Loads global address for variable at offset n by pushing SB + n onto the stack. This instruction is used for variables declared at program scope.

- LDLADDR n: Loads local address for variable at offset n by pushing BP + n onto the stack. This instruction is used for variables declared at subprogram scope.

Let's examine a CPRL example.

```
var    m, n : Integer;
var    c : Char;
const five := 5;

begin

    m := 7;
    n := five*m;
```

```
    c := 'X';
    writeln "n = ", n;
    writeln "c = ", c;

end.
```

After compiling and assembling this program, we can run the disassembler to see the actual layout of the object code with memory addresses as follows:

```
 0:    PROGRAM 10
 5:    LDGADDR 0
10:    LDCINT 7
15:    STOREW
16:    LDGADDR 4
21:    LDCINT 5
26:    LDGADDR 0
31:    LOADW
32:    MUL
33:    STOREW
34:    LDGADDR 8
39:    LDCCH 'X'
42:    STORE2B
43:    LDCSTR    "n = "
56:    PUTSTR
57:    LDGADDR 4
62:    LOADW
63:    PUTINT
64:    PUTEOL
65:    LDCSTR    "c = "
78:    PUTSTR
79:    LDGADDR 8
84:    LOAD2B
85:    PUTCH
86:    PUTEOL
87:    HALT
```

When this program is loaded into memory, register PC will be initialized to 0, register SP will be initialized to 87, and registers SB and BP will be initialized to 88. Execution of the first instruction will allocate space on the run-time stack for variables m, n, and c, and at that point, the three variables will have addresses as follows:

- m: relative address = 0 (absolute address = 88).

- n: relative address = 4 (absolute address = 92).

- c: relative address = 8 (absolute address = 96).

CVM uses relative addressing. The absolute addresses are provided for informational purposes.

The following diagram shows the layout of this program in memory after the first instruction has been executed:

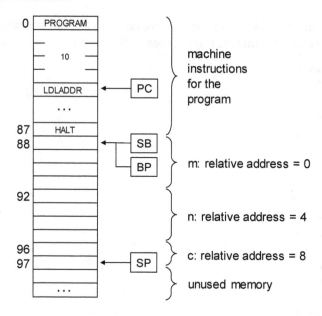

10.4 Using the Stack to Hold Temporary Values

The part of memory below the CVM instructions and global variables is used as a run-time stack that holds subprogram activation records (see Chapter 13) and temporary, intermediate values. As machine instructions are executed, the stack grows and shrinks. The run-time stack is empty at both the start and end of the each CPRL statement in the main program.

As an example showing the stack storing temporary values, let's assume the following:

- register SB has the value 100

- integer variable x has relative address 0

- integer variable y has value 5 and relative address 4

- integer variable z has value 13 and relative address 8

The CPRL assignment statement

```
x := 2*y + z;
```

will compile to the following CVM instructions:

```
LDGADDR 0
LDCINT  2
LDGADDR 4
LOADW
MUL
LDGADDR 8
LOADW
ADD
STOREW
```

We can visualize how the stack is used to store temporary values by using a sequence of diagrams showing the state of the stack after execution of each machine instruction.

The stack is empty at the start of the CPRL assignment statement.

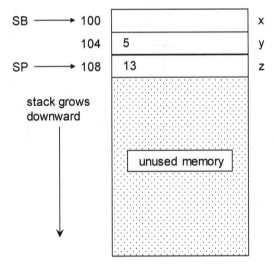

After execution of LDGADDR 0:

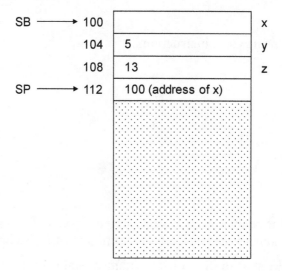

After execution of LDCINT 2:

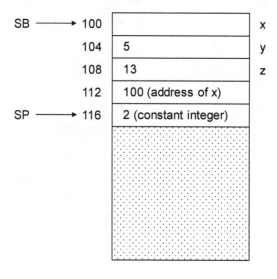

After execution of LDGADDR 4:

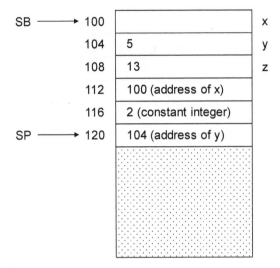

After execution of LOADW:

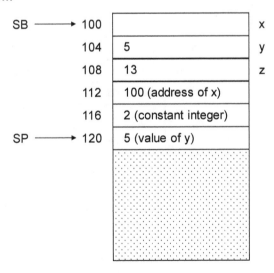

After execution of MUL:

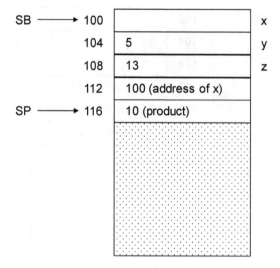

After execution of LDGADDR 8:

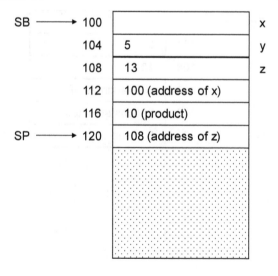

After execution of LOADW:

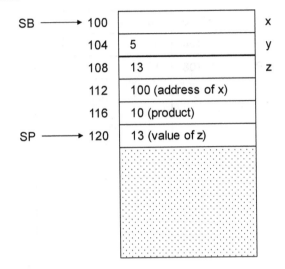

After execution of ADD:

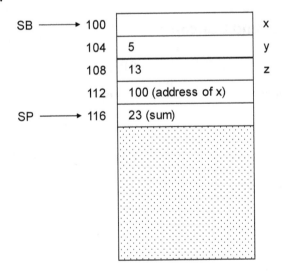

After execution of the final machine instruction STOREW:

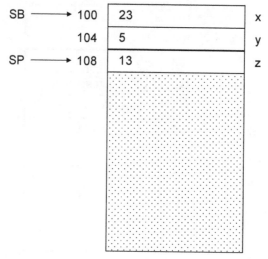

Note that at this point, variable x has now been assigned the value 23, and the run-time stack is empty again.

10.5 Essential Terms and Concepts

arithmetic opcodes   BP

compare/branch opcodes   I/O opcodes

logical opcodes   load/store opcodes

PC   program/procedure opcodes

relative address   SB

shift opcodes   SP

stack architecture   word (in CVM)

10.6 Exercises

1. What does it mean when we say that CVM uses a stack architecture? Explain and give an example (e.g., how does the ADD instruction work in CVM).

2. Name and describe the 4 internal/special purpose registers of CVM.

3. Fill in the blank relative to CVM.

    a. CVM has _____ internal (i.e., special purpose) registers. (How many?)

    b. A word consists of _____ byte(s). (How many?)

    c. Boolean values are represented using _____ byte(s). (How many?)

    d. Character values are represented using _____ byte(s). (How many?)

    e. Integer values are represented using _____ byte(s). (How many?)

    f. Each CVM opcode occupies _____ byte(s). (How many?)

    g. CVM is _____ -addressable. (Give a unit of memory.)

    h. All variable addressing is performed relative to _____ or _____. (Which registers?)

4. Suppose the first two declarations in a program are as follows:

```
var x, y : Integer;
var b : Boolean;
```

    a. What is the relative address of x?

    b. What is the relative address of y?

    c. What is the relative address of b?

Chapter 11
Code Generation

Code generation depends not only on the source language, but it also depends very heavily on the target machine, making it harder to develop general principles. However, we can describe some general guidelines and templates for generating code.

During code generation, we must never lose sight of the most important rule.

> **First Rule of Code Generation: The resulting object code must be semantically equivalent to the source program.**

> I remember vividly the first time I encountered a bug in a commercially-available compiler. From that point on I had difficulty trusting that compiler. Fortunately, this turned out to be a rare occurrence. While bugs might exist in commercially-available compilers, most of them don't manifest in normal, day-to-day software development.

11.1 Overview of Code Generation

Other than I/O errors, any errors encountered during code generation represent internal errors and should never occur. We will report any errors, but there will be no attempt at error recovery. Also, we occasionally use assertions to make sure that everything is consistent, but recall that assertions are used only to help us debug the compiler. They should never occur, and any related error messages are intended for the compiler writer, not for the programmer using the compiler.

In this chapter we will concentrate on code generation for the CPRL/0 subset (i.e., no subprograms or arrays). Chapters 13 and 14 will discuss details of constraint analysis and code generation for subprograms and arrays.

Using CVM as the target machine simplifies some aspects of code generation that must be addressed on most "real" machines, such as I/O and the efficient use of general purpose registers. Generating assembly language rather than actual machine language also simplifies code generation. For example, the assembler keeps track of the address of each machine instruction, maps labels to machine addresses, and handles the details of branch instructions. If we were targeting actual CVM machine code these functions would need to be performed by the compiler.

Method `emit()`

Code generation is performed by the `emit()` methods in the AST classes. Similar to the implementation of the `checkConstraints()` methods, most of the AST classes delegate some or all code generation to component classes within the tree. For example, class

StatementPart contains a list of statements. Code generation for class StatementPart is implemented simply as a for loop that calls emit() for each of the statements in the list.

```
@Override
public void emit() throws CodeGenException, IOException
    {
      for (Statement stmt : statements)
          stmt.emit();
    }
```

Class AST defines four methods that write assembly language to the target file as follows:

```
protected void emitLoadInst(Type t) throws IOException
protected void emitStoreInst(Type t) throws IOException
protected void emitLabel(String label)
protected void emit(String instruction)
```

These are the only methods that actually write to the file. Since all abstract syntax tree classes are subclasses (either directly or indirectly) of class AST, then all abstract syntax tree classes inherit these code-generation methods. All emit() methods involved in code generation must call one or more of these methods, or call another method that calls one or more of these methods, to write out the assembly language during code generation.

11.2 Labels and Branching

In the context of CVM assembly language, a label is simply a name for a location in memory. The compiler uses labels for branching, both forward and backward.

Here are a couple of examples.

- A loop statement needs to branch backward to the beginning of the loop.

- An if statement with an else part needs to branch to the else part if the condition is false. If the condition is true, it needs to execute the then statements and then branch over the else part.

Branches (a.k.a. jumps) are relative. The assembler computes the offset. For example, BR L5 could translate to "branch 8" (forward 8 bytes) or "branch -12" (backward 12 bytes).

Labels are implemented within the class AST. The key method is getNewLabel(), which returns a string to be used for a label.

```
/**
 * Returns a new value for a label number.  This method should
 * be called once for each label before code generation.
 */
protected String getNewLabel()
```

During code generation, the compiler keeps track of label numbers so that a new label is returned each time the method is called. Labels returned from getNewLabel() are strings of the form "L1", "L2", "L3", …

As an example, let's consider the implementation of emit() for a loop statement. The AST class LoopStmt uses two labels.

```
private String L1;    // label for start of loop
private String L2;    // label for end of loop
```

These labels are initialized within the constructor.

```
L1 = getNewLabel();
L2 = getNewLabel();
```

The actual values assigned to the labels by calls to getNewLabel() do not matter. What matters is that the values are unique and can be used as targets for branches. Note that L1 and L2 above are the local names for the labels within class LoopStmt. The actual string values of L1 and L2 could be different; e.g., "L12" and "L13".

CVM Branch Instructions

CVM has seven branch instructions as follows:

BR	unconditional branch
BNZ	branch if nonzero (branch if true)
BZ	branch if zero (branch if false)
BG	branch if greater
BGE	branch if greater or equal
BL	branch if less
BLE	branch if less or equal

Together with the CMP (compare) instruction, these branch instructions are used to implement control flow logic within a program or subprogram.

Emitting Code for an Unconditional Branch

An unconditional branch in CVM has the form

```
BR Ln
```

where Ln is the label of the instruction that is the target of the branch. The assembler converts

```
BR Ln
```

to a branch based the relative offset of the target instruction. For example, depending on the relationship of the label to the branch instruction, "BR L5" would be converted to something like "BR 12" (branch forward 12 bytes) or "BR -8" (branch backward 8 bytes). At the machine level for CVM, each branch instruction occupies 5 bytes: 1 byte for the opcode and 4 bytes for the offset.

The actual code to emit an unconditional branch looks like the following:

```
emit("BR " + L2);
```

In this example L2 is just the name of a string variable that holds the actual label value.

To simplify the analysis of disassembled code, all branch instructions in CVM add the offset to the address of the branch instruction. For example, a disassembled instruction of the form

```
128:   BR 85
133:
```

means that the address of the branch instruction is 128, and after execution of the branch instruction, the program counter will be 85 + 128 or 213.

On most real machines, the program counter would have already been updated to the address of the next instruction before the addition, and so execution of the branch instruction BR 85 would add 85 to the address of the instruction following the branch instruction; i.e., 85 + 133 or 218.

Emitting Code for Branch Instructions Based on Boolean Values

The conditional branch instructions are often preceded by a CMP instruction. This instruction removes two integers from the top of the run-time stack and compares them. It then pushes a byte representing -1, 0, or 1 back onto the stack depending on whether the first integer is less than, equal to, or greater than the second integer, respectively. The conditional branch instructions remove this byte value from the top of the run-time stack and use it to branch accordingly. For example, the instruction

```
BGE Ln
```

will branch to the specified label if the byte value is either 0 or 1. Since CMP compares only integers, boolean and character values will need to be "promoted" to integers before calling CMP.

In many situations, the code generated for a Boolean expression is followed immediately by a branch instruction. Consider as one example a relational expression used as part of a while condition in a loop.

```
while x <= y loop ...
```

In this case, if the condition evaluates to **false**, we want to generate code to jump over the statements in the body of the loop; i.e., we want to generate code similar to the following:

```
...  // emit code to leave the values of x and y on the top of the stack
CMP
BG L1
...
```

Consider as a second example the same relational expression used as part of an exit-when statement.

```
exit when x <= y;
```

In this case, if the condition evaluates to **true**, we want to generate code to branch to the end of the enclosing loop; i.e., we want to generate code similar to the following:

```
...  // emit code to leave the values
     // of x and y on the top of the stack
CMP
BLE L1
```

Note that in the first example we wanted to generate a branch if the relational expression was false, and in the second example we wanted to generate a branch if the relational expression was true.

In addition to the standard emit() method, which leaves the value of an expression on the top of the run-time stack, we introduce a helper method emitBranch() for expressions. The helper method emits code to produce a value on the run-time stack plus code that branches based on that value.

```
public void emitBranch(boolean condition, String label)
    throws CodeGenException, IOException
```

As pointed out in the previous examples, sometimes we want to emit code to branch if the expression evaluates to true, and sometimes we want to emit code to branch if the expression evaluates to false. The boolean parameter condition in method emitBranch() specifies which option we want to use.

The emitBranch() method is defined in class Expression and overridden in class RelationalExpr. The default implementation in class Expression works correctly for Boolean constants, Boolean named values, and "not" expressions.

Here is the implementation of emitBranch() for relational expressions.

```
public void emitBranch(boolean condition, String label)
    throws CodeGenException, IOException
  {
    Token operator = getOperator();

    emitOperands();
    emit("CMP");
```

```
        Symbol operatorSym = operator.getSymbol();

        if (operatorSym == Symbol.equals)
            emit(condition ? "BZ "  + label : "BNZ " + label);
        else if (operatorSym == Symbol.notEqual)
            emit(condition ? "BNZ " + label : "BZ "  +  label);
        else if (operatorSym == Symbol.lessThan)
            emit(condition ? "BL "  + label : "BGE " + label);
        else if (operatorSym == Symbol.lessOrEqual)
            emit(condition ? "BLE " + label : "BG "  + label);
        else if (operatorSym == Symbol.greaterThan)
            emit(condition ? "BG "  + label : "BLE " + label);
        else if (operatorSym == Symbol.greaterOrEqual)
            emit(condition ? "BGE " + label : "BL "  + label);
        else
            throw new CodeGenException(operator.getPosition(),
                        "Invalid relational operator.");
    }
```

11.3 Load and Store Instructions

Class AST provides two helper methods for emitting load and store instructions for various types. The code generated by both of these methods assumes that the target address for the load or store instruction is already on the top of the stack.

```
/**
 * Emits the appropriate LOAD instruction based on the type.
 */
public void emitLoadInst(Type t) throws IOException

/**
 * Emits the appropriate STORE instruction based on the type.
 */
public void emitStoreInst(Type t) throws IOException
```

Method emitLoadInst() emits the appropriate load instruction based on the size (number of bytes) of a type; i.e., it will emit one of the following load instructions:

- LOADB (load byte)

- LOAD2B (load 2 bytes)

- LOADW (load 4 bytes)

- LOAD (load n bytes)

Each of these instructions pops an address from the top of the stack and then pushes (loads) the appropriate number of bytes starting at that address onto the stack. While the general-purpose LOAD instruction (the fourth one above) could be used in all situations, the LOADB, LOAD2B, and LOADW instructions are shorter (no extra argument to specify the number of bytes), faster, and representative of the most common use case. As such, using the first three instructions represents a small performance improvement for the generated code. (See Chapter 12 for additional details on code optimization.)

Method emitLoadInst() is implemented as follows:

```
protected void emitLoadInst(Type t) throws IOException
  {
    int numBytes = t.getSize();

    if (numBytes == Constants.BYTES_PER_WORD)
        emit("LOADW");
    else if (numBytes == 2)
        emit("LOAD2B");
    else if (numBytes == 1)
        emit("LOADB");
    else
        emit("LOAD " + numBytes);
  }
```

Similarly, method emitStoreInst() emits the appropriate store instruction based on the size of a type; i.e., it will emit one of the following store instructions:

- STOREB (store byte)

- STORE2B (store 2 bytes)

- STOREW (store 4 bytes)

- STORE (store n bytes)

Each of these instructions pops an address from the top of the stack and then pops (removes) the appropriate number of bytes from the stack and stores them at memory locations starting at that address. Method emitStoreInst() is implemented similar to emitLoadInst() shown above.

11.4 Computing Relative Addresses

Since all addressing is performed relative to a register, we will need to compute the relative address (offset) for each variable plus the total number of bytes of all variables for the program and for each subprogram. In addition, for subprograms, we will need to compute the relative address for each parameter. Discussion of these computations for subprograms will be postponed to Chapter 13. Here we focus solely on computing the relative address for each variable declared at the program level. You should review the discussion of relative addressing in Section 10.2 before continuing.

Method setRelativeAddresses() in the AST class Program computes these values by looping over all single variable declarations as follows:

```
private void setRelativeAddresses()
  {
    // initial relative address is 0 for a program
    int currentAddr = 0;

    if (declPart != null)
      {
        for (InitialDecl decl : declPart.getInitialDecls())
          {
            // set relative address for single variable declarations
            if (decl instanceof SingleVarDecl)
              {
                SingleVarDecl singleVarDecl = (SingleVarDecl) decl;
                singleVarDecl.setRelAddr(currentAddr);
                currentAddr = currentAddr + singleVarDecl.getSize();
              }
          }
      }

    // compute length of all variables
    varLength = currentAddr;
  }
```

The instance variable varLength records the total number of bytes for all variables declared at the program level.

Code Generation for Variables

For variables (e.g., on the left side of an assignment statement), code generation must leave the address of the variable on the top of the run-time stack. The CVM instruction LDGADDR (load global address) will push the (global) address for a variable onto the top of the run-time stack. For CPRL/0, all variables can use this instruction since they all have PROGRAM scope.

Method emit() for class Variable (for CPRL/0) is implemented as follows:

```
public void emit() throws IOException
  {
    emit("LDGADDR " + decl.getRelAddr());
  }
```

For full CPRL, we will need to modify emit() for class Variable to correctly handle parameters, variables declared at SUBPROGRAM scope level, and index expressions for array variables. These details are covered in Chapters 13 and 14.

11.5 Expressions

For expressions, code generation must leave the value of the expression on the top of the run-time stack. The size (number of bytes) of the value will depend on the type of the variable; e.g.,

- 1 byte for a boolean

- 2 bytes for a character

- 4 bytes for an integer

- several bytes for a string literal (4 bytes for the length of the string plus 2 bytes for each character)

Code Generation for ConstValue

An object of class ConstValue is either a literal or a declared const identifier. Class ConstValue has a method getLiteralIntValue() that returns the value of the constant as an integer. We can use this method together with the appropriate "load constant" instruction to generate code for the value of the constant.

Method emit() for class ConstValue is implemented as follows:

```
@Override
public void emit() throws CodeGenException, IOException
    {
    Type exprType = getType();

    if (exprType == Type.Integer)
        emit("LDCINT " + getLiteralIntValue());
    else if (exprType == Type.Boolean)
        emit("LDCB " + getLiteralIntValue());
    else if (exprType == Type.Char)
        emit("LDCCH " + literal.getText());
    else if (exprType == Type.String)
        emit("LDCSTR " + literal.getText());
    else
        ...   // throw a CodeGenException
    }
```

Code Generation for Named Values

A named value is similar to a variable except that it generates different code. For example, consider the following assignment statement:

```
x := y;
```

The identifier "x" represents a variable, and the identifier "y" represents a named value. Class NamedValue is defined as a subclass of Variable. Code generation for NamedValue first calls emit() for its superclass Variable, which leaves the address of the variable on the top of the run-time stack. Then it calls emitLoadInst(), which pops the address off the stack and then pushes the appropriate number of bytes onto the stack, starting at that memory address.

Here is the implementation of method emit() for class NamedValue.

```
public void emit() throws CodeGenException, IOException
  {
    super.emit();    // leaves address on top of stack
    emitLoadInst(getType());
  }
```

Code Generation for Unary Expressions

A unary expression contains an operator and one operand, where the operand is an expression. There are only two types of unary expressions in CPRL, unary negation for integer expressions and not for boolean expressions. Note that the operand can be an arbitrary expression of the appropriate type. Code generation for both types of unary expressions follows the following pattern:

```
emit code for the operand
emit code to perform the operation
```

Code Generation for Binary Expressions

A binary expression contains an operator and two operands, each of which is an expression. Examples of binary expressions include addition for integer expressions and relational expressions for integers, characters, etc. (e.g., x <= y). Code generation for a binary expression usually follows the following pattern:

```
emit code for the left operand
emit code for the right operand
emit code to perform the operation
```

Note that we are generating code that will evaluate the expression using a "postfix" (a.k.a. "reverse polish") notation approach.

The implementation of method emit() for class AddingExpr follows this pattern.

```
public void emit() throws CodeGenException, IOException
  {
    Expression leftOperand  = getLeftOperand();
    Expression rightOperand = getRightOperand();
    Symbol     operatorSym  = getOperator().getSymbol();

    leftOperand.emit();
    rightOperand.emit();

    ...  // assert that the operator is plus or minus

    if (operatorSym == Symbol.plus)
        emit("ADD");
    else if (operatorSym == Symbol.minus)
        emit("SUB");
  }
```

Code Generation for Logical Expressions

In general, code generation needs to consider whether or not the language requires logical expressions to use short-circuit evaluation (a.k.a., early exit). Similar to most high-level languages, CPRL has such a requirement.

Here are some examples of short-circuit evaluation. In these examples, expr1 and expr2 can be arbitrary Boolean expressions consisting of multiple operators and operands.

Example 1. Given an expression of the form expr1 and expr2, the left operand (expr1) is evaluated. If the result is false, the right operand (expr2) is not evaluated and the truth value for the compound expression is considered to be false. Otherwise, the right operand (expr2) is evaluated and its value becomes the value for the compound expression.

Example 2. Given an expression of the form expr1 or expr2, the left operand (expr1) is evaluated. If the result is true, the right operand (expr2) is not evaluated and the truth value for the compound expression is considered to be true. Otherwise, the right operand (expr2) is evaluated and its value becomes the value for the compound expression.

Using a code generation approach similar to that for AddingExpr will not result in short-circuit evaluation. For example, in generating code for an "and" expression, we can't simply emit code for left operand, emit code for the right operand, and then "and" them together.

From a programmer's perspective, it is almost always preferable for a programming language to use short-circuit evaluation for logical expressions, and not simply for performance reasons. Consider the following Java excerpt:

```
if (person != null && person.getName().equals("John")
  {
    statement₁;
    statement₂;
  }
else
  {
    statement₃;
    statement₄;
  }
```

If the first condition in the if statement (person != null) is false, then we don't want to evaluate the second condition, since doing so would raise the dreaded null pointer exception. Try to rewrite the above logic without assuming short-circuit evaluation of logical expressions. First, you will need to use nested if statements. But beyond that, you will need to determine how to handle the else statement. The most straightforward approach for the else statement is simply to repeat it for both if statements.

Even if we disregard the possibility of null references or pointers, the problem still exists. Consider, for example the following logic:

```
if (y != 0 && x/y > 0)
  {
    statement₁;
    statement₂;
  }
else
  {
    statement₃;
    statement₄;
  }
```

If the first condition is false, then an attempt to evaluate the second condition would result in division by zero.

Here is the CPRL code template for logical and (with Short-Circuit Evaluation).

```
...  // emit code for the left operand
     // (leaves boolean result on top of stack)
```

```
    BNZ L1
    LDCB 0
    BR  L2
L1:
    ...  // emit code for the right operand
         // (leaves boolean result on top of stack)

L2:
```

When the instruction BNZ L1 above is executed, the boolean value on the top of the stack is popped off. The instruction LDCB 0 is needed to restore the expression value 0 (false) to the top of the stack. By default the assembler will optimize LDCB 0 to the single opcode instruction LDCB0.

11.6 Statements

Code generation for statements can be described by showing several representative examples of code templates or patterns, where a code generation template specifies some explicit instructions and delegates portions of the code generation to nested components. Code generation templates for control structures will often use labels to designate destination addresses for branches.

11.6.1 Code Generation for AssignmentStmt

Grammar Rule

```
variable ":=" expression ";" .
```

Here is a general description of the steps involved in code generation for an assignment statement.

- Emit code for the variable on left side of the assignment operator. This code should leave the variable's address on top of run-time stack.

- Emit code for the expression on right side of the assignment operator. This code should leave the expression's value on top of run-time stack.

- Emit the appropriate store instruction based on the expression's type. This code removes the value and the address from the top of the run-time stack and copies the value to the address using method emitStoreInst().

Code generation template for type Integer

```
    ...  // emit code for variable
    ...  // emit code for expression
    STOREW
```

Code generation template for type `Boolean`

```
...  // emit code for variable
...  // emit code for expression
STOREB
```

Method emit() for class `AssignmentStmt`

```
public void emit() throws CodeGenException, IOException
  {
    var.emit();
    expr.emit();

    emitStoreInst(expr.getType());
  }
```

11.6.2 Code Generation for a List of Statements

Grammar Rule

```
statements = ( statement )* .
```

Code generation template for a list of statements

```
for each statement in statements
    ...  // emit code for statement
```

Example: method emit() in class `StatementPart`

```
public void emit() throws CodeGenException, IOException
  {
    for (Statement stmt : statements)
        stmt.emit();
  }
```

11.6.3 Code Generation for `LoopStmt`

Grammar Rule

```
loopStmt = ( "while" booleanExpr )? "loop" statements "end" "loop" ";" .
```

Code generation template for loop without a `while` prefix

```
L1:
    ... statements nested within the loop
        (usually contain an exit statement)
    BR L1
L2:
```

Code generation template for loop with a while prefix

```
L1:
    ...  emit code to evaluate while expression
    ...  branch to L2 if value of expression is false
    ...  statements nested within the loop
    BR L1
L2:
```

Method emit() for LoopStmt

```java
@Override
public void emit() throws CodeGenException, IOException
  {
    // L1:
    emitLabel(L1);

    if (whileExpr != null)
        whileExpr.emitBranch(false, L2);

    for (Statement stmt : statements)
        stmt.emit();

    emit("BR " + L1);

    // L2:
    emitLabel(L2);
  }
```

11.6.4 Code Generation for readStmt

Grammar Rule

```
readStmt = "read" variable ";" .
```

Code generation template for a variable of type Integer

```
...  // emit code for variable
     // (leaves variable's address on top of stack)
GETINT
```

Code generation template for a variable of type Character

```
...  // emit code for variable
     // (leaves variable's address on top of stack)
GETCH
```

11.6.5 Code Generation for `ExitStmt`

Grammar Rule

```
exitStmt = "exit" ( "when" booleanExpr )? ";" .
```

The exit statement must obtain the end label number, say L2, from its enclosing loop statement.

Code generation template when the exit statement does not have a when boolean expression suffix

```
BR L2
```

Code generation template when the exit statement has a when boolean expression suffix

```
...   // emit code that will branch to L2 if the
      // "when" boolean expression evaluates to true
```

Method `emit()` for `ExitStmt`

```java
public void emit() throws CodeGenException, IOException
  {
    String exitLabel = loopStmt.getExitLabel();

    if (whenExpr != null)
        whenExpr.emitBranch(true, exitLabel);
    else
        emit("BR " + exitLabel);
  }
```

11.6.6 Code Generation for `IfStmt`

Grammar Rule

```
ifStmt = "if" booleanExpr "then" statements
        ( "elsif" booleanExpr "then" statements )*
        ( "else" statements )? "end" "if" ";" .
```

Code generation template for an `if` statement

```
      ...   // emit code that will branch to L1 if
            //     the boolean expression is false
      ...   // emit code for then statements
      BR L2
L1:
      ...   // emit code for elsif parts      (may be empty)
      ...   // emit code for else statements (may be empty)
L2:
```

Code generation template for an elsif part

```
(assumes L2 is the label for the end of the if statement)
    ... // emit code to branch to L1 if the elsif
        //     boolean expression is false
    ... // emit code for elsif statements
    BR L2
L1:
```

11.7 Disassembler

An **assembler** translates from assembly language to machine code. A **disassembler** is a program that translates from machine code (binary file) back to assembly language (text file). A disassembler for CVM is available for download at the book web site (see Java source file edu.citadel.cvm.Disassembler.java). While technically not required for the implementation of a compiler, the disassembler can be useful when debugging the generated code.

Here is an example showing the source code, disassembled object code, and an annotated version of the disassembled object code that illustrates more clearly how the source code statements are implemented in CVM. Note that the disassembler output has the machine address for each CVM instruction.

Code Generation Example

Source Code

```
var x : Integer;
const n := 5;

begin

    x := 1;

    while x <= n loop
        x := x + 1;
    end loop;

    writeln "x = ", x;

end.
```

Disassembled Machine Code

```
  0     PROGRAM 4
  5:    LDGADDR 0
 10:    LDCINT1
 11:    STOREW
 12:    LDGADDR 0
 17:    LOADW
 18:    LDCINT 5
 23:    CMP
 24:    BG 23
 29:    LDGADDR 0
 34:    LDGADDR 0
 39:    LOADW
 40:    INC
 41:    STOREW
 42:    BR -30
 47:    LDCSTR  "x = "
 60:    PUTSTR
 61:    LDGADDR 0
 66:    LOADW
 67:    PUTINT
 68:    PUTEOL
 69:    HALT
```

Note that, without optimization, the single opcode instruction LDCINT1 at memory address
10 would be LDCINT 1, and the INC instruction at memory address 40 would look like the
following:

```
LDCINT 1
ADD
```

Annotated Disassembled Object Code

```
// reserve 4 bytes for x
 0: PROGRAM 4

// x := 1;
 5: LDGADDR 0
10: LDCINT1
11: STOREW

// while x <= n loop
12: LDGADDR 0
17: LOADW
18: LDCINT 5
23: CMP
```

```
24: BG 23

// x := x + 1
29: LDGADDR 0
34: LDGADDR 0
39: LOADW
40: INC
41: STOREW

// end loop;
42: BR -30

// writeln "x = ", x
47: LDCSTR   "x = "
60: PUTSTR
61: LDGADDR 0
66: LOADW
67: PUTINT
68: PUTEOL

// end.
69: HALT
```

11.8 Essential Terms and Concepts

assembler

branching/branch instructions

emit() (method)

emitLoadInst(Type t) (method)

getNewLabel() (method)

named value

short-circuit evaluation

variable

binary expression

disassembler

emitBranch() (method)

emitStoreInst(Type t) (method)

label

relative addressing

unary expression

11.9 Exercises

1. **Project Assignment.** Implement **Project 6: Code Generation for CPRL/0** as described in Appendix A.

2. Give the opcodes and descriptions for the seven branch instructions in CVM.

3. Fill in the blanks.

   a. Code generation is performed by method _____ in the AST classes.

   b. A/An _____ translates from assembly language to machine code.

   c. A/An _____ translates from machine code to assembly language.

4. True or False (T or F)

   a. Code generation depends on both the source language and the target machine.

   b. Most AST classes delegate some of the code generation to component classes.

   c. Code generation for a variable (e.g., on the left side of an assignment statement) leaves the variable's address on the top of the stack.

   d. Code generation for an expression leaves the value of the expression on the top of the stack.

   e. CPRL requires logical expressions to use short-circuit evaluation.

   f. A label is a name for a location in memory.

   g. Method getNewLabel() returns a different label (string) every time it is called.

5. Explain the difference between the instruction LDCINT 1 and the instruction LDCINT1. Also, examine the set of CVM instructions defined in Appendix E for other similar instructions. (Hint: There are three additional instructions similar to LDCINT1.)

6. Suppose that programming language 1 supports short-circuit evaluation of logical operators "and" (or "&&") and "or" (or "||"), and that programming language 2 does not. That is, programming language 2 evaluates both operands before performing the logical operation. Consider the following skeletal code in programming language 1 (with short-circuit evaluation):

```
if condition_1 and condition_2 then
    ...  // statements
end if;
```

This skeletal code can be written equivalently in programming language 2 (without short-circuit evaluation) as follows:

```
if condition_1 then
   if condition_2 then
      ...  // statements
   end if;
end if;
```

Now suppose that you have the following skeletal code in programming language 1:

```
if condition_1 and condition_2 then
   ...  // statements 1
else
   ...  // statements 2
end if;
```

Rewrite this skeletal code in programming language 2 (without short-circuit evaluation).

Chapter 12
Code Optimization

Code optimization refers to code generation techniques and transformations that result in a semantically equivalent program that runs more efficiently; i.e., the program runs faster, uses less memory, or both. The term "optimization" is actually used improperly since the generated code is rarely optimal. A better name might be "code improvements," but the phrase "code optimization" is in widespread use, and we will continue to follow that practice.

No study of compilers would be complete without covering this topic, but the compiler project outlined in this book does not include an assignment on optimization. All target code is generated in the most straightforward manner. So, for example, when adding constant 1 to a variable, the instructions "LDCINT 1" and "ADD" are generated rather than the more optimized "INC" instruction. However, by default, some minor optimizations are performed by the assembler, and students are encouraged to study the assembler's Java source code to see how these optimizations are implemented. Students can also use the provided disassembler to examine the optimized code and compare it to the code generated by their compiler. It is not common for an assembler to perform optimizations, but it is common for a compiler to perform optimizations on a low-level representation of the source code, and we can consider CVM assembly language to be a low-level representation for CPRL source code. Assembler optimizations can be turned off with the command line switch "-opt:off" if desired.

Code optimization often involves a time-space tradeoff in that techniques that make the code faster often require additional memory, and conversely. However, there are usually some optimizations that improve both run-time performance and memory utilization. Most compilers perform at least some optimization, but some compilers devote significant resources to optimization. Such compilers are called "optimizing compilers." An optimizing compiler can often generate object code that will perform at a level equivalent to the best hand-coded assembly language.

12.1 Overview of Code Optimization

While a one-pass compiler might perform minor optimizations as part of code generation, most compilers perform optimization on intermediate representations of the program; e.g., on a high-level representation such as abstract syntax trees or on a low-level representation, possibly even on machine code.

Optimizations are often classified as local or global. A local optimization is one that examines only a few statements at a time, while a global optimization looks at an entire compilation unit. Local optimizations are common. Global optimizations are much more difficult to implement. Optimizing compilers do both.

Optimizations are sometimes classified as being either machine dependent or machine independent. Machine-independent optimizations are performed on an intermediate representation of the program without any specific knowledge of the target machine, while machine-dependent optimizations are customized for a specific machine.

William A. ("Bill") Wulf, a computer scientist who spent most of his adult life working on optimizing compilers, was often quoted as saying that "There is no such thing as a machine-independent optimization. Not one! People who use the phrase don't understand the problem! There are lots of semantics-preserving transformations that improve code size or speed for some machines under some circumstances. But those same transformations may be pessimizations for another machine!"

Code Optimization Issues

As with most software systems, compiler development must support a variety of conflicting objectives including minimizing the cost of implementation, minimizing the schedule for implementation, compilation speed, maximizing the run-time performance of the generated object code, and minimizing the size of the generated object code. Adding optimizations to a compiler can impact cost and schedule, and performing optimizations during compilation can impact compilation times. There is overhead involved in implementing compiler optimizations, and whole-program or global optimization is time consuming and often difficult or impractical. Remember that occasionally, especially during development, faster compile times can be more important that more efficient object code.

Personal Anecdote: The Ada programming language was accompanied by an extensive validation test suite, and one of the earliest validated compilers was developed by Digital Equipment Corporation (DEC). In a conversation with one of the compiler developers, he revealed that one of the test programs gave them a lot of problems. When they finally tracked it down, they discovered that the error was not in the Ada-specific part of the compiler but in a common global optimizer that was used for all of their compilers. They wrote an equivalent PL/I program, and sure enough, it had the same error. They corrected the error in the global optimizer, and both the Ada program and the PL/I program ran correctly.

One cost-effective approach to implementing compiler optimizations is to let someone else do it. For example, by using a common, low-level intermediate language such as the one provided by the LLVM project, compiler developers get compiler optimizations and code generation for most common computer architectures with little cost beyond the time required to understand the LLVM Intermediate Representation (IR). This concept is illustrated in the following figure.

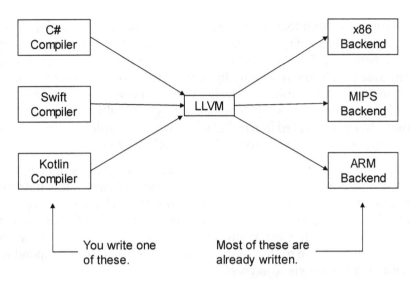

It is extremely difficult for a compiler to improve algorithmic complexity, and therefore the best source of optimization is often the programmer. No amount of compiler optimization is going to make a bubble sort run faster than a quick sort. Additionally, a programmer can use profiling to determine areas where optimization might have a significant impact and then rewrite time-critical code in assembly language.

There is an old programming adage that says you should "make the program correct before making it faster." With respect to compiler design, this means all optimizations should still produce semantically equivalent object code. Compiler results should be tested with and without optimizations to ensure that no optimization introduces an error.

Several common optimization themes have emerged over time and should be exploited by compiler developers. Here are just a few to think about.

- Optimize the common case even at the expense of a slow path. For example, suppose that there are two general approaches to implementing exception handling. One approach results in better overall performance of the generated code if no exceptions are thrown, but it results in slower performance whenever an exception is thrown and must be handled. The alternative approach implements the throwing and catching of exceptions more quickly, but it has a negative overall impact on the performance of the generated code if no exceptions are thrown. This guideline suggests that one should go with the first approach. (Note: This example involving exception handling was taken from a discussion the author had with a developer working on an actual commercial compiler.)

- Less code usually results in faster execution and lower product cost for embedded systems, where the code must be replicated in thousands of devices. If a compiler needs to make tradeoffs between faster execution and smaller code size, then there should be a compiler switch or pragma that the developer can use to give guidance as to which one is preferred over the other.

- Exploit the computer architecture of the target machine. For example, generate code to exploit the memory hierarchy – registers first, then cache, then main memory, then disk (virtual memory). Register allocation is discussed in the following section, but in general, the idea is to improve locality by keeping related code and data as close together in memory as possible. Similarly, compiler developers can exploit parallelization it two ways, first by taking advantage of multiple processors to allow computations to be performed in parallel and second by exploiting instruction pipelining; e.g., rearranging code to minimize pipeline hazards.

One interesting point about optimizations is that after some optimizations have been performed, additional potential optimizations can be more obvious. It is not uncommon for an optimization phase to make multiple passes over the code, with each pass looking for additional optimizations that might not have been detected during the previous pass. Compilers that implement extensive optimizations often provide a compiler switch or pragma that provides guidance to the compiler about how much time to spend in optimization, ranging from none to aggressive.

12.2 Common Optimizations

In this section we present several common optimizations that can be performed by a compiler.

Machine-Specific Instructions

The basic idea here is to make use of specific instructions available on the target computer. Here are some examples.

- Increment and decrement instructions are available on many computer architectures and can be used in place of add and subtract instructions. This is usually an optimization that has a small improvement in both run-time performance and memory utilization. Although a single replacement of "add 1" by "inc" might not seem like much, the overall improvement can be more significant if done inside loops that are executed thousands of times.

- Some architectures provide block move instructions and block search instructions that can usually outperform the best hand-coded loops. For example, on the Intel x86, a "rep" prefix can be added to a "move byte" or a "move word" instruction to implement a block move from one part of memory to another.

- Some architectures provide special addressing modes or instructions to improve the processing of arrays. Sometimes array index computation can be improved by using addition to a constant pointer, a fact often exploited directly in C source code.

- Some architectures provide specific pre/post increment instructions that can be useful in certain situations. The early C compilers were developed on such architectures, and the use of ++ as both prefix and postfix operators allowed the programmer to provide an optimization "hint" to the compiler, similar to the use of the `register` directive in C.

Register Allocation

Most computer architectures have general-purpose registers, and register allocation is the process of assigning program variables to these registers. Since accessing a variable stored in a register is much faster than accessing a variable stored in memory, the efficient use of registers can have a significant effect on run-time performance. The overall process involves both register allocation, selection of variables that will reside in registers (e.g., a loop index), and register assignment, selection of specific registers for the variables.

Register allocation is a very hard problem. One common approach uses a "graph coloring" algorithm, which is suitable for static compilation but often too time consuming for just-in-time (JIT) compilers, where the translation is performed at run time.

Constant Folding

Constant folding is simply the compile-time evaluation of arithmetic expressions involving constants. For example, consider the following assignment statement:

```
c = 2*PI*r;
```

Assuming PI has been declared as a named constant, evaluation of 2*PI can be performed by the compiler rather than computed at run time, and the resulting product can be used in the expression. Unless there is something very unusual going on in the instruction pipeline, this is one type of optimization that almost always results in better performance.

Algebraic Identities

Algebraic identities can often be used to simplify certain expressions. Examples include the following:

```
x + 0 = 0 + x = x
x - 0 = 0 - x = x
x*1 = 1*x = x
0/x = 0 (provided x ≠ 0)
```

But beware that not all algebraic identities from mathematics are applicable since arithmetic performed by computers is not always equivalent to the mathematical concepts. This is especially true for floating point computations, but it is also true for integer computations. Problems result from the fact that computers use a fixed number of bits to represent mathematical numbers, but there are infinitely many mathematical numbers.

Strength Reduction

Strength reduction involves replacing operations with simpler, more efficient operations. Use of machine-specific instructions as discussed previously can be considered a form of strength reduction. Here are some examples of this type of optimization.

```
i = i + 1 → inc i (use increment instruction)
i*2 or 2*i → i + i  (replace multiplication by 2 with addition)
x/8 → x >> 3  (replace division by 2n with right-shift n)
MOV EAX, 0 → XOR EAX   (usually smaller and faster in x86 assembly language)
```

Common Subexpression Elimination

The basic idea is to detect a common subexpression, evaluate it only once, and then reference the common value as needed.

For example, consider the two following sets of statements:

```
a = x + y;                          a = x + y;
...                                 ...
b = (x + y)/2;                      b = a/2;
```

These two sets of statements are equivalent provided that x and y do not change values in the intermediate statements, and the set of statements on the right would be more efficient under normal circumstances.

Loop-Invariant Code Motion (a.k.a. Code Hoisting)

For this optimization we try to move calculations outside of a loop (usually before the loop) when doing so does not affect the semantics of the program. This optimization also facilitates storing constant values in registers. Consider the following example taken from Wikipedia:

```
while j < maximum - 1 loop
    j = j + (4+a[k])*PI+5;   // a is an array
end loop;
```

The calculation of "maximum - 1" and "(4+a[k])*PI+5" can be moved outside the loop and precalculated. The optimized version of the code would look as follows:

```
int maxval  = maximum - 1;
int calcval = (4+a[k])*PI+5;
while (j < maxval) loop
    j = j + calcval;
end loop;
```

Peephole Optimization

This is not so much a specific optimization as it is an approach to implementing certain types of optimizations. This approach is usually applied to the generated target machine code or a low-level intermediate representation. In fact, this is the approach used by the CVM assembler for implementing optimizations. The basic idea is to analyze a small sequence of instructions at a time (the peephole) for possible performance improvements. The peephole is a small window into the generated code.

Examples of peephole optimizations include:

- Elimination of redundant loads and stores

- Elimination of branch instructions to other branch instructions

- Algebraic identities and strength reduction. These can be easier to detect in the target machine code.

Example. Peephole Optimization

Consider the following source code excerpt:

```
    ...
    loop
        ...

        exit when x > 0;
    end loop;
    ...
```

Straightforward code generation might result in something like the following, with the peephole shown as examining a sequence of three instructions:

```
    L4:
        ...
        LDLADDR 0
        LOADW
        LDCINT 0
        CMP
        BG  L5        peephole
        BR  L4
    L5:
        ...
```

As an optimization, we could replace the two instructions

```
    BG  L5
    BR  L4
```

with the single instruction

```
BLE L4
```

This example illustrates an actual example of an optimization performed by the assembler. The assembler would also replace the two occurrences of LDCINT 0 with the optimized LDCINT0.

12.3 Optimization in CPRL

As mentioned earlier in this chapter, none of the optimizations listed in the previous section are actually performed within the CPRL compiler project as outlined in this book, but several are performed by the assembler. The assembler for CPRL performs the following optimizations using a "peephole" optimizer:

- constant folding

- branch reduction (as illustrated in the above example)

- strength reduction: use "inc" and "dec" where possible

- strength reduction: use left (right) shift instead of multiplying (dividing) by powers of 2 where possible

It is possible to perform some optimizations within the abstract syntax tree. The general approach to implementing this is to add optimize() methods in each AST class. These methods "walk" the tree in a manner similar to the checkConstraints() and emit() methods. Earlier versions of the project compiler assignments actually did this, but the optimization assignments were removed to simplify the basic compiler project. In addition, another change that can simplify some optimizations within the abstract syntax tree is to add a parent reference to each node in the tree. In the current implementation, each AST object has references to its child objects, but the child objects don't maintain a reference to their parent.

12.4 Essential Terms and Concepts

algebraic identities

common subexpression elimination

global optimization

loop-invariant code motion

machine-independent optimization

peephole optimization

strength reduction

code optimization

constant folding

local optimization

machine-dependent optimization

machine-specific instructions

register allocation

12.5 Exercises

1. True or false (T or F)

   a. Optimizations that reduce the size of the object code will always result in faster run-time performance.

   b. According to William A. Wulf, there are usually lots of machine-independent optimizations.

2. Give some examples of machine-specific instructions the can be used for optimization.

Chapter 13
Subprograms

The term subprogram will be used to mean either a procedure or a function. We have already addressed subprograms and issues of scope within the scanner, parser, and identifier table, so most of the effort required to implement subprograms involves modifications of the AST classes. We begin with a review of relevant concepts.

13.1 Review of Subprograms, Scope, and Parameters

The grammar rules for subprograms give rise to the following methods in class `Parser` where the return values of the methods are either AST classes or lists of AST classes.

```
List<SubprogramDecl> parseSubprogramDecls()
SubprogramDecl parseSubprogramDecl()
ProcedureDecl parseProcedureDecl()
FunctionDecl parseFunctionDecl()
List<ParameterDecl> parseFormalParameters()
ParameterDecl parseParameterDecl()
ProcedureCallStmt parseProcedureCallStmt()
List<Expression> parseActualParameters()
ReturnStmt parseReturnStmt()
FunctionCall parseFunctionCall()
```

The following diagram depicts the inheritance hierarchy for relevant AST classes.

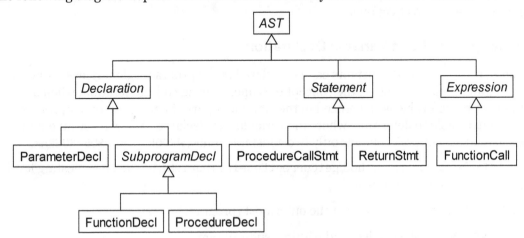

Variable Parameters and Value Parameters

The following example illustrates the use of parameters in CPRL:

```
var x : Integer;

procedure inc(var n : Integer) is
begin
   n := n + 1;
end inc;

begin
   x := 5;
   inc(x);
   writeln(x);
end.
```

What value is printed by this program? (Answer: 6) The integer parameter for procedure inc above is a variable parameter, meaning that the actual parameter is passed by reference. Any operation performed on the formal parameter n is effectively performed on the actual parameter x, so incrementing n inside the procedure will have the effect of incrementing x.

If "var" is removed from the parameter declaration, what value is printed? (Answer: 5) Removing "var" from the parameter declaration means that the actual parameter is passed by value; i.e., the value of the actual parameter x is copied into the formal parameter n, but thereafter x and n are completely independent of each other. Changing the value of n inside the procedure has no effect on x.

The Scope Level of a Variable Declaration

Recall that variables and constants can be declared at the program (global) level or at the subprogram level, introducing the concept of scope. During code generation, when a variable or named value is referenced in the statement part of a program or subprogram, we need to be able to determine where the variable was declared. We will use an enum class named ScopeLevel that has only two constant values, PROGRAM and SUBPROGRAM.

Class IdTable contains a method getCurrentLevel() that returns the block nesting level for the current scope. It returns

- PROGRAM for objects declared at the outermost (program) scope.

- SUBPROGRAM for objects declared within a subprogram.

When a variable is declared, the declaration is initialized with the current scope level.

```
ScopeLevel scopeLevel = idTable.getCurrentLevel();
varDecl = new VarDecl(identifiers, varType, scopeLevel);
```

The following example illustrates scope levels:

```
var x : Integer;    // scope level of declaration is PROGRAM
var y : Integer;    // scope level of declaration is PROGRAM

procedure P1 is       // scope level of declaration is PROGRAM
   var x : Integer;  // scope level of declaration is SUBPROGRAM
   var b : Integer;  // scope level of declaration is SUBPROGRAM
begin
   ... x ...     // x was declared at SUBPROGRAM scope
   ... b ...     // b was declared at SUBPROGRAM scope
   ... y ...     // y was declared at PROGRAM scope
end P1;

begin
   ... x  ...      //  x was declared at PROGRAM scope
   ... y  ...      //  y was declared at PROGRAM scope
   ... P1 ...      // P1 was declared at PROGRAM scope
end.
```

Note that procedure P1 is considered to be declared at PROGRAM scope. In the above example, procedure P1 does not have any parameters, but if it did, they would be declared at SUBPROGRAM scope.

Class IdTable supports the ability to open new scopes and to search for declarations, both within the current scope and in enclosing scopes. Class IdTable is implemented as a stack of maps, where each map is from identifier strings (names of things) to their declarations; i.e., the map key is the identifier string and the map value is declaration corresponding to the identifier. Note that, since we don't allow subprograms to be nested, our stack has at most two levels. However, some of the project exercises described in Appendix B would make use of additional stack levels.

When a new scope is opened, a new map is pushed onto the stack. When a scope is closed, the top map is popped off the stack. Within a subprogram, searching for a declaration involves searching within the current level (top map in the stack containing all identifiers declared at SUBPROGRAM scope) and then within the enclosing scope (the map under the top containing all identifiers declared at PROGRAM scope).

Here are several key methods in class IdTable.

```
/**
 * Opens a new scope for identifiers.
 */
public void openScope()
```

```
/**
 * Closes the outermost scope.
 */
public void closeScope()

/**
 * Add a declaration at the current scope level.
 * @throws ParserException if the identifier token associated with
 *                         the declaration is already defined in the
 *                         current scope.
 */
public void add(Declaration decl) throws ParserException

/**
 * Returns the Declaration associated with the identifier token.
 * Searches enclosing scopes if necessary.
 */
public Declaration get(Token idToken)

/**
 * Returns the current scope level.
 */
public ScopeLevel getCurrentLevel()
```

Constraint Rules for Subprograms

We close this section with a list of constraint rules for subprograms, where constraints are organized according to the various grammar rules and must be implemented in their corresponding AST classes.

- **Return Statement**
  - Type Rule: If the statement returns a value for a function, then the type of expression being returned must be the same as the function return type.
  - Miscellaneous Rule: If the return statement returns a value, then the return statement must be nested within a function declaration.
  - Miscellaneous Rule: If the return statement is nested within a function, then it must return a value.
  - Miscellaneous Rule: The return statement must be nested within a subprogram. (This rule is already handled by the parser using class `SubprogramContext`.)

- **Function Declaration**
  - Miscellaneous Rule: There should be no `var` parameters.
  - Miscellaneous Rule: There should be at least one return statement.

    – Miscellaneous Rule: All return statements must return a value.

- **Subprogram Call (for both procedures and functions)**
  - Type Rule: The number of actual parameters should be the same as the number of formal parameters, and each corresponding pair of parameter types should match.

- **Procedure Call**
  - Miscellaneous Rule: If the formal parameter is a var parameter, then the actual parameter must be a named value (not an arbitrary expression).

13.2 Run-time Organization for Subprograms

Understanding the run-time organization for subprograms involves the following four major concepts:

1. Activation records

2. Variable addressing

3. Passing parameters and returning function values

4. CVM instructions for subprograms

We start with a brief overview of the CVM instructions mentioned in the fourth bullet above. These instructions are used specifically in the implementation subprograms.

- PROC (procedure)

- LDLADDR (load local address)

- LDGADDR (load global address)

- CALL (call a subprogram)

- RET (return from a subprogram)

We will discuss these instructions as we work through this chapter. Additional details are provided in Appendix E. Note that CVM does not have separate instructions for procedures and functions. So, for example, the PROC, CALL, and RET are used in a similar manner for both. The three load instructions mentioned above are used in implementing parameters.

Active Subprograms

When a program is running, a subprogram is said to be ***active*** if it has been called but has not yet returned. When a subprogram is called, we need to allocate space on the run-time stack for its parameters and local variables. In addition, if the subprogram is a function, we need to allocate space on the run-time stack for the return value. When the subprogram returns, the allocated stack space is released. An active subprogram is one for which this space (activation record) is currently on the run-time stack.

13.3 Activation Record

An activation record (a.k.a., frame) is a run-time structure for each currently active subprogram.

Here is an important point. A new activation record is created every time a subprogram is called. If a subprogram is called recursively, there will be multiple activation records for that subprogram, one for each call.

The activation record consists of up to five parts as follows:

- The return value part. This part is only present for functions, not procedures.

- The parameter part, which may be empty if there are no parameters.

- The context part, which consists of the saved values for PC and BP. This part always uses two words (8 bytes) of memory on the run-time stack.

- The local variable part, which may be empty if there are no local variables.

- The temporary part, which holds operands and results as statements are executed. This part grows and shrinks as statements are executed, but it is always empty at the beginning and end of every statement of the subprogram.

Let's examine the parts of an activation record in more detail.

Return Value Part of an Activation Record

A function call must first allocate space on the run-time stack for the return value. The number of bytes allocated is the number of bytes for the return type of the function. Specifically, the emit() method in class FunctionCall contains the following code:

```
// allocate space on the stack for the return value
emit("ALLOC " + funcDecl.getType().getSize());
```

Parameter Part of an Activation Record

For each value parameter, a subprogram call must emit code to leave the value of the actual parameter on the top of the run-time stack. For each variable (var) parameter, a procedure call must emit code to leave the address of the actual parameter on the top of the run-time stack. The actual parameter must be a named value, not an expression. Details of parameter passing are covered later in this chapter.

Context Part of an Activation Record

The context part of an activation record is never empty – it always contains exactly two word values (8 bytes) as follows:

- The dynamic link – the base address (BP) of the activation record for the calling subprogram.

- The return address – the address of the next instruction following the call to the subprogram. This is simply the value of the program counter (PC) immediately before the call instruction is executed.

The context part of an activation record is managed by the CVM CALL and RET instructions. The CALL instruction saves (pushes) the calling subprogram values for BP and PC onto the stack, and the RET instruction restores (pops) them back into the appropriate registers.

Local Variable Part of an Activation Record

If local variables are declared in a subprogram, then space must be allocated on the run-time stack for those variables. The CVM instruction PROC (procedure) has an integer argument for the variable length of subprogram.

As an example, suppose that two integer variables and one boolean variable are declared in a procedure P2 as follows:

```
procedure P2 is
    var m, n : Integer;
    var b : Boolean;
begin
    ...
end P2;
```

Then this procedure will need to allocate nine bytes for local variables. The instruction PROC 9 will be emitted to allocate the necessary space on the run-time stack. An instruction of the form PROC 0 is used whenever a subprogram does not have any local variables.

Temporary Part of an Activation Record

The temporary part of an activation record is analogous to the use of the run-time stack to hold temporary values as described in Section 10.4. In fact, the temporary part of an activation record is simply the run-time stack as used by the subprogram for storing activation records of other subprogram calls and temporary, intermediate values of computations. As machine instructions for the subprogram are executed, the temporary part grows and shrinks, and it is empty at the start and end of each CPRL statement in the subprogram.

We illustrate with an example similar to the one in Section 10.4. Let's assume the following:

- register BP has the value 200

- local integer variable x has relative address 8

- local integer variable y has value 6 and relative address 12

The CPRL assignment statement

```
x := y + 1;
```

will compile to the following CVM instructions:

```
LDLADDR 8
LDLADDR 12
LOADW
LDCINT 1     // will be optimized to LDCINT1
ADD
STOREW
```

We visualize the growing and shrinking of the temporary part by using a sequence of diagrams showing the state of the temporary part after execution of each machine instruction.

The temporary part is empty at the start of the CPRL statement.

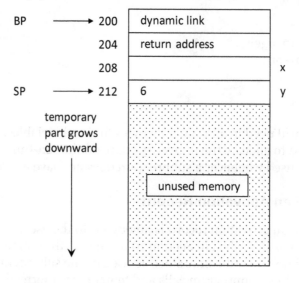

After execution of LDLADDR 8:

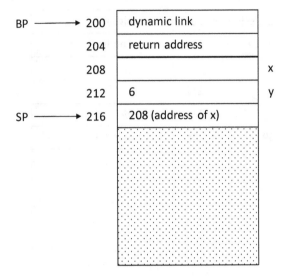

After execution of LDLADDR 12:

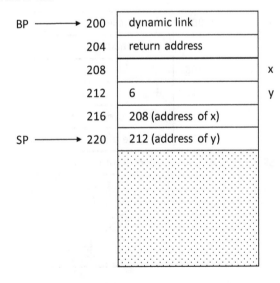

After execution of LOADW:

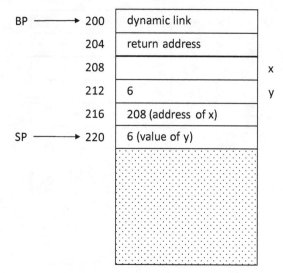

After execution of LDCINT1:

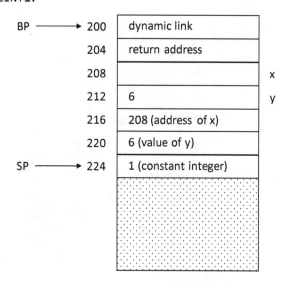

After execution of ADD:

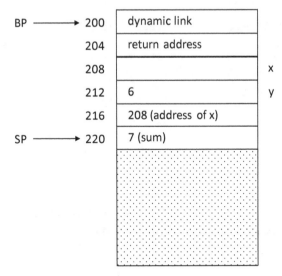

After execution of STOREW:

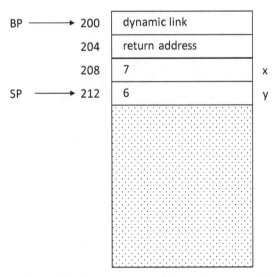

At this point the local variable x has been assigned the value 7, and the temporary part is empty again.

Example: Subprogram with Parameters

Now let's examine the complete layout of an activation record for the a procedure with parameters. Consider the following simple procedure:

```
var x : Integer;

procedure P3(a : Integer, b : Integer) is
    var n : Integer;
begin
    ...
end P3;

begin
    ...
    P3(2, 5);
    ...
end.
```

The activation record for procedure P3 is illustrated in the following diagram. Note that in this diagram, the memory addresses are shown as relative to the BP register and not in absolute values.

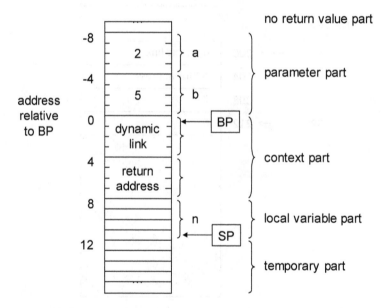

Recursion

Since a new activation record is created every time a subprogram is called, CPRL supports recursive calls. To illustrate, suppose that a program calls procedure P3, and then P3 makes a recursive call to itself. Each call to P3 has its own activation record, which means each call has its own copy of parameters, locally declared variables, etc.

The following diagram illustrates this situation:

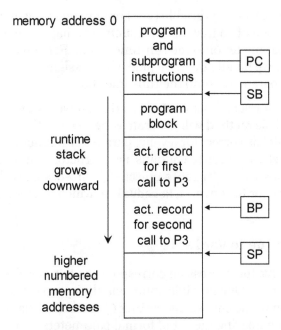

Note that recursion does not have to be direct; that is, procedure P3 does not have to call itself. The approach that we use for calling subprograms is easily extended to supports indirect recursion (a.k.a. mutual recursion), where a subprogram is called not by itself but by another subprogram that it called, either directly or indirectly.

Loading a Program

When a program is loaded into the CVM, the object code for the program is loaded into the beginning of memory starting at address 0. Register PC is initialized to 0, the address of the first instruction, and register SB is initialized to the address following the last instruction (i.e., the first free byte in memory). Register BP is initialized to the address of the byte following the last instruction (i.e., the same as SB). Register SP is initialized to BP − 1 since the run-time stack is empty.

13.4 Parameters

Functions can have only value parameters, but procedures can have both variable (var) and value parameters. The code to handle the passing of these two kinds of parameters as part of a procedure call is somewhat analogous to how you handle an assignment statement of the form "x := y", where we generate different code for the left and right sides. For the left side of an assignment statement, we generate code to leave the address on the run-time stack. For the right side of an assignment statement, we generate code to leave the value on the run-time stack.

As an analogy for parameters, for variable (var) parameters we generate code similar to the way we handle the left side of an assignment statement; that is, we want to push the address of the actual parameter onto the run-time stack. For value parameters, we generate code similar to the way we handle the right side of the assignment; that is, we want to push the value of the actual parameter onto the run-time stack.

When parsing the code for actual parameters, by default we always call parseExpression(). This method will generate code to leave the value of the expression on the run-time stack, which is correct for a value parameter but not for a variable parameter. Note that the code for class Variable contains a constructor that takes a single NamedValue object and uses it to construct a Variable object. When working with variable parameters, we will use this constructor to convert a NamedValue, which is a true expression value, to a Variable.

Converting NamedValue to Variable

When you have a NamedValue expression corresponding to a variable parameter, you need to convert it to a Variable. One possible approach, the approach that we adopt, is to perform the conversion in the checkConstraints() method of class ProcedureCall. When iterating through and comparing the list of formal parameters and actual parameters, if the formal parameter is a variable parameter and the actual parameter is not a NamedValue, then generate an error message since you can't pass an arbitrary expression to a variable parameter. However, if the formal parameter is a variable parameter and the actual parameter is a NamedValue, then convert the NamedValue to a Variable so that code will be generated to leave the variable's address on the top of the run-time stack.

Following is an excerpt from method checkConstraints() in class ProcedureCall that shows how we convert a NamedValue to a Variable:

```
for (int i = 0;  i < actualParams.size();  ++i)
  {
    Expression    expr  = actualParams.get(i);
    ParameterDecl param = formalParams.get(i);

    ...  // check that types match

    // check that named values are being passed for var parameters
    if (param.isVarParam())
      {
        if (expr instanceof NamedValue)
          {
            // replace named value by a variable
            expr = new Variable((NamedValue) expr);
            actualParams.set(i, expr);
          }
```

```
      else
        {
          throw error(expr.getPosition(),
          "Expression for a var parameter must be a variable.");
        }
    }
  }
```

13.5 Subprogram Calls and Returns

Calling a Subprogram

When a subprogram is called, we manage the non-temporary parts of its activation record as follows:

- For a function, space is allocated on the run-time stack for the return value.

- The actual parameters are pushed onto the run-time stack.

  - Push expression values for value parameters.
  - Push addresses for variable parameters.

- The CALL instruction pushes the context part onto the run-time stack.

- The PROC instruction of the subprogram allocates space on the run-time stack for the subprogram's local variables.

PROC Instruction versus ALLOC Instruction

For CVM, the PROC instruction and the ALLOC instruction are equivalent and can be used interchangeably. Both instructions simply move the stack pointer SP to allocate space on the run-time stack; e.g., for a function return value or a subprogram's local variable. In general we prefer to use PROC at the beginning of a subprogram to allocate space for its local variables and ALLOC elsewhere, but this preference is entirely arbitrary.

Returning from a Subprogram

The CVM return instruction indicates the number of bytes used by the subprogram parameters so that they can be removed from the stack. Here is an example.

```
  ret 8
```

When a return instruction is executed,

- BP is set to the dynamic link. This restores BP to point to the caller's activation record.

- PC is set to the return address. This restores PC to the instruction after the call.

- SP is set so as to restore the stack to its state before the call instruction was executed.

  – For procedures, SP is set to the memory address before the activation record.
  – For functions, SP is set to the memory address of the last byte of the return value. The return value remains on the stack.

Note that for functions, the space allocated on the run-time stack for the function's return value remains so that the return value can be used in an expression.

13.6 Computing Relative Addresses

Similar to what we did at the program level, we need to compute the relative address (offset) for each variable plus the total number of bytes of all variables for each subprogram. In addition, for subprograms, we will need to compute the relative address for each parameter. There is one minor difference in computing the relative address of variables of a subprogram. Since addressing is relative to the BP register, and since BP points to the first byte of the activation record, the starting relative address for the first variable is the number of bytes in a frame, not zero as it was for program-level variables.

Also, relative addresses for parameters are negative numbers since parameters are *above* BP in the stack. It is easier to compute relative addresses for parameters in reverse order, so we iterate backwards through the list of parameter declarations to compute their relative addresses.

Method setRelativeAddresses() in the AST class SubprogramDecl is defined as follows:

```
protected void setRelativeAddresses()
  {
    // initial relative address for a subprogram
    int currentAddr = Constants.BYTES_PER_FRAME;

    for (InitialDecl decl : initialDecls)
      {
        // set relative address for single variable declarations
        if (decl instanceof SingleVarDecl)
          {
            SingleVarDecl singleVarDecl = (SingleVarDecl) decl;
            singleVarDecl.setRelAddr(currentAddr);
            currentAddr = currentAddr + singleVarDecl.getSize();
          }
      }

    // compute length of all variables by
    // subtracting initial relative address
    varLength = currentAddr - Constants.BYTES_PER_FRAME;
```

```
      // set relative address for parameters
      if (formalParams.size() > 0)
        {
          // initial relative address for a subprogram parameter
          currentAddr = 0;

          // we need to process the parameter declarations in reverse order
          ListIterator<ParameterDecl> iter
              = formalParams.listIterator(formalParams.size());
          while (iter.hasPrevious())
            {
              ParameterDecl decl = iter.previous();
              currentAddr = currentAddr - decl.getSize();
              decl.setRelAddr(currentAddr);
            }
        }
    }
}
```

Referencing Variables and Parameters

Referencing Local Variables

The LDLADDR (load local address) instruction is used to reference variables local to the subprogram and the subprogram parameters. This instruction computes the absolute address of a local variable from its relative address with respect to BP and pushes the absolute address onto the run-time stack. From the perspective of the CVM machine, the definition of LDLADDR is as follows:

```
pushInt(bp + displ)
```

The use of LDLADDR with subprograms is similar to the use of LDGADDR for program variables except that the relative address of the first local variable is 8 instead of 0 since there are 8 bytes in activation record. Relative addresses can be negative to load the address of a parameter.

Referencing Global Variables

The LDGADDR (load global address) instruction is used within a subprogram to reference global variables; i.e., variables declared at the program level. This instruction computes the absolute address of a global variable from its relative address with respect to SB and pushes the absolute address onto the run-time stack. From the perspective of the CVM machine, the definition of LDGADDR is as follows:

```
pushInt(sb + displ)
```

Note that LDGADDR is equivalent to LDLADDR for programs that do not have subprograms since SB and BP will both have the same value (i.e., they both point to the same memory location).

Let's return to the example of an activation record for a procedure P3 as covered earlier in this chapter.

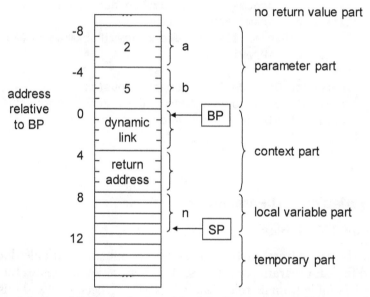

Recall that x is a global variable not depicted in this diagram. We illustrate the referencing of variables and parameters for procedure P3 with a few examples as follows:

- –   LDLADDR -8   loads (pushes) the address of parameter a onto the stack

- –   LDLADDR -4   loads (pushes) the address of parameter b onto the stack

- –   LDLADDR 8   loads (pushes) the address of local variable n onto the stack

- –   LDGADDR 0   loads (pushes) the address of global variable x onto the stack

Variable (var) Parameters

For variable (var) parameters, the address of the actual parameter is passed; i.e., the value contained in the formal parameter is the address of the actual parameter. As an example, consider the following program, where procedure P4 has a variable parameter named a.

```
var x : Integer;

procedure p4(var a : Integer, b : Integer) is
    var n : Integer;
begin
    ...
```

```
   end p4;

   begin
      x := 5;
      p(x, 6);
   end.
```

The call p(x, 6) passes the address of x into parameter a; i.e., the value contained in parameter a is the address of x. Loading the value contained in parameter a onto the run-time stack is equivalent to loading the address of x onto the stack.

Let's assume that the address of x is 325. Then the activation record for P4 is illustrated in the following diagram:

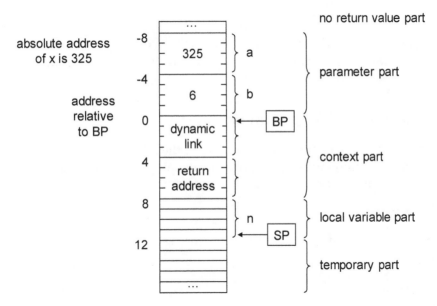

The two instructions

```
   LDLADDR -8
   LOADW
```

will push the address of the actual parameter x onto the run-time stack.

Based on the above discussion, we can implement method emit() for class Variable as follows:

```
@Override
public void emit() throws CodeGenException, IOException
  {
    if (decl instanceof ParameterDecl
        && ((ParameterDecl)decl).isVarParam())
      {
        // address of actual parameter is value of var parameter
        emit("LDLADDR " + decl.getRelAddr());
        emit("LOADW");
      }
    else if (decl.getScopeLevel() == ScopeLevel.PROGRAM)
        emit("LDGADDR " + decl.getRelAddr());
    else
        emit("LDLADDR " + decl.getRelAddr());
  }
```

Note that the above implementation of method emit() is incomplete in that it does not yet consider the case where the variable is an array. The next chapter will address the necessary modifications for array variables.

13.7 Example of Program Execution

In order to get a better understanding of the roles of the internal registers and run-time stack when executing subprograms, let's examine in detail the call of and return from a simple function. Consider the following CPRL program.

```
var x : Integer;

function abs(n : Integer) return Integer is
begin
    if n >= 0 then
        return n;
    else
        return -n;
    end if;
end abs;

begin
    x := -5;
    writeln abs(x);
end.
```

Let's assume that compiling this program yields the following assembly code:

```
        PROGRAM 4
        BR L5
L0:
        PROC 0
        LDLADDR -4
        LOADW
        LDCINT 0
        CMP
        BL L3
        LDLADDR -8
        LDLADDR -4
        LOADW
        STOREW
        RET 4
        BR L4
L3:
        LDLADDR -8
        LDLADDR -4
        LOADW
        NEG
        STOREW
        RET 4
L4:
L5:
        LDGADDR 0
        LDCINT 5
        NEG
        STOREW
        ALLOC 4
        LDGADDR 0
        LOADW
        CALL L0
        PUTINT
        PUTEOL
        HALT
```

After optimization and assembly, a disassembled version of the code would look as follows:

```
 0:    PROGRAM 4
 5:    BR 63
10:    PROC 0
15:    LDLADDR -4
20:    LOADW
21:    LDCINT0
22:    CMP
23:    BL 27
28:    LDLADDR -8
33:    LDLADDR -4
38:    LOADW
39:    STOREW
40:    RET 4
45:    BR 23
50:    LDLADDR -8
55:    LDLADDR -4
60:    LOADW
61:    NEG
62:    STOREW
63:    RET 4
68:    LDGADDR 0
73:    LDCINT -5
78:    STOREW
79:    ALLOC 4
84:    LDGADDR 0
89:    LOADW
90:    CALL -80
95:    PUTINT
96:    PUTEOL
97:    HALT
```

The "Handouts" directory on the book's web site contains a complete step-by-step execution trace of this code that shows memory contents, memory locations referenced by the registers, the run-time stack, etc. Here we present a subset of that execution trace. Note that before execution of the first instruction, PC has the value 0, BP has the value 98, SB also has the value 98, and SP has the value 97. We visualize this state as follows:

```
PC ->    0:    PROGRAM 4
         5:    BR 63
        10:    PROC 0
        15:    LDLADDR -4
        20:    LOADW
        21:    LDCINT0
        22:    CMP
        23:    BL 27
        28:    LDLADDR -8
        33:    LDLADDR -4
        38:    LOADW
        39:    STOREW
        40:    RET 4
        45:    BR 23
        50:    LDLADDR -8
        55:    LDLADDR -4
        60:    LOADW
        61:    NEG
        62:    STOREW
        63:    RET 4
        68:    LDGADDR 0
        73:    LDCINT -5
        78:    STOREW
        79:    ALLOC 4
        84:    LDGADDR 0
        89:    LOADW
        90:    CALL -80
        95:    PUTINT
        96:    PUTEOL
SP ->   97:    HALT
SB ->   98:    ?              <- BP
```

The first instruction, PROGRAM 4, allocates four bytes on the run-time stack.

```
            0:  PROGRAM 4
  PC ->     5:  BR 63
           10:  PROC 0
           15:  LDLADDR -4
           20:  LOADW
           21:  LDCINT0
           22:  CMP
           23:  BL 27
           28:  LDLADDR -8
           33:  LDLADDR -4
           38:  LOADW
           39:  STOREW
           40:  RET 4
           45:  BR 23
           50:  LDLADDR -8
           55:  LDLADDR -4
           60:  LOADW
           61:  NEG
           62:  STOREW
           63:  RET 4
           68:  LDGADDR 0
           73:  LDCINT -5
           78:  STOREW
           79:  ALLOC 4
           84:  LDGADDR 0
           89:  LOADW
           90:  CALL -80
           95:  PUTINT
           96:  PUTEOL
           97:  HALT
  SB ->    98:  ?          <- BP ┐  4 bytes allocated on stack for
           99:  ?                │  for x by the first instruction
          100:  ?                ├  (ignore current value)
  SP ->   101:  ?                ┘
```

After executing the branch instruction at address 5 we have the following:

```
              0:  PROGRAM 4
              5:  BR 63
             10:  PROC 0
             15:  LDLADDR -4
             20:  LOADW
             21:  LDCINT0
             22:  CMP
             23:  BL 27
             28:  LDLADDR -8
             33:  LDLADDR -4
             38:  LOADW
             39:  STOREW
             40:  RET 4
             45:  BR 23
             50:  LDLADDR -8
             55:  LDLADDR -4
             60:  LOADW
             61:  NEG
             62:  STOREW
             63:  RET 4
   PC ->     68:  LDGADDR 0
             73:  LDCINT -5
             78:  STOREW
             79:  ALLOC 4
             84:  LDGADDR 0
             89:  LOADW
             90:  CALL -80
             95:  PUTINT
             96:  PUTEOL
             97:  HALT
   SB ->     98:  ?          <- BP   ⌉
             99:  ?                  |  x (value not yet initialized)
            100:  ?                  |
   SP ->    101:  ?                  ⌋
```

Now let's fast-forward to the point where PC has the value 90, pointing it to the CALL instruction. At this point the integer variable x (at relative address SB + 0 or absolute address 98) has the value -5, the ALLOC instruction at address 79 has allocated space for the function return value, and the two instructions at addresses 84 and 89 have already pushed the value of the parameter (-5) onto the run-time stack.

```
           0:    PROGRAM 4
           5:    BR 63
          10:    PROC 0
          15:    LDLADDR -4
          20:    LOADW
                 ...
          45:    BR 23
          50:    LDLADDR -8
          55:    LDLADDR -4
          60:    LOADW
          61:    NEG
          62:    STOREW
          63:    RET 4
          68:    LDGADDR 0
          73:    LDCINT -5
          78:    STOREW
          79:    ALLOC 4
          84:    LDGADDR 0
          89:    LOADW
PC ->     90:    CALL -80
          95:    PUTINT
          96:    PUTEOL
          97:    HALT
SB ->     98:    -1        <- BP      ⎤
          99:    -1                   ⎥  x (value is -5)
         100:    -1                   ⎥
         101:    -5                   ⎦
         102:    ?                    ⎤  allocated space for function return
         103:    ?                    ⎥  value (ignore current value left
         104:    ?                    ⎥  over from previous instructions)
         105:    ?                    ⎦
         106:    -1                   ⎤
         107:    -1                   ⎥  value of x pushed on the stack
         108:    -1                   ⎥  as a parameter for the call
SP -> 109:    -5                      ⎦
```

Execution of the CALL instruction saves the context part of the activation record on the run-time stack; that is, it pushes the value of BP (98) and the address of the instruction following the call (95) onto the stack, and then adds -80 to the value of PC, which yields the following:

```
            0:   PROGRAM 4
            5:   BR 63
PC ->      10:   PROC 0
           15:   LDLADDR -4
           20:   LOADW
                 ...
           55:   LDLADDR -4
           60:   LOADW
           61:   NEG
           62:   STOREW
           63:   RET 4
           68:   LDGADDR 0
           73:   LDCINT -5
           78:   STOREW
           79:   ALLOC 4
           84:   LDGADDR 0
           89:   LOADW
           90:   CALL -80
           95:   PUTINT
           96:   PUTEOL
           97:   HALT
SB ->      98:   -1
           99:   -1              x (value is -5)
          100:   -1
          101:   -5
          102:   ?               allocated space for function return
          103:   ?               value (ignore current value left
          104:   ?               over from previous instructions)
          105:   ?
          106:   -1
          107:   -1              value of x pushed on the stack
          108:   -1              as a parameter for the call
SP -> 109:   -5
BP -> 110:   0
          110:   0               saved value of BP
          112:   0
          113:   98
          114:   0
          115:   0               saved value of PC
          116:   0
SP -> 117:   95
```

Execution of PROC 0 allocates 0 bytes on the run-time stack (i.e., it doesn't alter the stack).

Fast-forward again to the point where PC has the value 63, pointing it to the RET instruction at that address and giving us the following:

```
          0:   PROGRAM 4
          5:   BR 63
         10:   PROC 0
         15:   LDLADDR -4
         20:   LOADW
               ...
         60:   LOADW
         61:   NEG
         62:   STOREW
PC ->    63:   RET 4
         68:   LDGADDR 0
         73:   LDCINT -5
         78:   STOREW
         79:   ALLOC 4
         84:   LDGADDR 0
         89:   LOADW
         90:   CALL -80
         95:   PUTINT
         96:   PUTEOL
         97:   HALT
SB ->    98:   -1  ⎤
         99:   -1  ⎥  x (value is -5)
        100:   -1  ⎥
        101:   -5  ⎦
        102:   0   ⎤
        103:   0   ⎥  function return value (value is 5)
        104:   0   ⎥
        105:   5   ⎦
        106:   -1  ⎤
        107:   -1  ⎥  value of x pushed on the stack
        108:   -1  ⎥  as a parameter for the call
SP ->   109:   -5  ⎦
BP ->   110:   0   ⎤
        110:   0   ⎥  saved value of BP
        110:   0   ⎥
        113:   98  ⎦
        114:   0   ⎤
        115:   0   ⎥  saved value of PC
        116:   0   ⎥
SP ->   117:   95  ⎦
```

Execution of RET 4 removes the context part of the activation record from the run-time stack and restores the saved values of PC (95) and BP (98). It also adjusts the stack to remove the value of the parameter, which gives us the final execution snapshot that we want to show for this example.

```
          0:   PROGRAM 4
          5:   BR 63
         10:   PROC 0
         15:   LDLADDR -4
         20:   LOADW
         21:   LDCINT0
         22:   CMP
         23:   BL 27
         28:   LDLADDR -8
         33:   LDLADDR -4
         38:   LOADW
         39:   STOREW
         40:   RET 4
         45:   BR 23
         50:   LDLADDR -8
         55:   LDLADDR -4
         60:   LOADW
         61:   NEG
         63:   RET 4
         68:   LDGADDR 0
         73:   LDCINT -5
         78:   STOREW
         79:   ALLOC 4
         84:   LDGADDR 0
         89:   LOADW
         90:   CALL -80
PC ->    95:   PUTINT
         96:   PUTEOL
         97:   HALT
SB ->    98:   -1        <- BP  ┐
         99:   -1               │  x (value is -5)
        100:   -1               │
        101:   -5               ┘
        102:   0                ┐
        103:   0                │  return value from function
        104:   0                │  (value is 5)
SP ->   105:   5                ┘
```

13.8 Essential Terms and Concepts

activation record

context part (of an activation record)

local variable part (of an activation record)

pass by reference

referencing local variables

return address

returning from a subprogram

temporary part (of an activation record)

variable parameter

calling a subprogram

dynamic link

parameter part (of an activation record)

pass by value

referencing global variables

return value part (of an activation record)

scope level

value parameter

13.9 Exercises

1. **Project Assignment.** Implement **Project 7: Subprograms** as described in Appendix A.

2. True or False (T or F)

    a. A function can have variable parameter declarations.

    b. An expression value (e.g., a constant) can be passed as the actual parameter if the corresponding formal parameter is a variable parameter.

    c. If a return statement returns a value, then the return statement must be nested within a function declaration.

    d. CPRL supports recursion.

3. An activation record for a currently active subprogram consists of five parts. Name and briefly describe all 5 parts. (Note: Not every active subprogram contains all parts.)

4. Fill in the blanks.

    a. The scope level of a variable or parameter declaration can be one of two possible values, _____ or _____ .

    b. A subprogram is either a _____ or a _____ .

    c. What is the difference between the two CVM instructions PROC and ALLOC?

5. Select several type and miscellaneous rules for CPRL subprograms, and for each such rule, write two test programs in CPRL, one correct program that satisfies the rule and one incorrect program that does not satisfy the rule. After completing Project 7 (Appendix A), use the test programs to check if your compiler correctly implements the rules.

Chapter 14
Arrays

CPRL supports one-dimensional array types, but arrays of arrays can be declared. Array indices are integer values, and the index of the first element in the array is 0. An array type declaration specifies the array type name (an identifier), the number of elements in the array (which must be a positive integer literal or constant), and the type of the elements in the array.

14.1 Using CPRL Arrays

To create array objects, you must first declare an array type and then declare one or more variables of that type. Here are some examples.

```
type T1 = array[100] of Integer;
type T2 = array[10] of T1;
var a1 : T1;  // contains 100 integers; indexed from 0 to 99
var b1 : T2;  // contains 10 arrays of integers; indexed from 0 to 9
...

a1[0]      // the integer at index 0 of a1 (the first integer)
b1[3]      // the array at index 3 of b1 (the fourth array)
b1[4][3]   // the integer at index 3 of the array at index 4 of b1
```

Type Equivalence for Arrays

Some programming languages use structural equivalence for array types; i.e., two array objects are considered to have the same type if they have the same number of elements and the element types are the same. So, for example, two array objects each containing 100 integers would be considered to have the same type.

In contrast, CPRL uses name equivalence for array types. Array objects in CPRL are considered to have the same type only if they are declared using the same type name. Thus, two distinct array type definitions are considered different even though they may be structurally identical. Additionally, two array objects with the same type are assignment compatible. Two array objects with different types are not assignment compatible, even if they have identical structures. This concept is illustrated through several examples.

Examples. Array Assignment

```
type T1 = array[100] of Integer;
type T2 = array[10] of T1;
type T3 = array[100] of Integer;
```

```
var a1 : T1;
var a2 : T1;    // a2 has the same type as a1
var b1 : T2;
var b2 : T2;    // b2 has the same type as b1
var c1 : T3;    // c1 does not have the same type as a1
...


a1 := a2;    // legal (same types)
b1 := b2;    // legal (same types)
a1 := c1;    // *** Illegal in CPRL (different types) ***
```

Note than the assignment a1 := c1 above is illegal in CPRL even though a1 and c1 are both arrays of 100 integers.

Reference Semantics versus Value Semantics

CPRL uses value semantics for assignment of arrays. In contrast, Java uses reference semantics. The following diagram illustrates the difference between the two for an assignment statement of the form a1 := a2 involving arrays; i.e., both a1 and a2 are variables of the same array type.

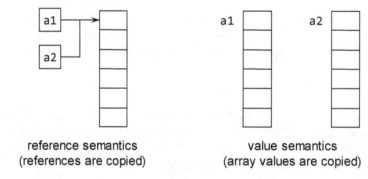

reference semantics   value semantics
(references are copied)   (array values are copied)

Consider the effect of modifying a2[0] after the assignment. If reference semantics is used for array assignment, then modifying a2[0] will also modify a1[0] since both a1 and a2 reference the same array object. With value semantics, both a1 and a2 are independent copies of the arrays, and therefore modifying a2[0] will have no effect on the data in a1.

Here are some additional examples of array assignment with comments to explain the fact that CPRL uses value semantics for array assignment.

```
type T1 = array[100] of Integer;
type T2 = array[10] of T1;
var  b1, b2 : T2;


...
```

```
b1 := b2;                  // array assignment (type T2)
                           // copies 1000 integers (4000 bytes)

b1[2] := b2[5];            // array assignment (type T1)
                           // copies 100 integers (400 bytes)

b1[2][7] := b2[5][0]       // Integer assignment
                           // copies 1 integer (4 bytes)
```

Passing Arrays as Parameters

As with parameters of other (non-structured) types, array parameters have semantics similar to assignment. Passing an array as a value parameter will allocate space for and copy the entire array. This can be an inefficient use of memory if you don't actually need to have a separate copy of the entire array. Passing an array as a variable (var) parameter will simply allocate space for the address of the array. Using a variable parameter has semantics similar to that of Java.

14.2 Implementing CPRL Arrays

We begin our discussion of implementing arrays by reviewing the relevant grammar rules, classes, parser methods, and constraints. Here are the four grammar rules relevant to arrays.

```
initialDecl = constDecl | arrayTypeDecl | varDecl .

arrayTypeDecl = "type" typeId "=" "array" "[" intConstValue "]" "of"
    typeName ";" .

typeName = "Integer" | "Boolean" | "Char" | typeId .

variable = ( varId | paramId ) ( "[" expression "]" )* .
```

These four grammar rules are implemented in four relevant parser methods for arrays as follows:

```
InitialDecl parseInitialDecl()
ArrayTypeDecl parseArrayTypeDecl()
Type parseTypeName()
Variable parseVariable()
```

Following is a diagram that shows the inheritance hierarchy of relevant AST classes and auxiliary classes.

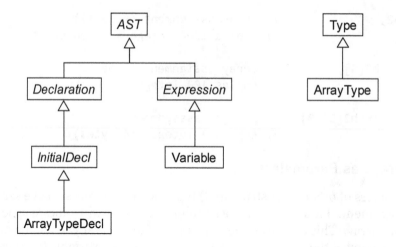

Class `ArrayType`

An array type declaration creates a new type – an array type. Class `ArrayType` encapsulates the following four properties of an array type.

- `name` – the name of the array type

- `numElements` – the number of elements in the array type

- `elementType` – the element type; i.e., the type of the elements in the array

- `size` – the size (number of bytes) of a variable with this type, which is computed as `numElements*elementType.size`

Array Object and Element Addresses

The relative address for a variable of an array type is the relative address of the first byte in the array. The relative address or offset for the element of the array at index n is the sum of the relative address of the array plus the offset of the nth element, computed as follows:

```
relAddr(a[n]) = relAddr(a) + n*elementType.size
```

Since the `Boolean` type uses a single byte, for an array of `Boolean` the relative address for the element at index n can be simplified to the following:

```
relAddr(a[n]) = relAddr(a) + n
```

Let's consider an example. Suppose we have the following declarations:

```
type T = array[100] of Integer;
var a : T;
```

We can visualize the layout of the array as shown in the following diagram:

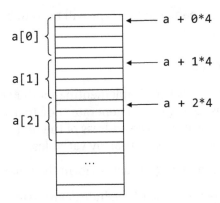

If the actual physical memory address of a is 60, then the actual address of a[0] is 60, the actual address of a[1] is 64, the actual address of a[2] is 68, etc.

Constraint Rules for Arrays

We close this section with a discussion of constraint rules and code generation for arrays. The constraints are organized according to two grammar rules and must be implemented in their corresponding AST classes.

- **Array Type Declaration**
    - Type Rule: The constant value specifying the number of items in the array must have type Integer, and the associated value must be a positive number.

- **Variable (and therefore also for Named Value)**
    - Miscellaneous Rule: Index expressions are permitted only for variables with an array type.
    - Type Rule: Each index expression must have type Integer.

This leads us to a discussion of the implementation for method checkConstraints() in class Variable. Consider the following declarations:

```
type T is array[10] of Integer;
var a : T;
```

Observe that a has type T, but a[i] has type Integer. Therefore, for each index expression, checkConstraints() must perform the following actions:

- Check that the type of the index expression is Integer.

- Check that the type of the variable is an array type.

- Set the type of the expression to the element type for the array. As an example, for an array of Boolean, each index expression has type Integer, but the result of indexing

into the array has type `Boolean`, and this type will need to be set in method
`checkConstraints()`.

Code Generation for Arrays

Here is a summary of the basic ideas for implementing method `emit()` in class `Variable`.
First, as with non-array types, `emit()` must generate code to leave the relative address of
the variable on the run-time stack (i.e., the address of the first byte of the array). There is
no change required to existing code for non-array variables.

Then, for each index expression, `emit()` must perform the following:

- Generate code to compute the value of the index expression.

  ```
  expr.emit();
  ```

- Generate code to multiply this value by the element type's size.

  ```
  emit("LDCINT " + arrayType.getElementType().getSize());
  emit("MUL");
  ```

- Generate code to add the result to the relative address of the variable.

  ```
  emit("ADD");
  ```

As an optimization, don't generate code for the second step above if the array's element
type has size 1 (e.g., if the element type is `Boolean`). Generating code for the second step
would simply multiply the value from the first step by 1.

14.3 Essential Terms and Concepts

array type declaration   class `ArrayType`

name equivalence for array types   reference semantics (for array assignment)

relative address of an array element   structural equivalence for array types

value semantics (for array assignment)

14.4 Exercises

1. **Project Assignment.** Implement **Project 8: Arrays** as described in Appendix A.
   This will complete your compiler for CPRL.

2. The following declaration is not permissible in CPRL. Explain why?

   ```
   var a : array[10] of Integer;
   ```

3. Explain the difference between reference semantics and value semantics for array assignment. Which one is used by CPRL? Which one is used by Java?

4. True or False (T or F)

    a. Array indices must be integer values.

    b. The index of the first element in an array is 1.

    c. Array assignment copies all values from the array on the right side of the assignment operator to the array on the left side.

    d. An array type declaration creates a new type.

5. Use the following declarations in the question below:

```
type T1 = array[100] of Integer:
type T2 = array[100] of Integer;
var a1 : T1;
var a2 : T2;
```

    Is the following assignment valid in CPRL (yes or no)?

```
a1 := a2;
```

6. Use the following declarations in the questions below:

```
type T1 = array[100] of Integer;
type T2 = array[10] of T1;
var a1 : T1;
var a2 : T2;
```

    a. What is the type of a1?

    b. What is the type of a1[5]?

    c. What is the type of a2[5]?

    d. What is the relative address (offset) of a1[5]?

    e. If the actual memory address of a1 is 100, what is the actual memory address of a1[5]?

    f. If the actual memory address of a2 is 500, what is the actual memory address of a2[5]?

7. Select one of the constraint rules (either a type or a miscellaneous rule) for CPRL arrays, and write two test programs in CPRL, one correct program that satisfies the rule and one incorrect program that does not satisfy the rule. After completing Project 8 (Appendix A), use the test programs to check if your compiler correctly implements the rules.

8. When passing an array as a parameter, the array can be passed as a value
   parameter or as a variable parameter. Explain an advantage of passing the array as
   a variable parameter even if the original array is not modified.

Appendix A
The Compiler Project

There are several general approaches for a compiler project in an academic course on compiler construction. One approach is to give detailed explanations and implementations about how to write a compiler for one source language but then concentrate the project around writing a compiler for a different source language. Another approach is to give explanations and partial implementations about how to write a compiler for a particular source language and then to concentrate the project around finishing the incomplete work and possibly extending the source language or targeting a different computer architecture. This book uses the latter approach.

The overall project of developing a compiler for CPRL is divided into 9 smaller projects as described below. For most of the projects, the book web site has lots of both complete and skeletal code to help you get started plus CPRL test programs that can be used to check your work. For each project you should test your compiler with both correct and incorrect CPRL programs as described in the projects below.

Organizational Structure of the Compiler Project

The compiler project is organized into three separate Eclipse projects, with explicit build-path dependencies among the projects. These three Eclipse projects correspond to three Java modules as defined in Java version 9 or later, and the Java module definitions, as defined in `module-info.java` files for the projects, are given below. While it is possible to place all classes in one Eclipse project, I recommend the following structure since it separates the architecture in a way that makes the dependencies transparent. If you are using an IDE other than Eclipse, there will be a similar way to organize the compiler project into different organizational units within that IDE.

1. Eclipse project `Compiler` contains classes that are not directly tied to the CPRL programming language and therefore are useful on any compiler-related project. Examples include classes such as `Position` and `Source` defined in package `edu.citadel.compiler` plus utility classes such as `ByteUtil` and `CharUtil` defined in package `edu.citadel.compiler.util`. There is also a package named `test` that contains a couple of test programs for the principal classes in the project. This project has no dependencies on other Eclipse projects. Its Java module definition is as follows:

    ```
    module edu.citadel.compiler
      {
        exports edu.citadel.compiler;
        exports edu.citadel.compiler.util;
      }
    ```

2. Eclipse project `CVM` contains classes that implement CVM, the virtual machine (emulator) for CPRL. It also contains classes that implement both a CVM assembler

and a CVM disassembler. This project has a dependency on the project `Compiler` as described in item 1 above. Its Java module definition is as follows:

```
module edu.citadel.CVM
    {
      exports edu.citadel.CVM;
      exports edu.citadel.CVM.assembler;
      exports edu.citadel.CVM.assembler.ast;
      requires transitive edu.citadel.compiler;
    }
```

3. Eclipse project `CPRL` contains the classes that implement the CPRL compiler. Complete source code is provided for the other two projects described above, but only portions of the source code are provided for this project. Although students will need to refer occasionally to the other two projects in order to understand the role their classes play in developing the CPRL compiler, all new development will take place only in this project. This project has a dependency on projects `Compiler` and `CVM` as described in items 1 and 2 above. Its Java module definition is as follows:

```
module edu.citadel.cprl
    {
      exports edu.citadel.cprl;
      exports edu.citadel.cprl.ast;
      requires edu.citadel.CVM;
      requires transitive edu.citadel.compiler;
    }
```

Since abstract syntax trees are not introduced until Project 4 below, the line

```
exports edu.citadel.cprl.ast;
```

can be commented out for Projects 0-3 as described below.

Project 0: Getting Started

- This is not a real project but more of an initialization of your working environment for the compiler project. Download files `bin.zip`, `doc.zip`, `examples.zip`, `src0-Compiler.zip`, and `src0-CVM.zip` from the book's web site and unzip them into a directory that you will use for your compiler implementation. Zip files with names beginning "`src…`" contain Java source files for the compiler project. Unzip the `src…` files and import them into your preferred IDE (e.g., Eclipse).

- File `bin.zip` contains sample Bash shell scripts and Windows command scripts for running and testing various stages of the compiler. When unzipped `bin.zip` will create two subdirectories named "`Bash`" and "`Windows`" that contain the Bash and Windows script files, respectively. For each Windows "`.cmd`" file there is a corresponding Bash "`.sh`" file; e.g., `cprlc.cmd` and `cprlc.sh`. Pick the collection of script files for your programming environment.

As an example of the contents of `bin.zip`, there is a script `cprlc.cmd` that will run the CPRL compiler on a single source file whose name is entered via standard input, and there is also a script `cprlc_all.cmd` that will run the compiler on all CPRL source files in the current working directory. Similarly there are two scripts `assemble.cmd` and `assemble_all.cmd` for running the assembler and two scripts `disassemble.cmd` and `disassemble_all.cmd` for running the disassembler. Scripts with the "_all" suffix are useful for testing the compiler against collections of correct and/or incorrect programs. There is a script `cprl.cmd` for running a single compiled CPRL program on the CVM, and there are two scripts `testCorrect.cmd` and `testCorrect_all.cmd` that can be used for testing correct programs and comparing the output with expected output. Additionally there are script files for testing the scanner and parser in the earlier projects.

There are two important steps for using these script files. First, you will need to edit your PATH environment variable to place the directory containing the script files in your path so that the operating system can find them when you enter their names on the command line. And second, you will need to edit the file `cprl_config.cmd` (or `cprl_config.sh`) so that your CLASSPATH environment variable "points to" the directories containing the Java class files for your project. Most of the other script files use `cprl_config.cmd` to set the class path appropriately. For example, my personal setup uses an Eclipse workspace with three Java projects in three separate directories named `Compiler`, `CPRL`, and `CVM`, and all Java class files are in subdirectories of these three directories named `classes` (not the default Eclipse name `bin`); e.g., `Compiler\classes`, `CPRL\classes`, and `CVM\classes`. When `cprl_config.cmd` is executed, it sets CLASSPATH to include the three `classes` directories.

- File `doc.zip` contains Javadoc-generated HTML files for the complete CPRL compiler as implemented by the author. These can be useful as a reference while working on the remaining projects.

- File `examples.zip` contains examples of correct and incorrect CPRL programs that can be used to test various parts of your compiler. There are three subdirectories in this zip file as follows:

    - `Correct` contains numerous correct CPRL programs. The programs are organized into four subdirectories for testing different projects as you progress though the compiler implementation. For example, there is a subdirectory containing only test programs for CPRL/0, the zero subset of CPRL (no subprograms or arrays) as outlined in Project 6 below. Testing should be performed cumulatively; i.e., you should always retest the CPRL/0 example programs when working later projects.

    - `Incorrect` contains numerous incorrect CPRL programs that will be used in testing error detection and recovery.

– ScannerTests contains both correct and incorrect files that can be used for testing your scanner as describe in Project 1 below. These are not necessarily complete CPRL programs. For example, one of the files contains every valid symbol in CPRL including all reserved words, operators, and numerous user-defined identifiers and literals.

You are strongly encouraged to develop additional test programs as you work though the remaining projects described below.

• File src0-Compiler.zip contains the classes for Eclipse project Compiler as described in Eclipse project 1 above. These classes are used by the other two Eclipse projects, and they are potentially reusable on other compiler projects. All of the classes in this zip file are complete and require no additional work for use on the compiler project.

• File src0-CVM.zip contains a complete implementation of CVM, the virtual machine (emulator) that will be used on subsequent projects to run CPRL programs. It also contains a complete implementation of a disassembler and a complete implementation of an assembler for CVM. You will run the assembler on assembly language files generated by your compiler to create machine code files that can be executed on the CVM. These classes are described in Eclipse project 2 above. All of the classes in this zip file are complete and require no additional work for use on the compiler project.

Project 1: Scanner

• Using the concepts from Chapter 5, implement a scanner for CPRL.

• Download file src-Scanner.zip from the book's web site, unzip the files, and import them into your preferred IDE. File src-Scanner.zip contains three classes in package edu.citadel.cprl. It has complete implementations for classes Symbol and Token plus a partial implementation of class Scanner. File src-Scanner.zip also contains a test driver that can be used together with the testScanner.cmd (or testScanner.sh) script file to "wrap" your scanner and run it against the example test files.

• **Complete the implementation for class Scanner.**

• Test your scanner with the scanner-specific test files and all correct CPRL examples.

Project 2: Language Recognition

• Using the concepts from Chapter 6, implement a parser that performs language recognition for the full CPRL language (not just the zero subset) based on the language definition in Appendix C and the context-free grammar in Appendix D.

• Download file src-ParserV1.zip from the book's web site, unzip the files, and import them into your preferred IDE. File src-ParserV1.zip contains two classes in package edu.citadel.cprl, a complete implementation for class IdTable as described in Chapter 6 and a partial implementation of class Parser that performs only language recognition. File src-ParserV1 also contains a test driver that can be used together with script files testParser.cmd (or testParser.sh) and testParser_all.cmd (testParser_all.sh) to "wrap" both your scanner and parser together and run them against the example test files. The zip file also contains a text file showing the results that you should expect when running this version of the parser against the incorrect test examples.

- **Complete the implementation for class Parser.**

- Do not implement error recovery for this project; i.e., when an error is encountered, simply report the error and exit compilation. Follow the examples for the parser methods with complete implementations.

- Test with all correct and incorrect examples. At this point the parser should accept all correct programs and reject all incorrect programs **except** those with type errors. Detection of type errors will be implemented in Project 5. Use the text file showing expected results as a guide.

Project 3: Error Recovery

- Using the concepts from Chapter 7, add error recovery to your parser.

- Download file src-ParserV2.zip from the book's web site and unzip the files. File src-ParserV2.zip contains only one class in package edu.citadel.cprl, a partial implementation of class Parser that demonstrates how to add error recovery to the parser methods. Do **not** import this class into your IDE since you already have an implementation for class Parser. Instead, use the class provided in this download as a guide to manually edit your existing parser in order to add error recovery. Use the test driver and script files from the previous project to run your parser against the example test programs. The zip file also contains a text file showing the results that you should expect when running this version of the parser against the incorrect test examples.

- **Edit your parser from the previous project to add error recovery.**

- Test with all correct and incorrect examples. At this point the parser should accept and reject exactly the same example programs as for the previous project, but this time your parser should report more than one error for some of the incorrect programs. Use the text file showing expected results as a guide.

Project 4: Abstract Syntax Trees

- Using the concepts from Chapter 8, add generation of abstract syntax trees to your parser. All parsing methods should return AST objects or lists of AST objects. From now on we will start referring to our implementation a "compiler" even though it doesn't yet generate code.

- Download file `src-ParserV3.zip` from the book's web site and unzip the files. File `src-ParserV3.zip` contains full or partial implementations of 40 AST classes in package `edu.citadel.cprl.ast`. Approximately half of the AST classes are implemented completely, while the remaining AST classes have only partial implementations. You should import the AST classes into your IDE and implement any unimplemented constructors. For now use empty bodies for methods `checkConstraints()` and `emit()` in the AST classes that are not fully implemented.

  File `src-ParserV3.zip` contains full or partial implementations of several classes in package `edu.citadel.cprl` as follows:

  - A complete implementation for class `Compiler`. You will start using class `Compiler` in the next project. It is included now for convenience since `src-ParserV3.zip` is the last zip file you will need to download.

  - Complete implementations for classes `LoopContext` and `SubprogramContext`. As described in Chapter 8, these classes are used to track entry to and exit from loops and subprograms. Use these classes to check `exit` and `return` statements.

  - A complete implementation for class `IdTable`. As described in Chapter 8, `IdTable` now stores references to an identifier's declaration. This class replaces the previous implementation of `IdTable` that we have been using in the previous two projects. Use the complete version of `IdTable` to check for declaration and scope errors. With this new implementation for `IdTable` your parser will now be able to detect additional scope errors when we implement subprograms in Project 7.

  - A complete implementation of a simple enum class `ScopeLevel` with two constants `PROGRAM` and `SUBPROGRAM` as described in Chapter 8. The scope level is used to keep track of the level at which identifiers were declared.

  - A complete implementation for class `Type` and a partial implementation for its subclass `ArrayType`. You should study these two classes and then complete the implementation for `ArrayType`, which is straightforward.

  - A partial implementation for class `Parser`. As described in Chapter 8, the important parsing methods now return AST objects or a lists of AST objects. Do **not** import this class into your IDE since you already have an implementation for class `Parser`. Instead, use the class provided in this download as a guide to manually edit your existing parser in order to add generation of AST classes.

- **Implement the missing constructors in the AST classes, complete the implementation of class `ArrayType`, and edit your parser from the previous project to add generation of AST classes or lists of AST classes.**

- Test your parser with all correct and incorrect examples. File `src-ParserV3.zip` contains a text file showing the results that you should expect when running this version of the parser against the incorrect test examples. The major differences in test results between versions 2 and 3 of your parser are that version 3 should also detect exit statements that are not nested within loops and return statements that are not nested within subprograms.

Project 5: Constraint Analysis for CPRL/0

- **Using the concepts from Chapter 9, implement checkConstraints() methods in the AST classes to perform full constraint analysis for the CPRL/0 subset (everything except subprograms and arrays).** In addition to the syntax and scope errors previously detected by your compiler, your compiler should also detect all type and miscellaneous errors for the CPRL/0 subset.

- Test with all correct and incorrect CPRL/0 examples. Henceforth you will use Compiler rather than TestParser to test your implementation with the CPRL examples. To invoke the compiler, use scripts cprlc.cmd/cprlc.sh or cprlc_all.cmd/cprlc_all.sh. At this point the compiler should accept all legal CPRL/0 programs and reject all illegal CPRL/0 programs. The examples directory contains a text file showing the expected results.

Project 6: Code Generation for CPRL/0

- **Using the concepts from Chapter 11, implement emit() methods in the AST classes to perform code generation for CPRL/0.** At this point you are actually generating assembly language for the CVM.

- Use the assembler provided in file src0-CVM (see Project 0 above) and script files assemble.cmd (assemble.sh) and assemble_all.cmd (assemble_all.sh) to generate machine code for all correct CPRL/0 examples.

- Use script files cprl.cmd/cprl.sh, testCorrect.cmd/testCorrect.sh, and testCorrect_all.cmd/testCorrect_all.sh to run and test all correct CPRL/0 examples.

Project 7: Subprograms

- **Using the concepts from Chapter 13, add constraint analysis and code generation for subprograms.**

- Test with all correct and incorrect subprogram examples. You should also retest all correct and incorrect CPPRL/0 examples.

Project 8: Arrays

- **Using the concepts from Chapter 14, add constraint analysis and code generation for arrays.** Completion of this project results in the final version of your compiler.

- Correct any remaining errors.

- Test with all correct and incorrect examples. Run all generated object code files on CVM to ensure that code is being generated properly.

Appendix B
Additional Project Exercises

For ambitious undergraduate students or for graduate students, below are a number of exercises, variations, and challenging extensions to the basic compiler project outlined in this book.

1. Create one or more CPRL test programs that test features of the language not covered in the test programs supplied with the book resources.

2. Add one or more new features to the CPRL language. Here are some ideas to get you started thinking along these lines.

   - Add a multiline comment along the lines of Java's /* ... */. Most languages have a form for comments that can extend over multiple lines as shown below.

     ```
     /* comment line 1
        comment line 2
        comment line 3 */
     ```

     One design issue here is whether or not multiline comments can be nested. Equivalently, does each opening comment tag require its own closing comment marker, or does the first closing comment tag end all "open" comments?

   - Allow integer literals to use underscores, as in 1_000_000 for 1 million.

   - Modify the definition of an assignment statement to allow multiple assignments, something along the lines of the following:

     ```
     x, y, z := 0;
     ```

     You will need to redefine the rule for an assignment statement so that comma separated list of variables can appear on the left side of the assignment symbol.

   - Add a for-loop. For example, the for-loop could look something like the following:

     ```
     for i in 1..10 loop
        ...
     end loop;
     ```

     Here are some possible grammar changes to consider.

     ```
     loopStmt = ( whilePrefix | forPrefix )? "loop" statements
                   "end" "loop" ";" .
     whilePrefix = "while" booleanExpr .
     forPrefix = "for" loopId "in" expression ".." expression .
     ```

     The idea here is that the for prefix serves as declaration for the loop identifier. Both expressions in the loop index range should have the same scalar type. The type of the loop identifier is the type of the expressions, which is often integer, but that is not required by the syntax. The loop identifier is declared in a new scope. This is roughly equivalent to the following:

```
// openScope
var loopId : <type of index range>;
loopId := <lower bound of index range>;
while loopId <= <upper bound of index range> loop
    ... // statements in body of loop
    loopId := loopId + 1;
end loop;
// closeScope
```

- Allow arbitrary expressions in `const` declarations. Currently `const` declarations allow only literals on the right side of the ":=" operator. This decision was made in order to simplify the compiler, since allowing expressions means that you have to perform compile-time arithmetic to computer the values. For example,

```
const i := 7;
```

is valid, but

```
const i := -7;
```

is not valid since technically -7 is an expression (unary minus followed by an integer literal) and not a literal.

- Add enumeration (`enum`) types. An enumeration type is defined by listing the identifiers that are the actual values of the type. Each enumerated identifier defines a constant value within the current scope. The predecessor (`pred`), successor (`succ`), and ordinal (`ord`) functions of an enumeration type T could be predefined in the run-time environment.

Examples

```
type Day = <Sun, Mon, Tue, Wed, Thu, Fri>;
type CardSuit = <Club, Diamond, Heart, Spade>;
// pred(Heart) is Diamond
// succ(Heart) is Spade
// ord(Heart) is 2
```

Possible grammar changes:

```
typeDecl = "type" typeId "=" typeDefn ";" .
typeDefn = enumTypeDefn | arrayTypeDefn .
enumTypeDefn = "<" idList ">" .
arrayTypeDefn = "array" "[" intConstValue "]" "of" typeName .
```

- Implement `String` as a full-fledged type in CPRL, so that we can declare variables of type `String`, use `String` types in assignment statements, return `String` values from functions, etc. Note that `String` is already a reserved word.

- Add records/structures similar to records in Pascal/Ada or structs in C/C++. Better yet, add classes similar to those in Java/C++.

- Allow mutually recursive subprograms; i.e., where subprogram A can call subprogram B, which in turn can call back to subprogram A. Currently CPRL does not support this since subprograms have to be fully declared and defined before being called. One way to do this is to separate subprogram declarations (signature only) and definitions, and to require only that declarations appear before calls to subprograms. The signature (name, parameter list, and possibly return type for a function) is all that is required to check that a call to the subprogram is valid. Feel free to look at an early definition of Pascal to see how that language was defined along these lines.

- Add bounds checking at run time for array indices. As implemented in Chapter 14, the compiler does not perform bounds checking when indexing into an array, and therefore it is possible to reference a value beyond the end of the array. As an example, if a is an array of 100 integers, it is possible to access a[150]. Of course the result would not be valid, but the implementation doesn't prevent this from happening. With bounds checking at run time, execution of the program would be halted and an error message would be printed. One way to simplify bounds checking for arrays is to add special instructions to the CPRL virtual machine. For example, the virtual machine implemented by Brinch Hansen [Hanson 1985] has an index instruction that performs bounds checking. Also consider storing the declared size of the array with the array itself, so that the offset of the first item in the array is 4 and not 0 as currently implemented.

- Add references/pointers and dynamic memory allocation (heap).

- Add a predefined environment with several built-in procedures and functions; e.g., make Boolean a predefined enum type, add functions inc (increment) and abs (absolute value) for integers, etc.

- Allow nested subprograms. CPRL allows subprograms to be declared within a program, but subprograms can't be declared within other subprograms. Many languages such as Pascal and Ada allow nested subprograms. Modify the definition of CPRL to allow subprograms to be declared within other subprograms. You will also need to address issues of scope, and the context part of an activation record will need to include a static link that references the activation record of the enclosing subprogram, similar to the way that the dynamic link references the activation record of the calling subprogram. See course references or other compiler texts for details.

3. Reduce the use of the value null in the parser. For example, create a subclass of Statement named EmptyStmt, which implements methods checkConstraints() and emit() by doing nothing (i.e., with an empty block). If parsing fails while parsing a

statement, return an empty statement rather than returning `null`. Do something similar for initial declarations and expressions.

4. Implement the compiler in a language other than Java. Languages that support recursion and object-oriented programming will work best with the approach used in this book. Examples include C++, C#, Python, Kotlin, Scala, and Swift.

5. Modify the target language/machine.

   - Target a real machine or the assembly language for a real machine (e.g., Intel x86).

   - Target the Java Virtual Machine (JVM) or assembly language for the JVM. (Yes, there is an assembler for the JVM.)

   - Target the Common Language Runtime (part of Microsoft's .NET Framework).

   - Target the C programming language. (Note that the first C++ "compilers" targeted C rather than a low-level language.)

6. Implement constraint analysis and code generation using the visitor design pattern.

7. Improve error recovery. For example, if a variable declaration contains an error after the list of identifiers, numerous error messages of the form "Identifier "x" has not been declared." can be generated. One approach to improving error handling for variable declarations is to declare the list of identifiers outside the try block in the parsing method `parseVarDecl()`. If an error occurs and the list of identifiers is not empty, declare each identifier in the list with a "special" type; e.g., "unknown." When comparing types for compatibility, allow type "unknown" so that spurious error messages are not generated. Similar problems and solutions exist when declaring constants and parameters.

8. Redesign code generation to allow for multiple targets.

   - Target a universal, machine-independent back end (e.g., LLVM).

   - Use design patterns to create a code-generation factory.

Appendix C
Definition of the Programming Language CPRL

Introduction

CPRL (for **C**ompiler **PR**oject **L**anguage) is a small but complete programming language with constructs similar to those found in Ada, Java, C++, and Pascal. CPRL was designed to be suitable for use as a project language in an advanced undergraduate or beginning graduate course on compiler design and construction. Its features illustrate many of the basic techniques and problems associated with language translation.

C.1 Lexical Considerations

General

CPRL is case sensitive. Upper-case letters and lower-case letters are considered to be distinct in all tokens, including reserved words.

White space characters (space character, tab character, and EndOfLine) serve to separate tokens; otherwise they are ignored. No token can extend past an end-of-line. Spaces may not appear in any token except character and string literals.

A comment begins with two forward slashes (//) and extends to the end of the line.

```
temp := x;    // swap values of x and y
x := y;
y := temp;
```

An implementation may define a maximum line length for source code files, but the maximum must be at least 255 characters.

Identifiers

Identifiers start with a letter and contain letters and digits. An identifier must fit on a single line, and all characters of an identifier are significant.

```
identifier = letter ( letter | digit )* .
letter = [A-Za-z] .
digit  = [0-9] .
```

Reserved Words

The following identifiers are keywords in CPRL, and they are all reserved.

and	array	begin	Boolean	Char	class	const
declare	else	elsif	end	exit	false	for

```
function   if         in        is        Integer    loop      mod
not        of         or        private   procedure  program   protected
public     read       readln    return    String     then      true
type       var        when      while     write      writeln
```

Note that some keywords such as "class", "for", "public", "private", "String", etc., are not currently used in CPRL but are reserved for possible future use. Such keywords are essentially terminal symbols in the context-free grammar that do not appear in any rule.

Literals

An integer literal consists of a sequence of 1 or more digits.

```
intLiteral = ( digit )+ .
```

A Boolean literal is either "true" or "false", and both of these words are reserved.

A character literal is a single character enclosed by a pair of apostrophes (sometimes called single quotes). Examples include 'A', 'x', and '''. A character literal is distinct from a string literal with length one.

Similar to Java and C++, CPRL uses the backslash (\) as a prefix character to denote escape sequences within character and string literals. The escape sequences used by CPRL are as follows:

\b	backspace
\t	tab
\n	linefeed (a.k.a. newline)
\r	carriage return
\"	double quote
\'	single quote (a.k.a. apostrophe
\\	backslash

```
charLiteral = "'" literalChar "'" .
literalChar    = printableChar | escapedChar .
printableChar = [^\u0000-\u001F\u007F-\u009F] .
escapedChar = "\\b" | "\\t" |"\\n" |"\\"" |"\\'" |"\\\\" .
```

A backslash is required for a character literal containing an apostrophe (single quote). Thus, '\'' can be used to represent a character literal consisting of a single quote, but ''' is not valid.

For convenience, we define a printable character as any 16-bit Unicode character that is not an ISO control character, although there are some 16-bit Unicode characters that are not ISO control characters that are also not printable. The Java method `isISOControl()` in class `Character` can be used to test this condition.

A string literal is a sequence of zero or more printable or escaped characters enclosed by a pair of quotation marks (double quotes).

```
stringLiteral = "\"" ( literalChar )* "\"" .
```

The word "String" is reserved, and string literals are allowed in constant declarations and output statements, but CPRL does not fully support a string type (e.g., you can't create a variable of type String).

Other Symbols

The following delimiters and operators are also recognized as CPRL symbols.

```
:   ;   ,   .   (   )   [   ]        // one character
+   -   *   /   <   =   >
:=   !=   >=   <=                     // two characters
<EndOfFile>                          // end of file
```

C.2 Types

CPRL is a statically typed language.

- Every variable or constant in the language belongs to exactly one type.

- Type is a static property and can be determined by the compiler.

In general, static typing allows better error detection at compile time as well as more efficient code generation.

Standard (predefined) Scalar Types

Type Boolean

The type `Boolean` is treated as a predefined type with two values, `false` and `true`. It is equivalent to type `boolean` in Java.

Type Integer

The type `Integer` is a predefined type that is equivalent to type `int` in Java.

Type Char

The type `Char` is a predefined character type that is equivalent to type `char` in Java.

Array Types

CPRL supports one dimensional array types (but arrays of arrays can be declared). An array type is defined by giving the number of elements in the array and the component type.

Examples

```
type T1 = array[10] of Boolean;
type T2 = array[10] of Integer;
type T3 = array[10] of T2;
```

Array indices are integers ranging from 0 to n-1, where n is the number of elements in the array.

C.3 Constants and Variables

General

Constants and variables must be declared before they can be referenced.

Constants

A constant provides a name for a literal value. Constants are introduced by declarations of the form

```
"const" constId ":=" literal ";"
```

The type of the constant identifier is determined by the type of the literal, which must be an integer literal, a character literal, a boolean literal, or a string literal.

Example

```
const maxIndex := 100;
```

Variables

Variables are introduced by declarations of the form

```
var varId₁, varId₂, ..., varIdₙ : typeName;
```

The type name must be one of the predefined types (such as Integer) or an identifier representing an array type. The type name cannot be a type constructor such as array constructor; i.e., the following is **not** allowed:

```
var x : array[100] of Integer;    // illegal in CPRL
```

Examples

```
var x1, x2 : Integer;
var found : Boolean;

type IntArray = array[100] of Integer;
var table : IntArray;
```

C.4 Operators and Expressions

Operators

The operators, in order of precedence, are as follows:

1. Boolean negation   not
2. Multiplying operators   *   /   mod
3. Unary adding operators   +   -
4. Binary adding operators   +   -
5. Relational operators   =   !=   <   <=   >   >=
6. Logical operators   and   or

Expressions

For binary operators, both operands must be of the same type. Similarly, for assignment compatibility, both the left and right sides must have the same type. Objects are considered to have the same type if and only if they have the same type name. Thus, two distinct type definitions are considered different even though they may be structurally identical. This is referred to as "name equivalence" of types.

Example

```
type T1 = array[10] of Integer;
type T2 = array[10] of Integer;

var x : T1;
var y : T1;
var z : T2;
```

In the above example, x and y have the same type, but x and z do not.

Logical expressions (expressions involving logical operators "and" or "or") use short-circuit evaluation. For example, given an expression of the form "$expr_1$ and $expr_2$", the left operand ($expr_1$) is evaluated, and if the result is false, the right operand ($expr_2$) is not evaluated and the truth value for the compound expression is considered to be false.

C.5 Statements

General

All statements terminate with a semicolon. Control flow statements are bracketed; e.g., "if" with "end if", "loop" with "end loop", etc.

Assignment Statement

The assignment operator is ":=". An assignment statement has the following form:

```
variable := expression;
```

Example

```
i := 2*i + 5;
```

The variable and the expression must have assignment compatible types. In general, CPRL uses named type equivalence, which means that two types are assignment compatible only if they share the same type name. Two array types with identical structure but different type names are not assignment compatible.

Example

```
type T1 = array[10] of Integer;
type T2 = array[10] of Integer;

var x : T1;
var y : T1;
var z : T2;
...

x := y;    // allowed
x := z;    // *** Illegal in CPRL ***
```

If Statement

An if statement starts with the keyword "if" and ends with the pair of keywords "end if". It may contain zero or more elsif clauses (note spelling of "elsif" without the second "e") and an optional else clause. A single "end if" marks the end of the if statement, regardless of the number of elsif clauses.

Examples

```
if x > 0 then
    sign := 1;
elsif x < 0 then
    sign := -1;
```

```
else
    sign = 0;
end if;

if a[i] = searchValue then
    found := true;
end if;
```

Loop and Exit Statements

A loop statement may be preceded by an optional "while" clause, but the body of the loop statement is bracketed by the keywords "loop" and "end loop". An exit statement can be used to exit the inner most loop that contains it. Note that an exit statement must be nested within a loop; it cannot appear as a standalone statement outside of a loop.

Example 1

```
while i < n loop
    sum := sum + a[i];
    i := i + 1;
end loop;
```

Example 2

```
loop
    read x;
    exit when x = SIGNAL;
    process(x);
end loop;
```

Input/Output Statements

CPRL defines only sequential text I/O for two basic character streams – standard input and standard output. I/O is provided by read, write, and writeln statements. The write and writeln statements can have multiple expressions separated by commas. Input is supported only for integers and characters.

Examples

```
read x;
writeln "The answer is ", 2*x + 1;
```

C.6 Programs and Subprograms

A program has an optional declarative part followed by a statement part. The declarative part starts with the reserved word "declare". The statement part is bracketed by reserved words "begin" and "end". A period (".") terminates the program.

Example 1

```
begin
   writeln "Hello, world.";
end.
```

Example 2

```
var x : Integer;
begin
   read x;
   writeln "x = ", x;
end.
```

Subprograms

As with Pascal and Ada, CPRL provides two separate forms of subprograms – procedures and functions. A procedure (similar to a void function in C or C++) does not return a value; it is invoked through a procedure call statement. A function must return a value and is invoked as part of an expression. Recursive invocations of subprograms are allowed. All subprograms must be declared before they are called, and all subprogram names must be distinct. The name of a subprogram must be repeated at the closing "end" of the subprogram declaration.

Procedures

Procedures are similar to those in Pascal except that explicit return statements (which must **not** be followed by an expression) are allowed within the statement part. Procedure calls are statements.

Example (Quick Sort)

```
procedure quickSort(var a : A, fromIndex : Integer, toIndex : Integer) is
   var i, j, pivot, temp : Integer;
begin
   i := fromIndex;
   j := toIndex;
   pivot := a[(fromIndex + toIndex)/2];

   // partition a[fromIndex]..a[toIndex] with pivot as the dividing item
   while i <= j loop
      while (a[i] < pivot) loop
         i := i + 1;
      end loop;

      while (a[j] > pivot) loop
         j := j - 1;
```

```
    end loop;

    if i <= j then
        // swap a[i] and a[j]
        temp := a[i];
        a[i] := a[j];
        a[j] := temp;

        // update i and j
        i := i + 1;
        j := j - 1;
    end if;
    end loop;

    if fromIndex < j then
        // sort top part
        quickSort(a, fromIndex, j);
    end if;

    if i < toIndex then
        // sort bottom part
        quickSort(a, i, toIndex);
    end if;

    end quickSort;
```

Assume that we have the following declarations:

```
const arraySize := 10;
type A = array[arraySize] of Integer;
var a : A;
```

Then we could call this procedure to sort the array as follows:

```
quickSort(a, 0, arraySize - 1);
```

Functions

Functions are similar to procedures except that functions can return values. Function calls are expressions. A function returns a value by executing a "return" statement of the following form:

```
return <expression>;
```

Example

```
function max(x : Integer, y : Integer) return Integer is
begin
   if x >= y then
      return x;
   else
      return y;
   end if;
end max;
```

Parameters

There are two parameter modes in CPRL – value parameters and variable parameters. Value parameters are passed by value (a.k.a. copy-in) and are the default. Variable parameters are passed by reference and must be explicitly declared using the "var" keyword.

Example

```
procedure inc(var x : Integer) is
begin
   x := x + 1;
end inc;
```

Functions cannot have variable parameters; only value parameters are permitted for functions.

Return Statements

A return statement terminates execution of a subprogram and returns control back to the point where the subprogram was called. A return statement within a function must be followed by an expression whose value is returned by the function. The type of the expression must be assignment compatible with the return type of the function. A return statement within a procedure must not be followed by an expression; it simply returns control to the statement following the procedure call statement.

A procedure has an implied return statement as its last statement, and therefore most procedures will not have an explicit return statement. A function requires one or more return statements to return the function value. There is no implicit return statement at the end of a function.

Appendix D
The CPRL Grammar

```
// Structural Grammar

program = declarativePart statementPart "." .

declarativePart = initialDecls subprogramDecls .

initialDecls = ( initialDecl )* .

initialDecl = constDecl | arrayTypeDecl | varDecl .

constDecl = "const" constId ":=" literal ";" .

literal = intLiteral | charLiteral | stringLiteral | booleanLiteral .

booleanLiteral = "true" | "false" .

arrayTypeDecl = "type" typeId "=" "array" "[" intConstValue "]"
    "of" typeName ";" .

varDecl = "var" identifiers ":" typeName ";" .

identifiers = identifier ( "," identifier )* .

typeName = "Integer" | "Boolean" | "Char" | typeId .

subprogramDecls = ( subprogramDecl )* .

subprogramDecl = procedureDecl | functionDecl .

procedureDecl = "procedure" procId ( formalParameters )? "is"
    initialDecls statementPart procId ";" .

functionDecl = "function" funcId ( formalParameters )? "return" typeName "is"
    initialDecls statementPart funcId ";" .

formalParameters = "(" parameterDecl ( "," parameterDecl )* ")" .

parameterDecl = ( "var" )? paramId ":" typeName .

statementPart = "begin" statements "end" .

statements = ( statement )* .

statement = assignmentStmt | ifStmt | loopStmt | exitStmt | readStmt
          | writeStmt | writelnStmt | procedureCallStmt | returnStmt .

assignmentStmt = variable ":=" expression ";" .

variable = ( varId | paramId) ( "[" expression "]" )* .
```

```
ifStmt = "if" booleanExpr "then" statements
        ( "elsif" booleanExpr "then" statements )*
        ( "else" statements )? "end" "if" ";" .

loopStmt = ( "while" booleanExpr )? "loop" statements "end" "loop" ";" .

exitStmt = "exit" ( "when" booleanExpr )? ";" .

readStmt = "read" variable ";" .

writeStmt = "write" expressions ";" .

expressions = expression ( "," expression )* .

writelnStmt = "writeln" ( expressions )? ";" .

procedureCallStmt = procId ( actualParameters )? ";" .

actualParameters = "(" expressions ")" .

returnStmt = "return" ( expression )? ";" .

expression = relation ( logicalOp relation )* .

logicalOp = "and" | "or" .

relation = simpleExpr ( relationalOp simpleExpr )? .

relationalOp = "=" | "!=" | "<" | "<=" | ">" | ">=" .

simpleExpr = ( addingOp )? term ( addingOp term )* .

addingOp = "+" | "-" .

term = factor ( multiplyingOp factor )* .

multiplyingOp = "*" | "/" | "mod" .

factor = "not" factor | constValue | namedValue | functionCall
        | "(" expression ")" .

constValue = literal | constId .

namedValue = variable .

functionCall = funcId ( actualParameters )? .

// A booleanExpr is simply an expression that has type boolean.
booleanExpr = expression .

// An intConstValue is simply a constValue that has type Integer.
intConstValue = constValue .

// All symbols above with a suffix of "Id" are simply identifiers.
constId = identifier .

varId = identifier .
```

```
paramId = identifier .

typeId = identifier .

procId = identifier .

funcId = identifier .

paramId = identifier .

// Common abbreviations used above:
//     declaration    -> decl
//     expression     -> expr
//     statement      -> stmt
//     parameter      -> param
```

```
//_____
//
// Lexical Grammar
// (Uses "\uxxxx" Unicode notation and regular expression character classes.)


// All quoted terminals in the structural grammar given above are
// considered to be symbols of the lexical grammar.  In addition, all
// reserved words listed in Appendix C, Section C1 are considered to be
// symbols of the lexical grammar even if they do not they appear as
// terminal symbols in the structural grammar.


// The following four rules also define terminal symbols for the parser.
identifier = letter ( letter | digit)* .

intLiteral = ( digit )+ .

charLiteral = "'" charLiteralElement | escapedChar "'" .

stringLiteral = "\"" ( stringLiteralElement | escapedChar )* "\"" .

// The remaining rules do not define terminal symbols for the parser.
letter = [A-Za-z] .

digit  = [0-9] .

// A graphic character is essentially any character that can be printed.
// For simplicity, the definition of graphic character excludes only ISO
// control characters, although some non-control characters might not
// actually be printable.  The ranges of allowable characters include
// space to tilde (~) plus NBSP to \uFFFF.
// NOTE: This rule is used only for descriptive purposes and can be omitted.
```

```
graphicChar = [\u0020-\u007E\u00A0-\uFFFF] .
    // equivalently, [ -~\u00A0-\uFFFF] or [^\u0000-\u001F\u007F-\u009F]

escapedChar = "\\" ("b" | "t" | "n" | "f" | "r" | "\"" | "\'" | "\\") .

// A char literal element is any graphic character except backslash (\) and
// single quote ('); i.e., includes space to ampersand, left paren to left
// bracket, right bracket to tilde, and NBSP to \uFFFF.
charLiteralElement = [\u0020-\u0026\i0028-\u005B\u005D-\u007E\u00A0-\uFFFF] .
    // equivalently, [ -&(-\[\]-~\u00A0-\FFFF]

// A string literal element is any graphic character except backslash (\) and
// double quote ("); i.e., includes space, exclamation point, pound sign to
// left bracket, right bracket to tilde, and NBSP to \uFFFF.
stringLiteralElement = [\u0020\u0021\u0023-\u005B\u005D-\u007E\u00A0-\uFFFF]
    // equivalently, [ !#-\[\]-~\u00A0-\uFFFF]
```

Appendix E
Definition of the CPRL Virtual Machine

E.1 Specification.

CVM (CPRL - Virtual Machine) is a hypothetical computer designed to simplify the code generation phase of a compiler for the Compiler PRoject Language (CPRL). CVM has a stack architecture; i.e., most instructions either expect values on the stack, place results on the stack, or both. Memory is organized into 8-bit bytes, and each byte is directly addressable. A word is a logical grouping of 4 consecutive bytes in memory. The address of a word is the address of its first (low) byte. Boolean values are represented in a single byte, character values use 2 bytes (Unicode Basic Multilingual Plane or Plane 0, code points from U+0000 to U+FFFF)), and integer values use a word (four bytes).

CVM has four 32-bit internal registers that are usually manipulated indirectly as a result of program execution. There are no general-purpose registers for computation. The names and functions of the registers are as follows:

- PC (program counter; a.k.a. instruction pointer): holds the address of the next instruction to be executed.

- SP (stack pointer): holds the address of the top of the stack. The stack grows from low-numbered memory addresses to high-numbered memory addresses. When the stack is empty, SP has a value of the address immediately before the first free byte in memory.

- SB (stack base): holds the address of the bottom of the stack. When a program is loaded, SB is initialized to the address of the first free byte in memory.

- BP (base pointer): holds the base address of the current frame; i.e., the base address for the subprogram currently being executed.

Each CVM instruction operation code (opcode) occupies one byte of memory. Some instructions take one or two immediate operands, which are always located immediately following the instruction in memory. Depending on the opcode, an immediate operand can be a single byte, two bytes (e.g., for a char), four bytes (e.g. for an integer or a memory address), or multiple bytes (e.g., for a string literal). The complete instruction set for CVM is given in the next section. Most instructions get their operands from the run-time stack. In general, the operands are removed from the stack whenever the instruction is executed, and any results are left on the top of the stack. With respect to boolean values, zero means false and any nonzero value is interpreted as true.

The following diagram illustrates a program is loaded into memory.

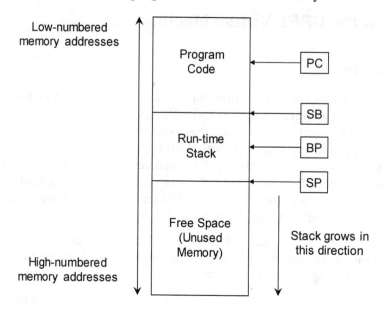

Variable Addressing

Each time that a subprogram is called, CVM saves the current value of BP and sets BP to point to the new frame (a.k.a., activation record). When the subprogram returns, CVM restores BP back to the saved value.

A variable has an absolute address in memory (the address of the first byte), but variables are more commonly addressed relative to a register. A local variable is addressed relative to the current BP. A global variable is addressed relative to value of SB.

Various load and store operations move data between the program code and the run-time stack.

E.2 CVM Instruction Set Architecture

Mnemonic	Short Description	Args	Definition
	Arithmetic Opcodes		
ADD	Add: Remove two integers from the top of the stack and push their sum back onto the stack.	none	$op_2 \leftarrow popInt()$ $op_1 \leftarrow popInt()$ $pushInt(op_1 + op_2)$
SUB	Subtract: Remove two integers from the top of the stack and push their difference back onto the stack.	none	$op_2 \leftarrow popInt()$ $op_1 \leftarrow popInt()$ $pushInt(op_1 - op_2)$
MUL	Multiply: Remove two integers from the top of the stack and push their product back onto the stack.	none	$op_2 \leftarrow popInt()$ $op_1 \leftarrow popInt()$ $pushInt(op_1 * op_2)$
DIV	Divide: Remove two integers from the top of the stack and push their quotient back onto the stack.	none	$op_2 \leftarrow popInt()$ $op_1 \leftarrow popInt()$ $pushInt(op_1 \div op_2)$
MOD	Modulo: Remove two integers from the top of the stack, divide them, and push the remainder back onto the stack.	none	$op_2 \leftarrow popInt()$ $op_1 \leftarrow popInt()$ $pushInt(op_1 \bmod op_2)$
NEG	Negate: Replace the integer at the top of the stack by its arithmetic negative.	none	$op \leftarrow popInt()$ $pushInt(-op)$
INC	Increment: Add 1 to the integer at the top of the stack.	none	$n \leftarrow popInt()$ $pushInt(n + 1)$
DEC	Decrement: Subtract 1 from the integer at the top of the stack.	none	$n \leftarrow popInt()$ $pushInt(n - 1)$

	Logical Opcodes		

NOT	Logical Not: Replace the byte at the top of the stack by its logical negation.	none	```op ← popByte()```
			```if op = 0```
			``` pushByte(1)```
			```else```
			``` pushByte(0)```

	Shift Opcodes		
SHL	Shift Left: Remove an integer from the top of the stack, shift the bits left by the specified amount using zero fill, and push the result back onto the stack. Note: Only the right most five bits of the argument are used for the shift.	amt (byte)	```op ← popInt()``` ```pushInt(op << amt)```
SHR	Shift Right: Remove an integer from the top of the stack, shift it right by the specified amount using sign extend, and push the result back onto the stack. Note: Only the right most five bits of the argument are used for the shift.	amt (byte)	```op ← popInt()``` ```pushInt(op >> amt)```
	Compare/Branch Opcodes		

CMP	Compare: Remove two integers from the top of the stack and compare them. Push a byte representing -1, 0, or 1 back onto the stack depending on whether the first integer is less than, equal to, or greater than the first integer, respectively.	none	```op₂ ← popInt()```
			```op₁ ← popInt()```
			```if op₁ = op₂```
			``` pushByte(0)```
			```else if op₁ > op₂```
			``` pushByte(1)```
			```else```
			``` pushByte(-1)```

BR	Branch: Branch unconditionally according to displacement argument (may be positive or negative).	displ (int)	`pc ← pc + displ`

BNZ	Branch if Nonzero: Remove one byte from the top of the stack. If it is nonzero then branch according to displacement argument (may be positive or negative); otherwise continue with the next instruction.	displ (int)	`op ← popByte()`
			`if op ≠ 0`
			`    pc ← pc + displ`

BZ	Branch if Zero: Remove one byte from the top of the stack. If it is zero, then branch according to displacement argument (may be positive or negative); otherwise continue with the next instruction.	displ (int)	`op ← popByte()`
			`if op = 0`
			`    pc ← pc + displ`

BG	Branch if Greater: Remove one byte from the top of the stack. If it is greater than zero then branch according to displacement argument (may be positive or negative); otherwise continue with the next instruction.	displ (int)	`op ← popByte()`
			`if op > 0`
			`    pc ← pc + displ`

BGE	Branch if Greater or Equal: Remove one byte from the top of the stack. If it is greater than or equal to zero, then branch according to displacement argument (may be positive or negative); otherwise continue with the next instruction.	displ (int)	`op ← popByte()`
			`if op ≥ 0`
			`    pc ← pc + displ`

BL	Branch if Less: Remove one byte from the top of the stack. If it is less than zero then branch according to displacement argument (may be positive or negative); otherwise continue with the next instruction.	displ (int)	```op ← popByte()
if op < 0
pc ← pc + displ```
BLE	Branch if Less or Equal: Remove one byte from the top of the stack. If it is less than or equal to zero then branch according to displacement argument (may be positive or negative); otherwise continue with the next instruction.	displ (int	```op ← popByte()
if op ≤ 0
PC ← PC + displ```
Load/Store Opcodes			
LOAD	Load multiple bytes onto the stack: The number of bytes to move is part of the instruction. Remove the absolute address from the top of the stack and push the n bytes starting at that address onto the stack.	n (int)	```addr ← popInt();
for i ← 0..n-1 loop
pushByte(mem[addr + i])```
LOADB	Load Byte: Loads a single byte onto the stack. The address of the byte is obtained by popping it off the top of the stack.	none	```addr ← popInt()
b ← mem[addr]
pushByte(b)```
LOAD2B	Load Two Bytes: Load two consecutive bytes onto the stack. The address of the first byte is obtained by popping it off the top of the stack.	none	```addr ← popInt()
b₀ ← mem[addr + 0]
b₁ ← mem[addr + 1]
pushByte(b₀)
pushByte(b₁)```

LOADW	Load Word: Load a word (four consecutive bytes) onto the stack. The address of the first byte is obtained by popping it off the top of the stack.	none	addr ← popInt() b_0 ← mem[addr + 0] b_1 ← mem[addr + 1] b_2 ← mem[addr + 2] b_3 ← mem[addr + 3] pushByte(b_0) pushByte(b_1) pushByte(b_2) pushByte(b_3)
LDCB	Load Constant Byte: Fetch the byte immediately following the opcode and push it onto the top of the stack.	b (byte)	pushByte(b)
LDCB0	Load Constant Byte 0: Optimized version of LDCB 0.	none	pushByte(0)
LDCB1	Load Constant Byte 1: Optimized version of LDCB 1.	none	pushByte(1)
LDCCH	Load Constant Character: Fetch the character immediately following the opcode and push it onto the top of the stack.	c (char)	pushChar(c)
LDCINT	Load Constant Integer: Fetch the integer immediately following the opcode and push it onto the top of the stack.	n (int)	pushInt(n)
LDCINT0	Load Constant Integer 0: Optimized version of LDCINT 0.	none	pushInt(0)
LDCINT1	Load Constant Integer 1: Optimized version of LDCINT 1.	none	pushInt(1)

LDCSTR	Load Constant String: The string (length plus characters) immediately follows the opcode. Fetch the length and push both the length and the starting address of the characters onto the top of the stack.	n (int)
		
		s (string)
			`pushInt(n)`
			`pushInt(pc)`
			`pc ← pc + 2*n`

LDLADDR	Load Local Address: Compute the absolute address of a local variable from its relative address [BP + displ] and push the absolute address onto the stack.	displ (int)	`pushInt(bp + displ)`
LDGADDR	Load Global Address: Compute the absolute address of a global (program level) variable from its relative address [SB + displ] and push the absolute address onto the stack.	displ (int)	`pushInt(sb + displ)`

STORE	Store n bytes: Remove n bytes from the top of the stack followed by an absolute address, and copy the n bytes to the location starting at the absolute address.	n (int)	`for i ← n-1..0 loop`
			`    data[i] ← popByte()`
			`addr ← popInt()`
			`for i ← 0..n-1 loop`
			`    mem[addr + i] ←`
			`data[i]`

STOREB	Store Byte: Store a single byte at a specified memory location. The byte to be stored and the address where it is to be stored are obtained by popping them off the top of the stack.	none	`b ← popByte()`
			`addr ← popInt()`
			`memory[addr] ← b`

STORE2B	Store Two Bytes: Store two bytes at a specified memory location. The bytes to be stored and the address where they are to be stored are obtained by popping them off the top of the stack.	none	`b₁ ← popByte()`
			`b₀ ← popByte()`
			`addr ← popInt()`
			`mem[addr + 0] ← b₀`
			`mem[addr + 1] ← b₁`

STOREW	Store Word: Store a word (4 bytes) at a specified memory location. The word to be stored and the address where it is to be stored are obtained by popping them off the top of the stack.	none	`b₃ ← popByte()`
			`b₂ ← popByte()`
			`b₁ ← popByte()`
			`b₀ ← popByte()`
			`addr ← popInt()`
			`mem[addr + 0] ← b₀`
			`mem[addr + 1] ← b₁`
			`mem[addr + 2] ← b₂`
			`mem[addr + 3] ← b₃`

ALLOC	Allocate: Allocate/reserve space on the stack for future use.	n (int)	`sp ← sp + n`
Program/Procedure Opcodes			
PROGRAM	Program: Initialize a program by setting the base pointer and then allocating space on the stack for the program's local variables.	varLen (int)	`bp ← sb` `sp ← bp + varLen - 1`
PROC	Procedure: Allocate space on the stack for a subprogram's local variables.	varLen (int)	`sp ← sp + varLen`

CALL	Call: Call a subprogram, saving the old values for BP and PC on the stack.	displ
		(int)
			`pushInt(bp)`
			`pushInt(pc)`
			`bp ← sp - 7`
			`pc ← pc + displ`

RET	Return: Return from a subprogram, restoring the old value for BP plus space on the stack that had been allocated for the subprogram's local variables and parameters.	parLen
		(int)
			`tempBP ← bp`
			`sp ← tempBP - parLen - 1`
			`bp ← getInt(tempBP)`
			`pc ← getInt(tempBP + 4)`

HALT	Halt: Stop the virtual machine.	none	`halt`

I/O Opcodes			

GETINT	Get Integer: Read digits from standard input, convert them to an integer, and push the integer value onto the top of the stack.	none	`s ← readStr()`
			`n ← toInt(s)`
			`pushInt(n)`

GETCH	Get Character: Read a character from standard input and push its value onto the top of the stack.	none	`c ← readChar()` `pushChar(c)`
PUTBYTE	Put Byte: Remove the byte at the top of the stack and write its value to standard output.	none	`b ← popInt()` `writeByte(b)`
PUTINT	Put Integer: Remove the integer at the top of the stack and write its value to standard output.	none	`n ← popInt()` `writeInt(n)`
PUTCH	Put Character: Remove the character from the top of the stack and write its value to standard output.	none	`c ← popChar()` `writeChar(c)`

PUTSTR	Put String: Remove the absolute address of the string and the string length from the top of the stack and write the characters to standard output.	none	`addr ← popInt()`
			`n ← popInt()`
			`for i ← 0..n-1 loop`
			`    writeChar(mem[2*i])`

PUTEOL	Put End-of-Line: Write a line terminator to standard output.	none	`write(EOL)`

Annotated Compiler References and Websites

What follows is not a comprehensive bibliography for compiler research but more of a listing of useful books and web sites that complement or extend many of the ideas presented in this book.

[Aho 2006] Alfred V. Aho, Monica S. Lam, Ravi Sethi, Jeffrey D. Ullman, *Compilers: Principles, Techniques, And Tools* (Second Edition – a.k.a. Purple Dragon), Addison Wesley, 2006, ISBN 978-0321486813.

> The Purple Dragon is a classic, and many people learned how to write compilers from the Purple Dragon or its predecessor, the Red Dragon. It goes into much more detail about almost every topic, and is therefore much better suited for a two-semester course for graduate students or very advanced undergraduates.

[ANTLR] ANTLR (ANother Tool for Language Recognition), http://www.antlr.org/.

> ANTLR is a parser generator for reading, processing, executing, or translating structured text or binary files. It provides support for generating scanners and parsers, for building parse trees, and for generating tree walkers that can be used to visit the nodes of those trees to execute application-specific code. See also https://github.com/antlr/, the GitHub web site for ANTLR, and [Parr 2013] below.

[Appel 2002] Andrew W. Appel and Jens Palsberg, *Modern Compiler Implementation in Java* (Second Edition), Cambridge University Press, 2002, ISBN 978-0521820608.

> This is a highly acclaimed and widely adopted text on writing compilers. This one uses Java as the implementation language, but there are parallel versions of the book that use implementation languages C and ML.

[Bloch 2018] Joshua Bloch, *Effective Java* (Third Edition), Addison-Wesley, 2018, ISBN 978-0134685991.

> This book has essentially nothing to do with compilers but everything to do with developing software using Java. Every Java programmer should own a copy of this book. I have owned copies of all three editions, and I refer them frequently.

[Campbell 2013] Bill Campbell, Swami Iyer, and Bahar Akbal-Delibas, *Introduction to Compiler Construction in a Java World*, CRC Press, 2013, ISBN 978-1439860885.

> This book uses Java exclusively. The source language being compiled is a subset of Java, the implementation language is Java, and the target machine is the JVM. The authors start by providing a working compiler, and most of the exercises are involved in updating the compiler to add new features to the language being compiled. There is also a chapter on translating JVM byte code to MIPS machine code.

[Coco/R] The Compiler Generator Coco/R, http://www.ssw.uni-linz.ac.at/Coco/.

> Coco/R is a tool for generating scanners and recursive-descent parsers based on a context-free grammar. It accepts LL(k) grammars for arbitrary k.

[CompOpt] Compiler Optimizations,
https://en.wikipedia.org/wiki/Category:Compiler_optimizations.

> This Wikipedia web page provides links to dozens of other Wikipedia web pages with details on specific compiler optimizations.

[Elder 1994] John Elder, *Compiler Construction: A Recursive Descent Model*, Prentice Hall, 1994, ISBN 978-0132911399.

> This is another excellent, very readable book whose scope and level of presentation are similar to the one taken in this book. The compiler source language Model is very similar to CPRL, and the implementation language is Modula-2.

[Hanson 1985] Per Brinch Hansen, *Brinch Hansen on Pascal Compilers*, Prentice Hall, 1985, ISBN 978-0130830982.

> Although somewhat out of date now, the book by Brinch Hansen presents a very readable introduction to compilers. Its scope and level of presentation are similar to the one taken in this book except that it uses Pascal as the implementation language and a subset of Pascal as the source language.

[ISO/IEC 14977] Information technology – Syntactic metalanguage – Extended BNF.

> ISO/IEC 14977 is an international standard for EBNF notation. Note that the notation in the standard is different from that used in this book. For example, the standard uses curly braces "{" and "}" to enclose syntax expressions that can be repeated zero or more times, and it uses square brackets "[" and "]" to enclose optional syntax expressions. A publicly-available PDF version of the standard can be downloaded at
> http://standards.iso.org/ittf/PubliclyAvailableStandards/index.html.

[LLVM] The LLVM Compiler Infrastructure, http://llvm.org/.

> LLVM is a professional grade collection of modular and reusable compiler tools. LLVM was originally written to be a replacement for the existing code generator in the GCC suite, and many of the GCC front ends have been modified to work with it. Apple's Swift, Mozilla's Rust, and many other programming language make use of LLVM as a back end. In 2012 the Association for Computing Machinery presented Vikran Adve, Chris Lattner, and Evan Cheng with the ACM Software System Award for their work on LLVM.

[Parr 2010] Terence Parr, *Language Implementation Patterns*, Pragmatic Bookshelf, 2010, ISBN 978-1934356456.

> Terence Parr has devoted most of his adult life to compiler research, teaching, and implementation. Personally I learned a lot from this book, and I highly recommend it to anyone interested in learning about compilers.

[Parr 2013] Terence Parr, *The Definitive ANTLR 4 Reference* (Second Edition), Pragmatic Bookshelf, 2013, ISBN 978-1934356999. (See also http://www.antlr.org/.)

> ANTLR is a tool for generating scanners and recursive descent parsers that is somewhat similar in scope to Coco/R described above. ANTLR was developed and is being maintained by Terence Parr. If you want to want to learn more about ANTLR, you will want to read this book. See also [ANTLR] above.

[ParseGen] Comparison of parser generators (Wikipedia), https://en.wikipedia.org/wiki/Comparison_of_parser_generators.

> This Wikipedia article provides a fairly comprehensive list of scanner and parser generators for various languages.

[RegEx1] Regular-Expressions.info, http://www.regular-expressions.info/.

> There are lots of good books and articles about regular expressions, but this web site probably has everything you need to know except possibly for details about how to use regular expressions in a specific programming language.

[RegEx2] Regular expression (Wikipedia), https://en.wikipedia.org/wiki/Regular_expression.

> Not surprisingly, Wikipedia also has a good treatment of regular expressions, which complements the web site listed above.

[Watt 2000] David A. Watt and Deryck F. Brown, *Programming Language Processors in Java: Compilers and Interpreters*, Prentice Hall, 2000, ISBN 978-0130257864.

> The book by Watt and Brown is similar in scope to this one, and it also uses Java as the implementation language. Its coverage of tombstone diagrams was the inspiration for much of Chapter 1. One key difference is that the book by Watt and Brown uses the visitor pattern to "walk" the abstract syntax trees. I highly recommend this book.

[Wirth 1996] Niklaus Wirth, *Compiler Construction*, Addison Wesley, 1996, ISBN 978-0201403534. (Available online at http://www.ethoberon.ethz.ch/WirthPubl/CBEAll.pdf.)

> Niklaus Wirth has been writing compilers and designing programming languages since the late 1960's. Notable languages designed by Wirth are Pascal, Modula-2, and Oberon. He was also the first person to propose the use of extended grammars, and the main parts of his notation were adopted by [ISO/IEC 14977] above. Wirth's

Compiler Construction is similar to this book in many ways except that it uses a subset of Oberon as both the source language and the implementation language for a compiler.

Index

CPSIA information can be obtained
at www.ICGtesting.com
Printed in the USA
LVHW012113010120
642203LV00008B/242/P